Evolution of Management Practice

Evolution of Management Practice

Edited by
J. Mark Munoz

DE GRUYTER

ISBN 978-3-11-131650-5
e-ISBN (PDF) 978-3-11-131698-7
e-ISBN (EPUB) 978-3-11-131716-8

Library of Congress Control Number: 2024947563

Bibliographic information published by the Deutsche Nationalbibliothek
The Deutsche Nationalbibliothek lists this publication in the Deutsche Nationalbibliografie;
detailed bibliographic data are available on the internet at http://dnb.dnb.de.

© 2025 Walter de Gruyter GmbH, Berlin/Boston
Cover design: Britta Zwarg, Berlin
Typesetting: Integra Software Services Pvt. Ltd.

www.degruyter.com
Questions about General Product Safety Regulation:
productsafety@degruyterbrill.com

Advance Praise for *Evolution of Management Practice*

"Everything in business has changed significantly over the last several decades, but there's a sense that management as a principle is foundational and therefore doesn't require constant evolution. In *Evolution of Management Practice*, a group of the smartest management thinkers and practitioners offer a 21st century framework for management."

> – *Johnny C. Taylor, Jr. President & CEO, SHRM, Society for*
> *Human Resource Management*

"There doesn't seem to be a single industry that AI will not impact in a significant way in the future and it already has in many. Leaders and management will be required to understand the full depth and breadth of the changes on the horizon and be prepared to transform their current strategies. *Evolution of Management Practice* picks up on these changes and begins to put in place a new framework of management."

> – *Mike Srdanovic, SVP Chief AI Architect, Northern Trust*

"A must read for leaders and managers who wish to mobilize their organizations in to-day's contemporary landscape. Today, organizations are asked to do more than ever in response to social needs such as sustainability goals, rapidly advancing disruptive technologies, and better digital data access and management. Contemporary management practice faces these fast-paced shifts in real time. *Evolution of Management Practice* is a beautifully edited book by a diverse group of authors that provide entrepreneurs, managers, policymakers, and scholars with fresh perspectives on shaping the future of management."

> – *Dr. Sharon Alvarez, Thomas Olofson Endowed Chair in Entrepreneurial Studies,*
> *Katz Graduate School of Business, University of Pittsburgh; Fellow, Strategic Manage-*
> *ment Society; Immediate Past President, Academy of Management*

https://doi.org/10.1515/9783111316987-202

Contents

Evolution of Organizing

Evolution of Controlling

J. Mark Munoz

1 Introduction: The Evolution of Management Practice

Abstract: The practice of management has traditionally been grounded on the quest for optimal organizational performance through effective planning, leading, organizing, and controlling. In recent years, the quest for operational efficiencies has been dampened by environmental factors such as the global pandemic, war, natural disasters, and financial crises, to name just a few. Other factors such as technological advancement and cultural shifts, among many others, have altered the business terrain. Amid this landscape, contemporary managers have to evolve and think and act in new ways.

Introduction

The practice of management has traditionally been grounded on the quest for optimal organizational performance through effective planning, leading, organizing, and controlling.

Over the years, the pathways to success of management practice have shifted in emphasis, covering a broad range of approaches in areas such as scientific methods, human behavior and motivation, quantitative and statistical systems, contingency planning and adaptation, strategic planning, quality improvement, leadership, globalization, sustainability and ethics, and diversity and inclusion, among others. The ideas of innovative thinkers such as Frederick Taylor, Henri Fayol, Abraham Maslow, Douglas McGregor, Frederick Herzberg, Peter Drucker, and Michael Porter made an impact on its practice.

In more recent times, the quest for organizational efficiencies has been dampened by environmental factors such as the global pandemic, war, natural disasters, and financial crises, to name just a few. Other factors such as demographic shifts, cultural and social transformation, globalization and diversity, sustainability consciousness, disruptive technologies, and changes in work attitudes, goals, and preferences have started to redefine the contemporary workplace.

Managers nowadays must weigh upon a multitude of emerging issues that could potentially derail organizational success. For instance, managers need to have a heightened sense of data privacy and security compared to past years. They need to navigate supply chain shortages and risks (Satariano and Yang, 2012; Jaeger 2019) and strategize through environmental issues such as drought in places like California (Cooley et al., 2015). They must elevate their performance in technological management (Minbaeva, 2018).

https://doi.org/10.1515/9783111316987-001

The multitude of changes brought about by a growingly global, digital, and highly unpredictable world necessitates a reassessment and refinement of traditional management practices. In past decades, written procedures and policies largely set the foundation for goals, resource allocation, and employee evaluation, as well as reward systems in organizations (Ouchi, 1980). At the current time, this may be challenging to implement since organizations constantly face numerous unpredictable external forces, talent and supply shortages, and intensifying global competition alongside a fast-paced technological environment.

Some of the management wisdom of the past still applies today. There is merit in planning, leading, organizing, and controlling in an efficient way. However, traditional management approaches need to be refined and reinvented to suit contemporary times. In fact, even management practices in the past underscore the importance of organizational adaptation in the environment in which they operate (DiMaggio and Powell, 1991). Furthermore, written rules cannot cover all possible operational scenarios (Ouchi, 1980).

The Contemporary Management Landscape

The intent of this book is to understand what management shifts and refinements are essential in the current business environment in order that organizational success may be found.

In a quest to understand where and what types of refinements are necessary, it is important to start with an assessment of the current operational terrain.

The contemporary business environment is characterized by the following:

Workplace disruption. In several industries, layoffs have become common. There has been corporate downsizing (Kalimo, 2003). As a result, productivity and morale are likely impacted. Some firms have seen a devolvement of work functions (Perry and Kulik, 2008). Other firms have started to outsource (Sparks et al., 2001). As a result, there has been a rise in job insecurity (De Witte, Pienaar, and De Cuyper, 2016).

Change in work attitudes. During the global pandemic, employees were introduced to the notion of working from home or doing remote work. Postpandemic, many employees found that remote work can result in a better work-life balance. Many companies have changed their policies to allow employees to work from home or remotely during some days of the week. Even prior to the pandemic, there has been a notable increase in workforce mobility (Green, Baldauf and Owen, 2009). Flexible work conditions have been noted (Joyce, Pabayo, Critchley and Bambra, 2010). Flexibility in human resource management practices leads to broader organizational flexibility (Chang et al., 2013). Communication technology advancements have set the stage for greater work mobility and freedom (Dewe and Cooper, 2012). Some organizations have learned that when they help employees find work and better life balance, they may end up rewarded with productivity enhancements (Schneider and Barbera, 2014).

Broad demographic mix. Some organizations have seen an aging workforce (Loretto and Vickerstaff, 2013). Managers are working with multiple generations in the workplace (Wesolowski, 2014). Contemporary managers must work with employees with a wide age range and a high extent of diversity.

High international context. Organizations have been impacted by global events and have also gained the ability to extend their influence in foreign locations. As a result, organizations have to adapt to both local and international contexts (Gress and Poon, 2007).

Reconfiguration of talent. Organizations have realized that talent can be a point of differentiation and a source of competitive advantage (Meara and Petzall, 2013). With regard to the management of talent, organizations have shifted from traditional approaches to more strategic models (Bersin, 2019).

Dynamic social construct. As a result of digital media, the social construct or organizations have changed. Information exchanges have taken on a new form, with the advent of social media requiring firms to carefully assess and plan their communication agenda as well as social interactions. There is an opportunity to enhance corporate engagement, but at the same time a heightened level of communication message sensitivity and careful planning is required. Firms have to navigate both formal and informal factors in contemporary organizations (Castel and Friedberg, 2010).

Skills and knowledge based. Organizations have seen the importance of cultivating knowledge and skills. Organizations need to boost employee engagement to increase productivity and performance (Macey et al., 2009). Organizations need to plan for and provide due attention to career management (Rowley and Jackson, 2011). Top management competencies set the framework for operational practices in firms (Foss, 2011). Well-planned and intentional approaches to training and retaining employees contribute to the attainment of organizational goals (Meara and Petzall, 2013). Knowledge management is growingly important (Boudreau and Cascio, 2017).

Technology grounded. Organizations have learned to unleash the power of technology to accomplish organizational goals. As a result, there is a growing need to better manage data and technology (Minbaeva, 2018).

Sustainability and wellness conscious. Organizations have found value in heightened corporate social responsibility and looking after the welfare of all stakeholders as well as the broader society. Improving the well-being of employees can have a positive impact on overall performance (Robertson and Cooper, 2011). There is merit in considering business sustainability (Lozano, 2015). Organizations need to provide due attention to employee well-being (Guest, 2017).

Sensitivity to cost and profit. Many organizations have felt the strain of inflationary pressures and intense competition. Restructuring and outsourcing have been ways companies employed to minimize cost (Gooderham et al., 2015).

Collaborative approach. Organizations have seen the value of internal and external collaborations. Close interdepartmental collaboration is essential (Rasmussen and Ulrich, 2015).

Quest for operational excellence. Organizations have actively sought ways to navigate countless challenges and enhance operations in order to find new pathways to goal attainment and profitability. Formal systems work best only under stable environments and when work output is measurable (Biancani et al., 2014), therefore necessitating adjustments and adaptation in the workplace. Clarity of work structures and knowledge management is growing important (Boudreau and Cascio, 2017).

The contemporary business environment is indeed one that pushes organizations to constantly assess markets and business environments, work through change, innovate, and create impactful strategies.

Pressure for change

There are several mounting challenges that organizations need to navigate. These challenges put pressure on organizations to change and become drivers of adaptation and management evolution. A few examples are given as follows:

Management of people. Organizations face the challenge of hiring, training, and keeping employees. They face challenges in talent management (Cardona and Morley, 2013). They need to work on issues relating to boosting morale, raising productivity, and boosting work efficiency (Ahmad and Allen, 2015). They need to be cognizant of workplace bullying (Woodrow and Guest, 2014) and ensure due emphasis is placed on the advancement of diversity, equity, and inclusion. Furthermore, organizations need to overcome difficulties relating to skill shortages (Garavan, McCarthy and Morley, 2016).

Management of process and systems. Some organizations have struggled with putting into place an effective process and system. Poor and ineffective leadership has been observed (Schyns and Schilling, 2013). Top management abilities have been deemed an important foundation of firm operations (Foss, 2011). Business ethics has been a concern in the practice of human resource management (Ghani, 2015). The way the organization runs, starting with the management team as drivers and process and structures as vehicles, would determine the course of the organizational journey.

Management of resources. Organizations need to have a mindset of resource conservation and optimization. Some organizations require employees to work under a fixed-hour arrangement and are not flexible (Karsten, 2013). Avenues to manage costs such as restructuring and outsourcing have been considered by some firms (Gooderham et al., 2015). While cost savings can be beneficial, organizations need to also evaluate how decisions can impact overall operational efficiency and profitability.

Management of technology. With rising technological innovation and digitalization, organizations grapple with ways to stay on top of technology and manage technological changes effectively. Technological changes have an impact on operations (Angrave et al., 2016). There is a growing need to better manage data and technology (Minbaeva, 2018). Cases of inconsiderate cyber usage have been observed (Coyne et al., 2016).

Management of international factors. With the acceleration of globalization, organizations have to find operational solutions to changing geopolitical climates, legal and regulatory obstacles, workforce internationalization, supply chain disruptions, and threats to cross-border investments and collaborations. Organizations have experienced intensified competition and a lack of operational predictability as a result of globalization (Elegbe, 2010). Among others, globalization has posed new challenges in human resource management (Alhartley, 2018).

These pressures for change have set the foundation for a new management paradigm.

Evolution of Management and the Way Forward

As the pressure to find optimal organizational performance grows, the ways in which management is practiced have changed. This has been evident in the four (4) key functions of management: planning, leading, organizing, and controlling.

Evolution of Planning. A heightened sensitivity to the needs and new demands and expectations of stakeholders, business ecosystem, and society are growingly emphasized in practice as compared to the past. Business sustainability is worth considering (Lozano, 2015). Contemporary managers need to strategically plan through unfolding technological changes as well as the fast-evolving business environment. There is a need to consider the external factors that impact the workplace (Guest, 2017) and plan accordingly.

Evolution of Leading. There has been a heightened sensitivity to culture, development, purpose, and work-life balance in organizations. Kropp, Cambon, and Clark (2021) highlighted the importance of empathy in contemporary management. Organizations should have approaches directed toward the enrichment of work (Wood and de Menezes, 2011). There is a need to pay due attention to employee well-being (Guest, 2017).

Building an employee pool comprising healthy and productive individuals is growing important (Kowalski, Loretto and Redman, 2015). Petriglieri (2020) underscored the importance of shifting the focus of contemporary management practice from speed and efficiency to one grounded on purpose, intentionality, and rationale of action.

Evolution of Organizing. Amid an environment with operational disruptions brought about by new technologies and geopolitical factors, contemporary managers need to organize structures, systems, and processes in unprecedented ways. It has become necessary to manage data and technology effectively (Minbaeva, 2018). Organizations have to work through supply uncertainty issues (Zhu, 2015) and have to design the appropriate policies, procedures, and resources to gain operational efficiencies

Evolution of Controlling. In an environment where there exist high levels of competition and consumer sophistication, organizations cannot be complacent. There is a strong push to innovate, benchmark, track performance, and quickly respond with corrective measures in order to be competitive. In the course of transformation, Nieto-Rodriguez (2023) emphasized the importance of clarity or aspiration and precisely what is to be gained in undertaking change initiatives. A broad and holistic strategic approach is necessary. Gherson and Gratton (2022) underscored the importance of skill development and the recalibration of work processes, systems, and roles in contemporary management.

Over the years, the practice of management has evolved in adaptation to contemporary challenges and opportunities. It will continue to evolve as business conditions change. The objective of this book is to capture and understand elements of this evolution at its current stage and to gain insights into possible trajectories into the future.

Management experts from diverse backgrounds were assembled in this book to provide fresh perspectives on the ways the practice of management has shifted in the current time.

This book will benefit managers and entrepreneurs from all walks of life worldwide. Those in academia would find the content helpful in shaping future research and theoretical frameworks. Consultants, government officials, and policy-makers would find the learned concepts applicable to diverse organizational structures and industries and valuable in policy creation and the setting of a developmental agenda.

The book aims to expand the conversation on the evolution of management and the quest toward finding optimal operational models for organizations. While not all areas pertaining to the changes in management practice are covered in this book, important discussions of contemporary transformations are highlighted.

The book is organized into 4 themes and 15 chapters. Chapter 1 – Introduction: The evolution of management practice (*J. Mark Munoz*); **Evolution of Planning**: Chapter 2 – Preparing for organizational change and business transformation (*Sara Junio*); Chapter 3 – Planning for technological change (*Syed Adeel Ahmed, Brendan Moore, and Cathy Rehfus-Wilsek*); Chapter 4 – Creating strategic value through digital reinvention *(Sunando Das and J. Mark Munoz);* Chapter 5 – Responsible and sustainable planning in contemporary organizations *(Duane Windsor);* **Evolution of Leading:** Chapter 6 – Preferred managerial leader behavior: Implicit and explicit theories *(Romie Frederick Littrell);* Chapter 7 – Human resource leadership in a technology-driven world *(Janet Kirby, Joshua Frye, and Anneliese Nash);* Chapter 8 – Preferred managerial leader behavior in a global and diverse world *(Romie Frederick Littrell);* Chapter 9 – Navigating the digital frontier: A model for effective leadership and virtual teams *(Lama Blaique);* **Evolution of Organizing:** Chapter 10 – Reorganization of enterprise business models with an AI and blockchain first approach *(Abhishek Kumbhat and J. Mark Munoz);* Chapter 11 – Incorporating design thinking into data-driven strategic management *(Diana Heeb Bivona and Kristine Mantey);* Chapter 12 – Organizing essential supply chain skills during a pandemic *(Albert Tan and Huay Ling Tay);* **Evolution of Controlling:** Chapter 13 – Innovation and operational control *(Syed Adeel Ahmed, Brendan Moore, and Cathy Rehfus-Wilsek);* Chapter 14 – Technology oversight for optimal corporate performance *(Oliver Degnan);* and Chapter 15 – Strategic control and its impact on efficiency, speed and innovation in organizations *(Manjula Salimath and Vallari Chandna).*

The practice of management has evolved in its appearance and function from what it was decades ago. It will continue to shift and change. In the coming years, there will be another generation of active practitioners with new ideas and agendas. While some of the methodologies and emphasis in its practice were somewhat modified, many of the traditional building blocks of management theory and its applications have remained relevant today. The human quest for betterment and advancement, at both the personal and organizational levels, continue to define the contemporary practice of management and will likely influence its further evolution in the future.

References

Aalbers, R., W. Dolfsma and O. Koppius (2014). Rich ties and innovative knowledge transfer within a firm, *British Journal of Management, 25*, 833–848.

Ahmad, M., & Allen, M. (2015). High performance HRM and establishment performance in Pakistan: An empirical analysis. *Employee Relations, 37*(5), 506–524.

Alharthey, B. K. (2018). Review on Globalization and Importance of Strategic Human Resource Management. *International Journal of Scientific Research and Management, 6*(3), 230–235. Accessed May 25, 2023. Available at: https://www.researchgate.net/publication/324090733_Review_on_Globalization_and_Importance_of_Strategic_Human_Resource_Management

Angrave, D., Charlwood, A., Kirkpatrick, I., Lawrence, M., & Stuart, M. (2016). HR and analytics: Why HR is set to fail the big data challenge. *Human Resource Management Journal, 26*(1), 1–11. https://doi.org/10.1111/1748-8583.12090

Aycan, Z. (2005). The interplay between cultural and institutional/structural contingencies in human resource management practices. *International Journal of Human Resource Management, 16*, 1083–1119.

Bersin, J. 2019. The Company as A Talent Network: Unilever and Schneider Electric Show the Way. Accessed May 25, 2023. Available at: https://joshbersin.com/2019/07/the-company-as-a-talent-network-unilever-and-schneider-electric-show-the-way/

Biancani, S., McFarland, D. A., & Dahlander, L. (2014). The semiformal organization. *Organization Science*, *25*, 1306–1324.

Boudreau, J., & Cascio, W. (2017). Human capital analytics: Why are we not there?- *Journal of Organizational Effectiveness: People and Performance*, *4*(2), 119–126. https://doi.org/10.1108/JOEPP-03-2017-0021

Cardona, P., & Morley, M. (2013). *Manager-subordinate Trust: A Global Perspective*. London, UK: Routledge.

Castel, P., & Friedberg, E. (2010). Institutional change as an interactive process: The case of the modernization of the French cancer centers. *Organization Science*, *21*, 311–330.

Chang, S., Y. Gong, S. A. Way, and L. Jia. (2013). Flexibility-Oriented HRM Systems, Absorptive Capacity, and Market Responsiveness and Firm Innovativeness. *Journal of Management*, *39*(7), 1924–1951. doi:10.1177/0149206312466145.

Cooley, Heather, Kristina Donnelly, Rapichan Phurisamban, and Madhyama Subramanian. (2015). *Impacts of California's Ongoing Drought: Agriculture*, Oakland, CA: Pacific Institute. 24.

Coyne, I., Farley, S., Axtell, C., Sprigg, C., Best, L., & Kwok, O. (2016). Understanding the relationship between experiencing workplace cyberbullying, employee mental strain and job satisfaction: A disempowerment approach. *International Journal of Human Resource Management*, *28*, 945–972. doi:10.1080/09585192.2015.1116454

Dewe, P., & Cooper, C. (2012). *Well-being and Work: Towards a Balanced Agenda*. Basingstoke: Palgrave Macmillan.

De Witte, H., Pienaar, J., & De Cuyper, N. (2016). Review of 30 years of longitudinal studies on the association between job insecurity and health and well-being: Is there causal evidence? *Australian Psychologist*, *51*, 18–31. doi:10.1111/ap.12176

DiMaggio, P. J., and W. W. Powell. (1983). The Iron Cage Revisited: Institutional Isomorphism and Collective Rationality in Organizational Fields. *American Sociological Review*, *48*(2), 147–160. doi:10.2307/2095101.

Elegbe, J. (2010). *Talent Management in the Developing World*. London: Routledge.

Foss, N. J. (2011). Why micro-foundations for resource-based theory are needed and what they may look like, *Journal of Management*, *37*, 1413–1428.

Garavan, T., McCarthy, A., & Morley, M. (2016). *Global Human Resource Development: Regional and Country Perspectives*. London: Routledge.

Ghani, B. (2015). Advance ethical practices in Human Resource Management: A case study of health care company. *Journal of Resource Development and Management*, *5*(1), 8–14.

Gherson, D., and Gratton, L. (2022). Managers can't do it all. *Harvard Business Review*. Accessed May 29, 2023. Available at: https://hbr.org/2022/03/managers-cant-do-it-all

Gooderham, P. N., M. J. Morley, E. Parry, and E. Stavrou. (2015). National and Firm-Level Drivers of the Devolution of HRM Decision Making to Line Managers. *Journal of International Business Studies*, *46*(6), 715–23. doi:10.1057/jibs.2015.5.

Green, A. E., Baldauf, B., & Owen, D. (2009). *Study on workers' mobility. Lot 2: Short-term international assignments* (Short-term mobility Final report). European Commission. February, 2009.

Gress, D., & Poon, P. H. (2007). Firm networks and Korean subsidiaries in the United States. *Growth and Change*, *38*, 396–418.

Guest, D. E. (2017). Human resource management and employee well-being: Towards a new analytic framework. *Human Resource Management Journal*, *27*, 22–38. doi:10.1111/1748-8583.12139

Jaeger, Jaclyn. 2019. Top 10 Supply Chain Risks for 2019. *Complianceweek*, May 7.

Joyce, K., Pabayo, R., Critchley, J. A., & Bambra, C. (2010). Flexible working conditions and their effects on employee health and wellbeing. *Cochrane Database of Systematic Reviews* (Report No. 2), doi:10.1002/14651858.CD008009.pub2

Kalimo, R. (2003). The effects of past and anticipated future downsizing on survivor well-being: An Equity perspective. *Journal of Occupational Health Psychology, 8*, 91–109.

Karsten, L. (2013). *Globalization and Time*. Oxon: Routledge.

Kowalski, T. H. P., Loretto, W., & Redman, T. (2015). Call for papers: Special issue of international journal of human resource management: Well-being and HRM in the changing workplace. *The International Journal of Human Resource Management, 26*, 123–126. doi:10.1080/09585192.2014.969973

Kropp, B., Cambon, A., Clark, S. (2021). What does it mean to be a manager today? *Harvard Business Review*. Accessed May 29, 2023. Available at: https://hbr.org/2021/04/what-does-it-mean-to-be-a-manager-today

Loretto, W., & Vickerstaff, S. (2013). The domestic and gendered context for retirement. *Human Relations, 66*, 65–86. doi:10.1177/0018726712455832

Lozano, R. (2015). A holistic perspective on corporate sustainability drivers, *Corporate Social Responsibility and Environmental Management, 22*, pp. 32–44.

Macey, W., Schneider, B., Barbera, K., & Young, S. (2009). *Employee Engagement: Tools for Analysis, Practice and Competitive Advantage*. Chichester: Blackwell Publishing.

Meara, B., & Petzall, S. (2013). *The Handbook of Strategic Recruitment and Selection: A Systems Approach*. Bingley: Emerald Group Publishing Limited.

Minbaeva, D. B. (2018). Building credible human capital analytics for organizational competitive advantage. *Human Resource Management, 57*(3), 701–713. https://doi.org/10.1002/hrm.21848

Nieto-Rodriguez, A. (2023). Organize your change initiative around purpose and benefits. Accessed May 29, 2023. Available at: https://hbr.org/2023/05/organize-your-change-initiative-around-purpose-and-benefits

Ouchi, W. G. (1980). Markets, bureaucracies, and clans. *Administrative Science Quarterly, 25*, 129–141.

Perry, E. L., & Kulik, C. T. (2008). The devolution of HR to the line: Implications for perceptions of people management effectiveness. *International Journal of Human Resource Management, 19*, 262–273. doi:10.1080/09585190701799838

Petriglieri, G. (2020). Are our management theories outdated? *Harvard Business Review*. Accessed May 29, 2023. Available at: https://hbr.org/2020/06/are-our-management-theories-outdated

Rasmussen, T., & Ulrich, D. (2015). Learning from practice: How HR analytics avoids being a management fad. *Organizational Dynamics, 44*(3), 236–242. https://doi.org/10.1016/j.orgdyn.2015.05.008

Robertson, I., & Cooper, C. (2011). *Well-being: Productivity and Happiness at Work*. Basingstoke: Palgrave Macmillan.

Rowley, C., & Jackson, K. (2011). *Human Resource Management*. New York, NY: Routledge.

Satariano, J., and Yang, A. (2012). Apple Iphone 5's Thin Display Drives Supply Shortfall. *Bloomberg Businessweek*, September 25.

Schneider, B., & Barbera, K. (2014). *The Oxford Handbook of Organization Climate and Culture*. Oxford, UK: Oxford University Press.

Schyns, B., & Schilling, J. (2013). How bad are the effects of bad leaders? A meta-analysis of destructive leadership and its outcomes. *The Leadership Quarterly, 24*, 138–158. doi:10.1016/j.leaqua.2012.09.001

Sparks, K., Faragher, B., & Cooper, C. L. (2001). Well-being and occupational health in the 21st century workplace. *Journal of Occupational and Organizational Psychology, 74*, 489–509. doi:10.1348/096317901167497

Wesolowski, P. (2014). Melding a multi-generational workforce: Communication technology is part of the problem – And the solution. *Human Resource Management International Digest, 22*, 33–35. doi:10.1108/HRMID-04-2014-0041

Wood, S., & de Menezes, L. M. (2011). High involvement management, high-performance work systems and well-being. *The International Journal of Human Resource Management, 22*, 1586–1610. doi:10.1080/09585192.2011.561967

Woodrow, C., & Guest, D. E. (2014). When good HR gets bad results: Exploring the challenge of HR implementation in the case of workplace bullying. *Human Resource Management Journal, 24*, 38–56. doi:10.1111/1748-8583.12021

Zhu, Stuart X. (2015). Analysis of dual sourcing strategies under supply disruptions. *International Journal of Production Economics, 170*, 191–203.

Evolution of Planning

Sara Junio

2 Preparing for Organizational Change and Business Transformation

Abstract: In the ever-evolving landscape of business management, organizations grapple with the need for transformation. This chapter explores change management strategies, drawing insights from theoretical perspectives, real-world case studies, and the dynamic shifts of Industry 4.0 and Industry 5.0. As we navigate this evolutionary journey, effective change management becomes paramount for organizational resilience and success.

Introduction

In the early 1970s, research that focused on how to grow organizations started to appear in publications. This was a time period in which computers were just being introduced for more automation in assembly lines, also known as the Third Industrial Revolution or "Industry 3.0" (Mohajan, 2021). This automation created efficiencies but also growth opportunities due to lower operating costs. This was the beginning of a change in the workforce that required behavior to be modified.

The late 1980s and early 1990s marked a pivotal era in the evolution of management practices, particularly in the domain of organizational change. It was during this time that the global business landscape underwent profound transformations, compelling organizations to rethink their change management strategies. Scholarly literature from this period, such as the works of Fennell and Alexander (1993) and Armenakis and Bedeian (1999), captures the essence of this shift. These publications not only reflect the growing recognition of change management as a critical organizational competency but also contribute to the theoretical and practical frameworks that guide contemporary change initiatives.

The Fourth Industrial Revolution, or "Industry 4.0," introduced machine learning, artificial intelligence, and the onset of big data in 2011. Requirements for the competitive market are increasing and new technologies are required for organizations to be or even remain relevant (Ahmed & Pathan, 2019). Organizations are required to build a competitive advantage and continuously build upon that advantage to survive. The building blocks for supporting the operational process include the collection of data, software to analyze the data, and a strategy and action plan for managing data. The process includes methods for introducing a competitive advantage through coupling data with innovation and speed. Organizations now find they need to continuously evaluate people, process, products, performance, and profitability to remain innovative, nimble, and competitive.

https://doi.org/10.1515/9783111316987-002

The availability of new technology, the expansion of data for decision-making, the increased customer demands, and the shareholder expectations for cost containment position organizations well to transform in the industrial revolution. This Industrial Revolution is no longer a new phenomenon. Hence, organizations must adapt to keep their business competitive (Hanelt et al., 2021) and assist employees through a psychological aspect as part of moving through a transition of change (Bridges, 2004).

Theoretical Perspectives on Organizational Transformation

The field of change management has evolved significantly over the decades, beginning with foundational models like Kurt Lewin's Change Management Model, which was introduced in the 1940s. Lewin's model is built on the concept of unfreezing, changing, and refreezing. The "unfreezing" stage involves preparing an organization to accept that change is necessary, "changing" involves the transition process where new behaviors and practices are introduced, and "refreezing" solidifies the new state as the norm within the organization. Lewin's model emphasizes the importance of creating a perceived need for change, managing the transition phase carefully, and ensuring that the new practices are embedded into the organization's culture to prevent regression (Cummings, Bridgman, & Brown, 2016).

In the 1990s, William Bridges introduced his Transition Model, which focuses on the psychological transitions that individuals experience during organizational change. Bridges' model outlines three stages: ending, neutral zone, and new beginning. The "ending" phase involves letting go of old ways and identities, which can be a challenging emotional process. The "neutral zone" is a critical transitional period where the old has gone, but the new hasn't fully taken hold, often characterized by confusion and uncertainty. Finally, the "new beginning" phase sees individuals embrace new identities, roles, and ways of working. Bridges' model underscores the importance of addressing the human side of change, recognizing that organizational change is not just a structural process but also an emotional and psychological one (Bridges, 2009).

John Kotter's Eight-Step Change Model, introduced in his 1996 book "Leading Change," is one of the most widely recognized frameworks in change management. Kotter's model outlines a sequential process for leading change: 1) establishing a sense of urgency, 2) forming a powerful coalition, 3) creating a vision for change, 4) communicating the vision, 5) empowering broad-based action, 6) generating short-term wins, 7) consolidating gains to produce more change, and 8) anchoring new approaches in the culture. This model is designed to prevent common pitfalls that can derail change initiatives, such as insufficient buy-in or lack of sustained momentum. Kotter emphasizes the importance of strong leadership and clear communication throughout the change process, ensuring that changes are not only implemented but also sustained over the long term (Kotter, 1996).

The ADKAR model was developed by Prosci, Inc. in the mid-1990s. This was around the time change management programs were being introduced across the nation as well, such as Total Quality Management and Six Sigma (Helms-Mills et al., 2008). Prosci recognized three components were needed in their methodology. The ADKAR model is one component of the overall Prosci Methodology used to manage change within an organization. The other two components are the Change Triangle Model (addressing organizational readiness) and the Three-Phase Process (addressing the process in which change occurs within the organization). The three phases of a transition, commonly referred to in various models, are based on Lewin's theories of change (Rosenbaum, 2018).

These models have collectively shaped modern change management practices, providing frameworks that address both the structural and human elements of change. Lewin's model offers a clear, three-phase process; Bridges emphasizes the psychological journey individuals undergo; and Kotter provides a comprehensive, step-by-step guide for organizational leaders. Each model has contributed to a deeper understanding of how to manage change effectively, highlighting the need for strategic planning, strong leadership, and attention to the human aspects of transition.

Drivers of Change

Organizational transformation involves fundamentally altering how an organization operates and provides value to its stakeholders. This can include changes in structure, culture, processes, governance, and external relationships. Organizations may undergo transformation to adapt to market changes, new technologies, regulatory shifts, or evolving societal norms and expectations (Christou & Piller, 2024). Despite its benefits, Industry 4.0 introduced challenges such as rapid technological advancements, changing workforce dynamics, and the need for upskilling (Ahmed & Pathan, 2019). Effective change management became crucial for addressing these disruptions. Leaders need to manage resistance, foster adaptability, and ensure smooth transitions. The focus shifted from merely adopting technology to managing its impact on people, processes, and culture.

The onset of Industry 5.0 emphasizes human roles alongside technology. This era recognizes that sustainable progress requires balancing automation with human creativity. Industry 5.0 aims for compatibility, sustainability, and resilience, emphasizing critical thinking and well-being. Organizations must adopt change management strategies that empower employees, nurture innovation, and foster collaboration. The goal is not just about using data but using it intelligently while prioritizing sustainability (Nahavandi, 2019).

Today's organizations have more complex and interdependent changes than ever before, which drives the need for change management practices. The biggest driver of change management comes from the onset of organizations undergoing a digital transformation (Hanelt et al., 2021). The digital transformations involve organizations implementing new technology, an ecosystem of data-enriched capabilities, that affect business operating models and deliver new forms of value creation to stakeholders (Hanelt et al., 2021; Stouten et al., 2018).

Advancements in technology with the automation of operational areas and machine learning impact an organization's processes and its people. The automation moves rote, routine tasks performed by a human to now performed by a machine. Additionally, the evolution of technology created the opportunity for organizations to compete globally. Operating in a dynamic environment with shifting global trends and market demands necessitates resilience and adaptability, which are fostered by effective change management (Hanelt et al., 2021). The complexity of operating on a global scale while upskilling or reskilling employees to enhance their critical thinking capabilities represents a significant transition for the workforce. Managing change effectively will facilitate this transition by providing structured approaches to address resistance, promote adaptability, and ensure that employees are adequately prepared for new roles and responsibilities, ultimately leading to smoother and more successful organizational transformations (Christou & Piller, 2024).

Challenges and Pitfalls

Change is not easy. Human nature is to resist change and hold on to the past. Employees cling to what is comfortable and controllable in their environment (Christou & Piller, 2024). Resistance is one of the most common challenges found during a transformation or an organizational change. It can be difficult to help employees through the psychological transitions in the transformation because they move at a pace that is specific to them (Bridges, 2004). Even if they had the desire to change behavior, the lack of a clear vision from the leadership can prevent them from understanding why they need to change or what they are moving toward (Hubbart, 2023). Additionally, when the culture of an organization does not support a learning or an entrepreneurial environment, it is perceived as having a lack of support for organizational changes and transformations. The lack of support for the workers wanting to change becomes problematic. "A culture that values learning and encourages experimentation and risk-taking is more likely to facilitate learning than a culture that is resistant to change" (Christou & Piller, 2024, p. 307).

Motivational factors to address challenges and pitfalls can vary widely depending on the nature of the work, the experience of the employees, the type of organization, and the structure of the organization. According to Phillips and Phillips (2019), there are common themes to increase motivation: provide recognition for team and individual accomplishments; treat employees with respect; empower the employees to take action; provide immediate and timely feedback and coaching; build trust with employees; and involve the employees in decisions as they have a vested interest in the outcome.

When the team is struggling, there can be a sense of helplessness by the team members. It is easy to stay caught up in the negative and simply apply the "blame game" when ultimately it is a signal the employees are resisting change. According to Wheelan et al. (2021), this is known as the fundamental attribution error, where people attribute the actions of others to personality characteristics without taking other factors into account. The team should be held accountable for the situations in which they can control and seek assistance from the leader to remove obstacles.

Regardless of how the employees and team members articulate their resistance to change, the leadership of the organization sets the tone and the probability for the success of the organizational change. If the sponsors of the change are not aligned with stakeholders or there is no acceptance or "buy-in" across the entire organization, there is a low likelihood of the transformation being a success (Hubbart, 2023).

Approach to Managing Change

As noted earlier, there are different models for managing change within the workforce. Ensuring the success of a transformation involves several key components. First, the sponsor of the transformation needs to establish a clear vision. Describing the future state the organization is striving to achieve is essential to help employees understand the new direction (Stouten et al., 2018). Stephen Covey famously wrote in his book, *The 7 Habits of Highly Effective People* (1989), that beginning with the end in mind provides a guiding direction for all decisions. The vision should align the change strategy with organizational goals and values. Executives and sponsors communicate the vision through the interplay of storytelling narratives that resonate with the workforce at every level of the organization (Robinson, 2022). The messages are delivered multiple times in many different channels, such as individual conversations, written media (newsletters, email), intranet platforms, town hall work base meetings, and even daily operational meetings. The more the message is delivered in a consistent manner throughout the entire transformation period in a way that resonates with the employees, the more likely the message will be received, supported, and championed by internal change agents to advance the message across the cross-functional teams (Stouten et al., 2018). Additionally, the sponsor delivering the message needs to behave in a manner that supports the desired behavior of the organization. This may require them to self-reflect on their leadership style and evaluate where changes need to be made before asking employees to change their behaviors.

The second part of this preparation is assessing the organization's readiness for change. This includes evaluating the current state of the culture, the leadership capabilities, and the engagement levels of employees (Christou & Piller, 2024; Stouten et al., 2018). Aniefiok Gilead Robinson (2022) captures the essence of assessing the organization's readiness through the definition of social intelligence in change management practices. Robinson describes this as a set of practices by managers in their daily habits that include situational and organizational awareness, social skills, and empathy for individuals about embarking on the change journey. The objective of assessing the readiness of the organization is to determine where there are barriers to the change, such as employee resistance, technological support, or capacity within the workplace for the transformation, to develop plans and activities to address those barriers early in the process (Stouten et al., 2018).

Building a change coalition is the third component of a successful change management practice. Employees may be aware of the need to transform and change, but until they "buy in" to the vision and see the benefits that impact them personally, it will be difficult to engage them or keep them engaged. A cross-functional team of leaders (not necessarily just a manager) that are champions for change will aid in the acceleration of the adoption of the new way of operations, the transformation itself. This team should represent all levels and departments in the organization so that employees can see they are represented when it comes to managing and delivering information to and from the workforce with the transformation sponsors. These are the leaders that can help a sponsor or a program manager leading the transformation fundamentally alter the mindset of those involved in the change (Hanelt et al., 2021). Ramadan et al. (2023) summarize the role of the coalition or change agents, described as those who ensure the teams are well prepared to respond to the transformation and make their organizations more agile.

Training and skill development are also critical components of a successful change management practice. Firstly, they ensure that employees possess the necessary skills and knowledge to adapt to new processes, technologies, and roles. Without adequate training, employees may struggle to understand and implement changes, leading to decreased productivity and increased resistance. Effective training programs help bridge the gap between current competencies and the skills required in the transformed organization. This preparation not only facilitates a smoother transition but also boosts employee confidence and engagement, which are crucial for the successful adoption of change.

Investing in training and skill development demonstrates the organization's commitment to its employees' growth and development. This investment can enhance job satisfaction and loyalty, reducing turnover during the transition period. By equipping employees with the tools they need to succeed in the new environment, organizations can foster a culture of continuous learning and improvement. This proactive approach not only addresses immediate training needs but also prepares the workforce for future changes, making the organization more resilient and adaptable in the long run (Kotter, 1996).

Finally, the last component of a change management practice is rewards and reinforcement. When implementing a change management practice, focusing on reinforcement is key to ensuring the changes are sustained and embedded within the organization. Reinforcement helps solidify new behaviors, processes, and practices, preventing regression to old habits. This focus on reinforcement includes providing ongoing support, recognizing and rewarding desired behaviors, and continually communicating the benefits and successes of the change. By reinforcing the change, organizations can maintain momentum, address any emerging resistance, and ensure that the change becomes a lasting part of the organizational culture. This sustained effort is essential for achieving long-term success and realizing the full benefits of the change initiative (Kotter, 1996).

Case Studies and Best Practices

The following three case studies exemplify successful change adoption techniques. The cases highlight how empowering employees and engaging them early in the process can drive transformation success. Building on the critical components of change management such as training, skill development, and reinforcement, these case studies demonstrate the practical application of these principles. By granting employees a sense of ownership and actively involving them from the outset, these organizations not only mitigated resistance but also harnessed the collective insights and innovations of their workforce.

The approaches seen in each case fostered a collaborative environment where change was not merely imposed but embraced, leading to sustainable and impactful organizational transformation.

Case Study #1

An academic medical center in New York City used the ADKAR change model when they adjusted their facility to the ACC patient care model (Wong et al., 2019). This large-scale initiative required years of preplanning the communication plans, change resistance plans, and transition action plans with newly created cross-functional teams. They recognized the first step in building awareness was to start the planning process early with constituents that would be impacted by the change.

According to Wong, this was a 2-year process of building cross-functional planning teams. "Our goal was to ensure that all our future nursing teams have the tools and competencies needed to appropriately care for patients on the newly formed AAC units" (Wong et al., 2019, p. 32). Next, they focused on the desired stage of the ADKAR model by allowing the teams to have more control over their functions than in the past. By empowering them with more control, they were able to "see" where changes needed to be made. The knowledge-building stage started with a small group of teams building the story of the end-state. A good story will help individuals see how they fit in and help them determine "how" to change. They focused on adding new resources and training for the ability stage of the ADKAR model. Finally, the reinforcement stage addressed finding ways to build cohesive teams. "In response [to a reoccurring theme of the lack of cohesiveness], nurse managers held regular unit-based team cohesion sessions with their staff, utilizing the tools learned to facilitate team development" (Wong et al., 2019, p. 35).

Case Study #2

The Federal Financial Management Community (FFMC) implemented a new customer-centric operating and servicing model. The new operating model meant the bureaucratic hiring process needed to change to be more flexible, more innovative, and more supportive of the customer. The leadership created a program that attracted, developed, and retained leading talent. The program is based on the Learning Enhancement, Advancement, and Development Model, also known as the LEAD model (Vineyard et al., 2020). FFMC's transformation involved implementing the program with the LEAD model to achieve the objectives of the new operating and servicing model. The leadership selected the Prosci ADKAR model to implement the change because of its strength in working with the psychological aspects of employee behavior. "While many employees fear the implementation of technology poses a threat to jobs, it will not replace the traditional, human workforce" (Vineyard et al., 2020, p. 46). Three change management lessons learned by FFMC are to (1) establish expectations with a high level of transparency; (2) provide a platform to evaluate success; and (3) give employees flexibility in their career growth direction, trajectory, and speed (Vineyard et al., 2020).

The key to engaging in a successful transformation is giving power to the employees and engaging them early. A learning organization builds on the knowledge of its employees in the learning process and empowers them to help build the future state of the organization. Helms-Mills et al. (2008) found that a learning culture creates a learning organization. FFMC's success was predicated on the learning culture implemented to support the transformation to the new operating model.

Case Study #3

Borough of Manhattan Community College, which serves 27,000 students as part of the City University of New York system, created a new strategic direction for its enrollment management program. Historically, the program simply managed the onboarding of new students. The new strategy was designed to enhance the entire student experience, from onboarding to achieving their educational goals (Walleser, 2020). The Prosci ADKAR model was followed to aid in the transition to the future state of the program.

The common theme among research cases studied with the Prosci ADKAR model is the preplanning with cross-functional teams to engage and empower employees early in the process. "We put together a cross-functional work team to survey training needs and to make recommendations regarding what was needed" (Walleser, 2018, p. 11). Walleser states, in this case, the lessons learned were: (1) Identify the barrier point to the change; (2) Listen and understand objectives; (3) Remove obstacles; (4) Make a personal appeal; (5) Hold employees accountable; and (6) Convert the strong dissenters (by challenging or redirecting their power).

The strategies for success employed in these cases have a common theme. These themes are noteworthy considerations for contemporary managers.

Each change was a success because of the extensive amount of planning ahead of the implementation with cross-functional teams and the method by which behaviors were reinforced. Employees were given more control and more power over their environment and became more engaged in the outcome. The following approaches were notable:

Planned Engagement. The academic medical center in New York was successful in building a new facility designed around the patient because of the extensive planning and engagement by cross-functional teams. The reinforcement came from the removal of obstacles and the development of a cohesive team.

Planned Cultural Change. The FFMC was successful because it focused on the human element of managing change and planned for resistance. It set expectations (a clear vision), focused on employee development, and reinforced behavior by creating a learning culture.

Planned Collaboration. The Borough of Manhattan Community College was successful because of its cross-functional planning and removal of obstacles.

All three cases recognized the power employees had in the transformation and harnessed that perceived power into a launching point for their respective changes.

Conclusion

The evolution of change management practices is a reflection of broader shifts in management principles over the years. Initially, management focused on optimizing efficiency and productivity through structured, top-down approaches, as seen in early models like Lewin's. However, as organizations and their environments became more complex, the need for more adaptive and human-centric approaches emerged. Models like those of Bridges and Kotter highlight a growing recognition of the psychological and cultural dimensions of change, emphasizing the importance of leadership, communication, and employee engagement.

With the advent of Industry 4.0 and the transition to Industry 5.0, management principles have further evolved to integrate digital advancements with a renewed focus on human creativity and well-being. This evolution underscores the shift from purely mechanistic views to more holistic and agile management practices that value the contributions of employees at all levels. Training, skill development, and reinforcement are now seen as essential components of successful change initiatives, reflecting a deeper understanding of the need to support and empower employees through continuous learning and engagement.

By embracing these evolved management principles, organizations can navigate the complexities of modern business environments more effectively, ensuring that technological and human elements are harmoniously integrated to drive sustainable growth and innovation. This journey from rigid structures to dynamic, people-centered strategies marks a significant transformation in how management is practiced and perceived, aligning with the overarching goal of achieving long-term organizational success in an ever-changing world.

Ultimately, the key to thriving in today's dynamic environment lies in bridging the gap between strategy and execution, prioritizing both technological and human elements to achieve lasting and meaningful change.

References

Agrawal, S., Agrawal, R., Kumar, A. & Luthra, S., Garza-Reyes, J. A. (2023). Can industry 5.0 technologies overcome supply chain disruptions? – a perspective study on pandemics, war, and climate change issues. *Operations Management Research*. https://doi.org/10.1007/s12063-023-00410-y

Ahmed, M. & Pathan, A. K. (2019). *Data Analytics: Concepts, Techniques, and Applications*. CRC Press. Taylor & Francis Group.

Bridges, W. (2004). *Transitions: Making Sense of Life's Changes*. Da Capo Press.

Cannavacciuolo, L., Capaldo, G., & Ponsiglione, C. (2023). Digital innovation and organizational changes in the healthcare sector: Multiple case studies of telemedicine project implementation, *Technovation (120)*. 102550. ISSN 0166-4972, https://doi.org/10.1016/j.technovation.2022.102550.

Christou, E. & Piller, F. (2024). Organizational transformation: A management research perspective. In: Letmathe, P. et al. (2024). *Transformation Towards Sustainability*. Springer, Cham. https://doi.org/10. 1007/978-3-031-54700-3_11

Covey, S. R. (1989). *The 7 Habits of Highly Effective People*. Simon & Schuster (formerly Free Press).

Cummings, S., Bridgman, T., & Brown, K. G. (2016). Unfreezing change as three steps: Rethinking Kurt Lewin's legacy for change management. *Human Relations, 69*(1), 33–60.

Da Veiga, A. (2018). An approach to information security culture change combining ADKAR and the ISCA questionnaire to aid transition to the desired culture. *Information and Computer Security, 26*(5), 584–612. http://dx.doi.org/10.1108/ICS-08-2017-0056

Derricks, J. (2018). Effective internal monitoring and auditing for change management. *The Journal of Medical Practice Management: MPM, 34*(2), 77–80.

Fennell, M. L. & Alexander, J. A. (1993). Perspectives on organizational change in the US medical care sector. *Annual Review of Sociology, 19*, 89–112. http://www.jstor.org/stable/2083382

Hanelt, A., Bohnsack, R., Marz, D. & Antunes Marante, C. (2021). A systematic review of the literature on digital transformation: Insights and implications for strategy and organizational change. *Journal of Management Studies, 58*(5), 1159–1197. https://doi.org/10.1111/joms.12639

Harrison, R., Fischer, S., Walpola, R. L., Chauhan, A., Babalola, T., Mears, S., & Le-Dao, H. (2021). Where do models for change management, improvement and implementation meet? A systematic review of the applications of change management models in healthcare. *Journal of Healthcare Leadership, 13*, 85–108.

Helms-Mills, J., Dye, K., & Mills, A. J. (2008). *Understanding Organizational Change*. Taylor & Francis Group.

Hubbart, J. A. (2023). Organizational change: Considering truth and buy-in. *Administrative Sciences, 13*(3). https://doi.org/10.3390/admsci13010003

Kotter, J. P. (1996). *Leading Change*. Harvard Business Review Press.

Mohajan, H. (2021). Third industrial revolution brings global development. *Journal of Social Sciences and Humanities, 7*(4), 239–251.

Nahavandi, S. (2019). Industry 5.0: A human-centric solution. *Sustainability, 11*(16), 4371.

Patterson, K., Grenny, J., Maxfield, D., McMillan, R., & Switzler, A. (2000). *Influencer*. McGraw-Hill Professional Publishing.

Phillips, P. P., & Phillips, J. J. (2019). Combining motivational forces to deliver team performance and a positive ROI. *Strategic HR Review, 18*(3), 109–115. https://doi.org/10.1108/SHR-03-2019-0015

Ramadan, M., Zakhem, N.B., Baydoun, H., Daouk, A., Youssef, S., Fawal, A.E., Elia, J., & Ashaal, A. (2023). Toward digital transformation and business model innovation: The nexus between leadership, organizational agility, and knowledge transfer. *Administrative Sciences Journal, 13*(185), 1–21. https://doi.org/10.3390/admsci13080185

Robinson, A. G. (2022) Social intelligence and successful strategic change management: A study of Jubilee Syringe Manufacturing Co. Ltd, Akwa Ibom State, Nigeria. *International Journal of Business and Management Review, 10*(3), 1–19.

Rosenbaum, D., More, E., & Steane, P. (2018). Planned organisational [sic] change management. *Journal of Organizational Change Management, 31*(2), 286–303. http://dx.doi.org/10.1108/JOCM-06-2015-0089

Stouten, J., Rousseau, D., & De Cremer, D. (2018). Successful organizational change: Integrating the management practice and scholarly literatures. *Academy of Management Annals, 12*(2), 752–788. https://doi.org/10.5465/annals.2016.0095

Suddaby, R., & Foster, W. M. (2017). History and organizational change. *Journal of Management, 43*(1), 19–38. https://doi.org/10.1177/0149206316675031

Vineyard, S., Fitz, D., Larkins, L., & Parker, A. (2020). Reimagine the financial management workforce for success in an age of innovation. *The Journal of Government Financial Management, 68*(4), 44–49.

Walleser, D. K. (2018). Managing change in a new enrollment management culture. *Strategic Enrollment Management Quarterly, 6*(3), 7–13.

Wheelan, S.A., Akerlund, M., & Jacobsson, C. (2021). *Creating Effective Teams: A Guide for Members and Leaders* (6th ed.). Los Angeles, CA: Sage Publications. ISBN: 9781544332970.

Wong, Q., Lacombe, M., Keller, R., Joyce, T, & O'Malley, K. (2019). Leading change with ADKAR, *Nursing Management (Springhouse), 50*(4), 28–35. doi: 10.1097/01.NUMA.0000554341.

Syed Adeel Ahmed, Brendan Moore, and Cathy Rehfus-Wilsek
3 Planning for Technological Change

Abstract: In this chapter, we cover ways in which leadership models have changed and been innovated upon. Because of recent changes in globalization, international regulations, supply chain disruptions, technological breakthroughs, and organizational cultural shifts, leaders must adapt their leadership styles and how they approach leading their teams and organizations. We outline as a response to these changes a competency, skills-based approach to leadership development as well as needs-based assessments of talent development needs of employees.

Introduction

Business leaders often struggle with the timing and extent of adopting technological changes. This challenge brings anxiety about balancing cost reduction and efficiency gains. As Satell (2013) observes, new technologies often enter the market with great fanfare, but disappointment soon sets in until practices and processes catch up, unleashing new value. Whether a business can take advantage of this new value depends on how well leaders can avoid chasing the "next shiny object," stick to a well-thought-out plan, and position their business for success. In this chapter, we explore challenges and opportunities surrounding technological change and give recommendations on strategic planning approaches for leaders and managers navigating the complexities of technological change.

Throughout this chapter, we suggest solutions business leaders and managers can adopt to better plan for technological change. This involves strategic planning, environmentally scanning your business' industry for opportunities for digitization and new technologies, avoiding evaluating technologies on their own merits, and reviewing the strategy for implementation.

Technological change is inevitable. Nobel (2014) points out that Swiss watchmakers were industry leaders for centuries until the 1970s when Japanese manufacturers introduced affordable, precise quartz watches. In some cases, like Swiss watches or fountain pens, older or retro technologies may be chosen for their nostalgic and aesthetic appeal rather than their cost-effectiveness, efficiency, or practicality.

While in most cases of substantial innovation, technological change involves a definitive step, in some cases outdated technologies will still be used. Retro-mechanical watches are one such example. Vinyl records, old video games, and fashion are other industries where fads can still occur. However, when purely considering efficiency in cost and training surrounding and utilizing technology for business purposes, rather than nostalgic or stylistic purposes, a technological change rarely reverts to an older,

https://doi.org/10.1515/9783111316987-003

previously used technology. In other words, if the business practices do not stay up to date and leadership adapts to tech-savvy practices, the inferior technology will disappear over time, creating new challenges and opportunities.

Challenges and Opportunities

One opportunity that arises when a market transformation happens is a business can become an early adopter and springboard into integrating the created value of the new technology into their product and services. Kelly-Detwiler (2013) suggests that once a market is changed, the benefits are permanent, and the outdated technology is eventually phased out, while the new technology serves as a foundation for further advancements and market growth. An example is the movement from written Emergency Medical Records (EMR) and Emergency Health Records (EHR), shifting from handwritten documents to electronic, digital formats stored in databases, such as Oracle or EPIC. Record digitization enables hospitals to communicate between one another more quickly about patient records and medical history while also cutting down costs surrounding document storage for the Human Resources and Legal departments. Technological changes surrounding digitization across all industries are technological changes that business leaders, employees, and managers often view as critical.

A case study from MIT indicated that digital transformation will be critical in the coming years, so companies should brainstorm in the current context how digitization will affect their businesses. Fitzgerald et al. (2013) reported that nearly 80% of respondents believed digital transformation would be crucial for their organizations within the next 2 years. Besides digitization, businesses are moving to cloud computing software solutions for their storage and service needs. While it is possible larger companies can better manage risk since they have significant resources, impact can be greater on smaller businesses because adopting and utilizing technological changes enables them to better compete in their industry.

Smaller businesses, such as clinics, compared to larger hospital systems, cannot afford to develop in-house security software and patient information storage protections affordably, so many move to cloud computing. McAfee (2012) suggests that existing business models are quickly becoming obsolete as a result of cloud computing, new security challenges, and consumers' demands for superior access to information. Customer demands are often shaped by their experience with other companies. For example, a customer who is used to interfacing with Amazon's online web interface might find a company's sales portal challenging to navigate if it differs significantly from other companies they interact with. Integrating business processes around a technological change is important. One effective way businesses can ensure an integrated approach includes departmental voices is through the creation of a strategic plan.

When done well, a strategic plan can define for leaders and employees a shared direction the company can take in the coming years. Generally, the company's vision, mission, and values are reflected in its business approach and the types of products and services it offers. Aligning the department, division, and teams' technology portfolio with the company's goals will help define what technological changes need to be planned for.

However, some technological changes are unplanned, and teams are forced to adapt quickly to shifting industry practices. Green and Hedges (2012) point out that even well-crafted strategic plans rarely unfold exactly as intended. Flexibility, adaptability, and resiliency are qualities that need to be thought of ahead of time before a disaster recovery scenario occurs. In the next section, we will discuss models for success and how to best evaluate technology and assess its compatibility with organizational goals.

Model for Success

Often, managers and leaders will look around at their competition and assume they should simply adopt whatever technology has the best marketing potential, regardless of their business needs. Davidson (2019) argues that a technology's value should be assessed based on how its implementation enables a business to achieve things that its competitors cannot rather than on its own merits. While following the latest and greatest technologies in an industry seems like a good decision and easy to justify as an expense, leaders and managers should examine their current technology portfolios and compare their business and organizational needs with their current technology performance. The increased costs might not justify the upgrade or slight improvement, company-wide. However, sometimes new technologies can reduce cost and a business can tap into the value added by the technological change immediately.

Costs should always be taken into account. Davidson (2019) points out that new technologies can paradoxically be both a significant source of expenses for a business and a means of eliminating its greatest costs. For example, Zoom and Microsoft Teams have quickly replaced webinar applications, phone calls, and older videoconferencing applications, such as Skype and other competitors for many companies. This is because these platforms provide more robust features, better usability, and integrated collaboration tools at a lower cost than traditional solutions. Involving the IT department and other stakeholders in any technological change is important. Consider the following before implementing organizational changes:

1. Digital first: Prioritizing digital investments is essential for successful digital transformation. As Fitzgerald et al. (2013) reported, nearly 80% of respondents believed digital transformation would be crucial for their organizations within the next 2 years, emphasizing the need to integrate digital initiatives into the overall strategy.

2. Strategically integrated: Digital transformation requires a company-wide effort rather than isolated experiments. Green and Hedges (2012) point out that even well-crafted strategic plans rarely unfold exactly as intended, underscoring the importance of flexibility and adaptability in the face of changing circumstances.
3. Highlight strengths: Companies should focus on their unique strengths and differentiators when developing their digital strategy. Davidson (2019) suggests that the value of a technology lies in its ability to enable a business to achieve things that its competitors cannot rather than its intrinsic merits.
4. Leverage Information Technology: Engaging IT teams early and often is crucial for successful digital initiatives. Satell (2013) highlights the importance of collaboration between different groups within the organization, citing IBM's Global Director of Public Safety, Mark Cleverley, who sees his role as extending analytical capabilities to a wider range of nonspecialist employees.
5. Prepare to change course: Companies should be willing to pivot or stop digital initiatives that are not working. Nisen (2012) argues that not every digital initiative will succeed, and that's acceptable. The key is to learn from failures and continue moving forward, emphasizing the importance of adaptability in the face of setbacks.

Information technology professionals can help communicate upcoming technological changes to the rest of the company's departments, leaders, and employees. Integrating the technological change into orientation and training through the human resources department will help set employee expectations regarding acceptable use policy for the technology. Additionally, organizational meetings and discussions on the subject will provide an opportunity for those who resist change or reject adoption to provide feedback and suggestions.

The technological change process should be inclusive. All stakeholders and departments need to be involved before a company-wide adoption of a new technology. A key benefit of this collaborative approach is to reconcile and integrate the diverse technological needs of departments. For example, given the different business needs of clinic vs. corporate offices for a hospital, an all-encompassing enterprise resource management software (ERMS) would not serve the needs of both. The clinic would need to ensure that patient information is private and protected (e.g., does not violate Health Insurance Portability and Accountability Act of 1994 [HIPAA] requirements), and this necessity may be overlooked by the human resources and operations departments. There could be many instances where big data analytics can be misused in organizations when organizational perspectives are limited.

Another area of technological change concern pertains to the use of big data analytics in customer research. If used incorrectly, leaders and managers might end up collecting useless data. Big data needs to be used to give users valuable information. Satell (2013) notes that big data is now facilitating a new type of consumer dialogue that employs natural language processing to analyze and interpret consumer feedback. Similar to HIPPA's requirement for privacy mentioned previously, all stakeholders need to be involved when implementing a new technology and its analytical practices. In the case of healthcare, even if data is collected from a large sample size, in instances where a rare disease is present, patient anonymity may not be possible in accordance with HIPPA guidelines.

Leaders need to determine whether they want to be an early or late adopter of technology. It is important to ask questions such as: Who are early adopters and influencers? Who are secondary adopters? And how would adoption impact the product created and value proposition (Krippendorgg, 2011)?

Aside from these questions, other questions relating to the industry and environment should be analyzed. Uncertainties and assumptions about customer persona, journey, and suppliers should be put in perspective and aligned with strategy. Green and Hedges (2012) advise paying close attention to uncertainties when monitoring the business environment and questioning the validity of assumptions made about markets and customers. If the business is operating effectively, being a secondary adopter might be best. However, if the approach is not working as expected, consider how a technological change can improve metrics surrounding customers' demands. Consider senior consultants and experts who can help transform collected data and turn it into useful business information.

Oftentimes, businesses have an internal marketplace of useful expertise that is not tapped into. For example, a manager at a hospital who wonders how to reduce patient flow or the intake process has experts in their organization who are accessible. They are called the frontline personnel. Satell (2013) points out that one of the significant challenges for management is facilitating effective communication between different groups within the organization, which is why IBM's Global Director of Public Safety, Mark Cleverley, sees a major part of his role as extending analytical capabilities to a wider range of nonspecialist employees. It is important to consider the input of frontline workers since they work directly with customers and are users of the products.

The fundamental economics of an organization must be sound. The value a firm adds for the customer must be less than the cost (financial, social, and environmental) it takes to provide the product or service. Additionally, ensuring the technological change serves customers and aligns well with the vision, mission, and values of the company will ensure that a good reputation is upheld. Pozen (2013) emphasizes that despite the constant changes in our world, economic fundamentals and personal integrity have remained constant principles over the centuries. When planning for technological change, ensure that the technology being implemented reduces cost, enhances customer service, and improves product quality. Utilizing a well-structured approach to planning for technological change should include strategic planning, environmental scanning of the industry for opportunities for digitization and new technologies, avoidance of evaluating technologies on their own merits, and reviewing the strategy for implementation.

Even with a well-structured approach, some technological changes may end up unplanned, and teams are forced to adapt quickly to shifting industry practices. Green and Hedges (2012) point out that even well-crafted strategic plans rarely unfold exactly as intended due to numerous internal and external factors, necessitating some degree of change during implementation. Being flexible, adaptable, and resilient are qualities that need to be thought of ahead of time before a disaster recovery scenario occurs or unforeseen change in current business practices. It is important to develop organizational strategies such as fostering a culture of continuous learning, investing in cross-functional collaboration, or building redundancy into critical systems.

The following case studies demonstrate how companies from different industries have successfully navigated technological change by leveraging their core competencies, investing in innovation, and adapting their business models. These real-world examples provide valuable insights into the strategies and approaches that can help organizations thrive in the face of technological disruption. By examining the experiences of General Electric, Netflix, and Fujifilm, we can draw lessons and best practices that are applicable to businesses across various sectors.

Mini-Case Study 1: General Electric (GE) and the Industrial Internet of Things

Background: General Electric, a multinational conglomerate, recognized the potential of connecting industrial machines and equipment to the Internet, enabling real-time data collection, analysis, and optimization.

Leveraging Core Competencies: GE leveraged its expertise in industrial machinery and developed the Predix platform, an operating system for the Industrial Internet of Things (IIoT). This allowed customers to monitor and optimize their industrial assets.

Results: By embracing IoT technologies, GE has helped its customers improve efficiency, reduce downtime, and drive innovation across various industries such as aviation, healthcare, and energy. GE successfully navigated this technological shift by building on its core competencies.

Mini-Case Study 2: Netflix's Transition from DVD Rentals to Streaming

Background: Netflix, once known for its DVD-by-mail rental service, faced a changing landscape as internet speeds improved and consumer preferences shifted toward streaming video.

Paradigm Shift: Netflix recognized the disruptive potential of streaming technology early on. They invested heavily in developing their streaming platform, partnered with content providers, and began producing original content.

Results: By proactively embracing this technological change, Netflix successfully transformed from a DVD rental company to a global leader in video streaming, with over 200 million subscribers worldwide. Netflix exemplifies how anticipating and decisively acting on technological shifts can redefine a business.

Full Case Study 3: Fujifilm's Transformation from Film to Healthcare Imaging

Background: Fujifilm, a Japanese photography company, faced a significant threat with the rise of digital photography in the late 1990s and early 2000s.

Diversification Strategy: Fujifilm made a strategic decision to diversify its business and explore new industries where its imaging expertise could be applied, particularly healthcare and medical imaging. They invested in R&D to develop cutting-edge medical imaging technologies.

Strategic Partnerships: Fujifilm made key acquisitions and partnerships to accelerate its entry into the healthcare market. This included acquiring Toyama Chemical, a pharmaceutical company, and partnering with Hitachi Medical Corporation on advanced medical imaging systems.

Continuous Innovation: Fujifilm continued to innovate, introducing products like the FDR D-EVO II wireless digital X-ray detector and AI-powered imaging processing software. This established Fujifilm as a leader in medical imaging.

Results: Healthcare is now one of Fujifilm's core business segments, generating significant revenue and growth. Fujifilm's medical imaging and diagnostic equipment are used worldwide, contributing to improved patient care. Fujifilm's successful transformation offers valuable lessons for businesses facing technological change. First, it is crucial to anticipate and embrace technological change, proactively identifying potential disruptions and opportunities. Second, when diversifying into new markets, companies should leverage their core competencies and existing expertise to create value in new domains. Third, investing in continuous innovation is essential to stay ahead of the curve and maintain a competitive edge. Finally, pursuing strategic partnerships and acquisitions can accelerate entry into new markets, providing access to complementary skills and resources that help drive growth and success in the face of technological change. Partnerships and acquisitions aid in the acceleration of entry into new markets.

Fujifilm's successful transformation illustrates how a company can thrive amid disruption by leveraging its expertise to create value in new markets through adaptability, innovation, and strategic decision-making.

The case studies of General Electric, Netflix, and Fujifilm demonstrate how companies from different industries have successfully navigated technological change by embracing key principles. These organizations recognized the need to anticipate and adapt to disruptions, leveraging their core competencies to create value in new markets. They invested in continuous innovation, developed strategic partnerships, and made bold decisions to transform their business models. By doing so, they not only survived but thrived in the face of technological change, setting powerful examples for other companies to follow.

In this chapter, we explored challenges and opportunities surrounding technological change and gave recommendations on strategic planning approaches for leaders and managers navigating the complexities of technological change.

Market transformations provide a unique opportunity for companies to become early adopters of innovative technologies and gain a competitive edge. However, top leadership support is essential for any technological change. Environmental scans can aid in the planning process, and the use of a strategic plan would be helpful.

We discussed the benefits of strategic planning but also recognized that even utilizing planning tools cannot prevent disruption in every industry. However, flexibility, adaptability, and resiliency were emphasized as ways a company can adapt to unforeseen technological changes.

Concerning models of success, we discussed the pitfalls of immediately adopting new technologies. Ensuring technology is evaluated based on how it helps the organization achieve its goals rather than on its own merits is crucial. We used examples to emphasize that costs should always be evaluated and that sound economic fundamentals and personal integrity should be preserved. We provided guidelines and key considerations for leaders and managers to decide when and how to adopt new technologies. Utilizing a business' internal talent marketplace can provide valuable expert insights into the organization's needs.

Overall, we recommend a well-structured approach to planning for technological change that involves several key components. First, strategic planning is crucial to set a clear direction and align organizational efforts. Second, environmental scanning of the industry helps identify potential opportunities and threats posed by emerging technologies. Third, it is important to avoid evaluating technologies in isolation and instead consider their fit and impact within the broader organizational context. Finally, regularly reviewing strategy implementation allows for necessary adjustments and ensures that the organization stays on track in its technological adoption journey.

Future research could analyze macro-level case studies on the misconceptions and pitfalls of adopting technologies too early or too late. While this chapter aimed to provide practical tools and guidelines for business professionals, insights into the benefits and uses of outdated technologies for niche products and services could also be useful. It is noteworthy that what we have presented could work for various businesses across industries, but leaders and managers must examine their own industry and business practices before applying any model to ensure it is well aligned with their organizational goals.

Contemporary Management Implications

The practice of management has evolved. What were viable approaches in past decades may no longer work in the contemporary, technologically driven business environment. Contemporary managers need to consider the following in the context of technological change:

– Digital transformation is critical and business leaders must navigate these changes effectively.

- Strategic planning and environmental scanning help identify opportunities and align technology with business goals.
- Avoid evaluating technologies in isolation; consider organizational fit and impact.
- Engage all stakeholders early in the process for successful implementation.
- Learn from case studies of companies that successfully navigated technological shifts.
- Remain flexible and adaptable as even the best-laid plans can be disrupted.
- Leverage internal expertise and frontline insights when assessing new technologies.
- Ensure sound economic fundamentals and alignment with company values.
- Continuously review and adjust strategy based on changing circumstances.

By thinking through and building on these key considerations, contemporary business leaders can confidently steer their organizations through the complexities of techno-logical change.

References

Davidson, E. (2019). The Advantages of New Technology for Businesses, *Chron, Business and Technology*. Retrieved January 15, 2024. https://smallbusiness.chron.com/advantages-new-technology-businesses-4047.html

Fitzgerald, M., Kruschwitz, N., Bonnet, D., and Welch, M. (2013). Embracing Digital Technology: A New Strategic Imperative, *MIT Sloan Management Review*, October, 7. https://sloanreview.mit.edu/projects/embracing-digital-technology/

Green, H., Hedges, K. (2012). Strategy Ain't What it Used to Be, *Forbes, Leadership*, September 11. https://www.forbes.com/sites/work-in-progress/2012/09/11/strategy-aint-what-it-used-to-be/?sh=6b3727026cd6

Kelly-Detwiler, P. (2013). How Walmart And G.E. Are Leading A Transformation In The Energy Market, *Forbes, Innovation-Sustainability*, September 30. https://www.forbes.com/sites/peterdetwiler/2013/09/30/walmart-ge-and-lighting-a-case-study-in-market-transformation/?sh=6e2b8a154ba3

Krippendorff, K. (2011). The Flow of Technology Adoption Reverses, *Fast Company*, May 26. https://www.fastcompany.com/1755281/flow-technology-adoption-reverses

McAfee, A. (2012). Leverage Technology for Business Transformation, *Harvard Business Review*, August 17. https://hbr.org/2012/08/leverage-technology-for-busine

Nisen, M. (2012). There's A Big Misconception About How Companies Become Tech-Savvy, *Business Insider, Strategy*, November 14. https://www.businessinsider.com/theres-a-big-misconception-about-how-companies-become-tech-savvy-2012-11

Nobel, C. (2014). Technology Re-emergence: Creating New Value for Old Innovations, *Harvard Business Review, Leadership*, January 6. https://www.forbes.com/sites/hbsworkingknowledge/2014/01/06/technology-re-emergence-creating-new-value-for-old-innovations/?sh=2d47b11f30ed

Pozen, R. C. (2013). Embrace Change, But Still Stand for Something, *Harvard Business Review, Career Planning*, January 3. https://hbr.org/2013/01/embrace-change-but-still-stand

Satell, G. (2013). Yes, Big Data Can Solve Real World Problems, *Forbes, Tech*, December 3. https://www.forbes.com/sites/gregsatell/2013/12/03/yes-big-data-can-solve-real-world-problems/?sh=17c94f858896

Sunando Das and J. Mark Munoz

4 Creating Strategic Value through Digital Reinvention

Abstract: The digital economy is huge, with a significant contribution and potential from AI. However, there is quite a distance to go on the success rate of AI initiatives. This chapter will talk about authors' perspectives on different ways AI can drive sizeable business impact/benefits as well as recognition of where human creativity will still hold the fort, hence the required management evolution in the reinvention of existing practices and recalibration of organizational structures to realize these benefits.

Introduction

The digital economy contributed $2.6 trillion to the $25.7 trillion US economy in 2022 (Bureau of Economic Analysis, US Department of Commerce,2023). The digital economy grew an average of 7.1% from 2017 to 2022 and generated 8.9 million jobs in 2022 (Bureau of Economic Analysis, 2023) in the United States alone. The substantial size of the digital economy is not limited to the United States but is a global phenomenon, with growth further accelerating in the last 2 years. This is evident from the fact that the contribution of digitally transformed enterprises increased from $13.5 trillion in 2018 to a projected $53.3 trillion of the global nominal GDP in 2023, accounting for more than half of the overall global nominal GDP (Taylor, 2024). This sizable contribution of the digital economy and digitally transformed enterprises underscores the need for firms to strengthen and refine their digital strategy to stay competitive. Artificial intelligence (AI) and machine learning (ML) have been established to be key enablers for the successful development and deployment of a digital strategy.

However, the success rate of AI and ML applications in driving business impact leaves a lot to be achieved, despite huge progress and advancements. Boston Consulting Group (BCG) had estimated in 2018 that AI and ML applications in the consumer product goods (CPG) industry can drive annual incremental growth by 10%+. However, the conundrum is that the industry growth (excluding inflation) was far lower than 10% in many CPG sectors during 2020–2022, let alone the component of growth enabled by ML and AI applications. This is due to a proportion of underperformance of the AI models since the start of disruptions 3 to 4 years back (first COVID-19, followed by macroeconomic uncertainty due to inflation). As per the McKinsey (2020) state of AI report, a significant proportion of respondents from AI high performers stated that their models underperformed

Note: This chapter represents the views of Sunando Das and J. Mark Munoz based on the body of work over the last decade and does not represent the views or work of any particular organization.

https://doi.org/10.1515/9783111316987-004

within business functions where AI is used most. This underperformance was across business functions, with varying rates of underperformance by function.

With the advent of generative AI, adoption of AI has increased significantly. As per the McKinsey State of AI in Early 2024 report, AI adoption in organizations (i.e. organizations that have adopted AI in at least one business function) has increased from an average of 50% in the last 6 years to 72% in 2024 driven by generative AI adoption. However, this higher adoption has not translated to a commensurate business impact yet. In an Oliver Wyman (2024) report, while 55% of employees use generative AI, 61% of users do not find it trustworthy. The *Wall Street Journal* 2024 article 'Generative AI Isn't Ubiquitous in the Business World—at Least Not Yet' the title speaks for itself. Oliver Wyman's 2024 report, 'How Generative AI is Transforming Business and Society,' estimates that the full potential of generative AI's productivity gains is 6 to 10 years away.

These pose two questions to enable strategic value creation through digital transformation specifically focusing on the role of AI and ML within digital transformation:

- **Reinvention**: How to drive a reinvention of AL and ML applications to increase success rates of AI initiatives? This will enable a higher business impact of AI initiatives.
- **Holistic Convergence**: How to carefully select generative AI use cases, understand where generative AI can drive strategic impact vs where not, and how to converge generative AI with broader AI capabilities for holistic business cases and drive business impact sooner? This will enable a successful move from the pilot euphoria stage to the business-as-usual deployment stage.

A strategic operational recalibration is essential (Munoz, 2021). The benefits of reinvention and holistic convergence cannot be realized without organizational recalibration on people skill sets and organizational structures.

In this chapter, we will delve into these two topics of reinvention and holistic convergence and outline how to increase the success rate of AI initiatives to enable value creation from strategic digital transformations. Furthermore, we will discuss how organizational recalibration will be required in enabling reinvention and holistic convergence. These activities will enable a higher success rate and business impact of AI initiatives, be it broader AI capabilities existing before the advent of generative AI or the specific generative AI capability. For this chapter, the word 'AI (Artificial Intelligence)' will refer to all AI applications (which have existed even before the advent of generative AI) excluding generative AI, and the word 'generative AI' will refer to generative AI/large language models (LLMs)/small language models (SLMs).

Value Creation through Digital Reinvention

There are six strategic reinvention approaches that firms can implement to increase the success rate of machine learning (ML) and artificial intelligence (AI) initiatives and accelerate the value creation of digital transformation programs.

1) Design Thinking Beyond AI

AI and ML algorithms learn from past data patterns to predict the future, which is a fundamental tenet of AI and ML. For instance, in the manufacturing sector, AI can have an impact on the monitoring and correction of the manufacturing process, supply chain, and production planning (PWC, 2017). However, with disruptions over the last 4 years (first COVID-19, followed by unprecedented economic disruptions and inflationary pressures), it takes time for data to build up before algorithms can even predict based on learning from the initial data and improve over time. Hence, the need to move from predicting the future of a known past to predicting the future of an unknown past.

This is where generating proxies from different data sources, especially digital data, creating multiple small ML/AI models feeding into a bigger model, and combining game theory with ML can tackle the challenges. It is about smart, creative thinking to design and approach the problem in a holistic way considering the limitations of data and algorithms.

Firms should find a convergence of expertise across AI/ML algorithms and behavioral economics to foresee the future and bring certainty to the uncertainty in business decisions.

2) Explainable AI at scale

There are AI algorithms such as neural networks, which are very good at prediction but are data-hungry models and are not good at explaining the reasons for the prediction. On the other hand, there are algorithms (such as classification models like XGBoost, support vector machines, and many more), which are good at explanations with reasonable accuracy including high accuracy in many business contexts.

In a business context, without having a good explanation and reasons for the prediction, it is difficult to act on the findings emerging from an AI model. For example, predicting the demand for products, predicting the rate at which consumers, channels, and categories will evolve, predicting the impact of advertising and new product launches, or predicting the likely churn rate are all extremely valuable. However, these predictions become much more useful when the drivers of these predictions are included to help understand what is accelerating or decelerating the predictions. These will enable firms to move from prediction to shaping growth, which will determine the business impact of AI initiatives. In other words, explainable AI will help move from prediction to incremental demand generation. Explainable AI is no longer an optional nice-to-have but a must-have to drive the impact of AI initiatives.

Explainable AI is as much about human expertise as it is about algorithmic evolutions. Even with deep neural networks, there are ways to get to explanations today till algorithmic evolutions can enable that in the future, for example, harnessing Shapley to get diagnostics around the drivers of the neural network prediction or having multiple specific models with explainable algorithms feeding into a final neural network model.

3) Connecting and augmenting organizational siloes for an integrated, holistic view:

There can be multiple AI initiatives running in parallel by different business functions within an organization. AI can be helpful in predicting sales (Huang and Rust, 2021), and this activity is intertwined with several other business activities, for example, pricing, consumer promotion, media mix optimizations, and creative excellence. However, these are interconnected – pricing strategy will have an impact on consumer promotion strategy as well as on the magnitude of impact media can drive. The key is to integrate these initiatives for a holistic view and an overall organizational drive. Without such integrations, the different outcomes from different AI models and initiatives will not be in consonance, i.e., strategies deployed from one model can reduce the impact of the strategies deployed from another model, resulting in the overall return on investments declining.

Similarly, outcome from an AI model of one business function can feed into the AI model of another business function. For example, demand prediction by the strategic planning team can feed into the supply chain team for procurement and production planning.

4) Big Data vs Small Data to Smart Big Data:

While big data is important and there are ample big data sources within any organization, the ability to act is often limited by the depth of the big data, for example, if there is a transactional database of 15 million customers of a retailer with the database having purchase histories and demographics of each customer – it is useful but only to a limited extent. The database would become more valuable if the database had details for each customer on their share of wallet and behavior with competition retailers, media consumption habits and response to historical campaigns, interest areas based on web behavior, and, hence, propensity to buy different brands and categories. It is extremely difficult to acquire all these details for each customer deterministically and cost-efficiently. However, the depth of the big database can be increased to incorporate these details through a combination of deterministic and probabilistic data. For example, the data on the share of wallet and behavior with competition retailers can be acquired on a sample of customers via survey. The survey data on a sample of customers can be projected to the entire customer database through propensity modeling harnessing ML. This is an example of increasing the depth of big data through a combination of deterministic and probabilistic data, thereby making the big data smarter to enable business impact. Technology has a big role to play here – for example, media consumption habits, interest areas, and responses to past campaigns can be integrated via harnessing third-party probabilistic digital data at scale.

Beyond smart modeling and technology, the partnership ecosystem also has a significant role here. For example, if a first-party customer database does not have sales data (industries without access to sales data at the customer level such as some consumer product goods manufacturers), the ability to showcase value and drive the power of digital intervention strategies becomes limited. This is where partnerships with retailers can help augment first-party data with sales data harnessing the power of technology such as clean rooms.

Increasing the probability of success of AI initiatives starts with data strategy. As illustrated above, harnessing technology, partnership ecosystems, and modeling using ML can help transform isolated big and small datasets into smart, integrated big data, which can help increase the impact of AI initiatives.

5) From thorough measurements with high latency to early warning indicators with low latency

The utopia of continuous learning closed-loop AI models is not achievable for all models in the immediate term due to data and infrastructure challenges. Some of the measurement systems, albeit very thorough, still have high latency to be useful for ongoing business decisions. Hence, the use of proxies from unstructured data as predictive lead indicators of changes in consumer behavior can help close this gap. These predictive lead indicators can feed into AI models to enable continuous-learning closed-loop systems, which will enable interventions in real time to drive business impact. The challenge for firms is to manage the balance between purists and pragmatists, as the margins of error will be higher when working with such proxies.

6) Transference between industries:

While there are significant differences between industries, necessitating domain-specific expertise and applications, there is also transferability of applications between industries.

The concept of driving retention, cross-sell, up-sell, and acquisition propensity models has been prevalent in the financial services and retail sectors for decades but was not possible earlier in consumer product goods industries at the individual consumer or segment level at scale. However, this can be made possible with the model development and consumer activation synchronized, converging first-party data integrations with either panel data or retailer data partnerships. Such synchronization can facilitate the move from past behavior proxies to predictive future behavior proxies as the basis of activation.

Learning from different industries can help conceptualize and implement new applications that were not possible before, thereby expanding the role of AI in driving business impact.

AI initiatives need to be aligned with strategy (Brock and Von Wangenheim, 2019). These six reinvention strategies will help increase the success rate of AI initiatives and, hence, drive value from digital programs. These six reinvention strategies imply company leadership needs to drive organizational culture change at three levels:

- **Human before machine**: 'Design thinking beyond AI' and 'Explainable AI at scale' reinvention strategies imply the need for encouraging and rewarding creative thinking in applying AI algorithms to drive the success of AI initiatives. This has an implication for the mix of skill sets and profiles in the crafting of data, analytics, or AI/ML teams.
- **Integrated view:** 'Smart big data', 'From thorough measurements with high latency to early warning indicators with low latency', and 'Transference between industries' reinvention strategies imply the need for a holistic, integrated view across data strategy, modeling, and business applications. This integrated view implies the need for leadership to design organizational structures that will enable technology, partner ecosystem, and data science teams working in tandem to create much deeper datasets for higher impact. The integrated view also implies that encouraging a mindset of calculated risks and perfection can be the enemy of progress to enable continuous digital intervention without perfection and drive timely impact as well as bringing the outside in from other industries.
- **Connected organization**: 'Connecting organizational siloes to drive impact' reinvention strategy demonstrates the need for leadership to create a connected organization with AI initiatives connected across business functions as well as some of the individual business unit AI initiatives collapsing into organization-wide initiatives transgressing across functions.

AI enhances operational reliability and contributes to ease of scale (Balasubramanian, Ye and Xu, 2022). At the heart of these reinventions is the ability to learn and foresee the future consumer decision-choice process. Without having adequate knowledge of the consumer decision-choice process, a data scientist alone will not be able to drive the reinventions. Similarly, a consumer insights/digital/marketing expert cannot conceptualize the need for these reinventions without being conversant with the art of the possible in AI.

The key task for organizations is to achieve the knowledge convergence of data scientists, consumer insights, and digital and strategy experts. The prerequisite for the knowledge convergence to shape is for the data scientists to acquire knowledge of the different facets of consumer behavioral dynamics and for consumer insights, digital, and strategy experts to acquire knowledge of the art possible in AI/ML. This recalibration of skill set should transcend across organizational hierarchies for it to bear fruit and realize the benefits of the reinvention possibilities.

Value Creation through Holistic Convergence

The steps outlined for value creation through AI/ML reinvention will increase the probability of AI initiatives driving business impact. For example, due to its potential impact on cost reduction, AI can boost ROI (Torres and Mejia, 2017). However, these efforts will not necessarily help increase the probability of driving the business impact of generative AI initiatives. To understand, how to drive the success of generative AI initiatives across industries, it is necessary to look at how generative AI can drive incremental commercial impact in three different ways. These three ways of driving business impact with generative AI correspond to the reinvention of AI applications as these are new business applications of AI not delivered before.

There are three dimensions on which generative AI (large language models/ LLMs) can drive catalytic business impact:

1) **Efficiency/Productivity gains**: For example:
- **Data Science/Data Engineering**: Data science/ML/AI/data engineering teams can reduce significant time by harnessing the benefits of coding assistants such as GitHub Copilot. This will enable unlocking the resource constraints, helping to do more with the same.
- **Creative/Content Development**: Generative AI can harness the historical data across campaigns to create future content such as generating the best executional elements for a content theme, generating the best text for e-commerce end-of-funnel content, evaluating the fit of talent with a brand, developing creative variations for contextual targeting, and driving production efficiencies. These will help drive significant efficiencies in content development.
- **New Product Development**: Generative AI can harness billions of unstructured text/image social media data, search data, and ratings and reviews data to uncover ideas for new product development to enable incremental growth. This is not a new application of AI. AI has been harnessed since 2015–2016 to drive this application. What generative AI is doing is bringing significant efficiencies in driving this application. Before the advent of generative AI/large language models, specific natural language processing (NLP) models were developed and applied to the data, which required high training and tuning effort. Any changes implied significant time in model retuning. Generative AI provided generalized large language models with fast fit-for-purpose adaptations, which drove significant efficiencies in deploying this application.
- **Customer Experience**: Generative AI can enable more accurate chatbots enabling faster, personalized, and better customer support query resolution, thereby driving customer satisfaction. And it is not just customer support query resolution where generative AI can transform customer experience; there are other applications too. For example, creating conversational interfaces to enable tailored and personalized content discovery in real time.

2) **Intelligence**, that is, enabling applications that were not possible before or transforming existing applications. For example:

- **Sparse data**: In many AI models, the challenge is the magnitude of missing data or the sparseness of data. Generating and harnessing reliable synthetic data is one of the ways of overcoming this challenge in many models. LLMs can be harnessed to create reliable synthetic data to train a customized fit-for-purpose AI model. This improves the data coverage in AI models, which in turn improves the reliability of the AI models.

- **Transforming existing applications**: For example, companies spend millions in testing marketing stimuli such as testing creative concepts and products before launch to assess the probability of in-market success and, accordingly, refine plans. With the databases of historic in-market launches/relaunches, in-market performance, investments to support the launches/relaunches, and each launch/relaunch decoded into a set of features, LLMs can predict the likely success of any new marketing stimuli without the need for testing. Such an LLM engine will work for a large majority of stimuli unless the stimulus is a catalytically new one and does not resemble any of the past launches/relaunches, in which case traditional testing will be the only solution. With the LLM engine, there will still be a need for a specific proportion of testing every year to augment the database to remain relevant going forward. However, for a large majority of the stimuli, LLM can predict the likely success without the need for any testing.

- **Connected Applications**: LLM can help in connecting different AI applications, thereby creating a connected holistic organizational viewpoint. For example, the optimal price pack architecture emerging from a price optimization model can feed into the supply chain, product development, procurement, and factory planning. Such models can help connect multiple parts of the organization with an always-on platform to understand the implications of changes in strategy in one part of the organization on another part of the organization in real time and, accordingly, deploy necessary interventions quickly. For example, if the revenue growth management team recommends a new pack size with cost-benefit analysis, it feeds into product development work plans, which feeds into procurement work plans followed by product development (packaging team) work plans, and factory planning, with a feedback mechanism incorporated between different teams but all these are happening in real time. These applications require the combination of LLMs and knowledge graphs, both of which are recent advancements in AI and have transformed how we process and comprehend information.

3) **User Experience**, that is, enhancing user experience and democratizing AI applications. For example:

- **Chatbots/Virtual Agents**: LLMs can not only drive efficiencies in addressing customer support queries but also enhance user experience with fast, accurate, and

personalized human-like responses, thereby increasing satisfaction and revenue per customer.
– **Personalized experiences**: LLMs can enable personalized product recommendations, personalized content creation, and tailored content discovery in real time to enhance user experience and facilitate search. These have applications across media and advertising, online retail, financial services, telecom, educational, and healthcare sectors.

There is no doubt that the opportunities are immense with LLMs (generative AI). However, this begs the question as to why the business impact of generative AI initiatives is still below its potential, as outlined in the 'Introduction' section. Business impact can be either in terms of incremental revenues, i.e., driving more impact, or decreased costs, i.e., driving the same impact for lower costs. Company leadership can enable four recalibrations to enable a higher business impact.

Better together: Often generative AI is not an application in isolation but has to be combined with existing practices including existing AI models for an overall framework. This can be done only when one is cognizant of what generative AI can do vs. what it cannot do. Without this knowledge, there is likely to be an overpromise of the possibilities of generative AI, which can lead to expectation-delivery mismatch. For example, if we take the area of content development, generative AI can drive combinatorial applications, i.e., combining and identifying from existing data. This can enable the development of executional elements given a content theme, end-of-funnel conversion content, and creative variations for contextual targeting and personalization. However, it cannot drive a transformative new content theme based on uncovering a new consumer need to drive relevance and differentiation of the brand. This transformative new content theme will still need to be based on existing insights practices where the role of humans will be critical. As this example of content development illustrates, it is about knowing when generative AI can play a role vs when not and harnessing the power of 'Man + Machine' for a full-funnel content development program. Organizational leadership needs to inculcate this thinking of 'better together' among its workforce at all levels. Social and organizational structures need to be reformed in the digital transformation process (Selander and Jarvenpaa, 2016). The process affects operational models as well as the organization's ecosystem (Reis and Melao, 2023).

Invest in training and technology and not only technology: Given a new field with unfamiliarity and misperceptions coexisting with excitement, it is imperative to invest in training with customized training programs by business functions alongside technology investments. Organizational leadership needs to empower and expand its learning organization with tangible, measurable metrics to evaluate the progress of workforce skill sets in this area. A McKinsey (2018) report noted the importance of digitally knowledgeable leaders, future capability planning, people empowerment, digital tools upgrades, and effective communication as essential to digital transformation success.

Training LLMs with own data and developing applications: While open-source generative AI platforms can enable a lot of knowledge and information search, strategic applications can be achieved by training generalized LLMs with their own custom data, which takes time and effort. This has an implication on the skill sets required within organizations, be it for developing such applications internally or evaluating the offerings of vendors. This can imply bringing in new talents and skill sets. Organizational leadership needs to account for a change in the shape of the workforce in the coming years and gradually prepare for the same. Digital leadership commitment is essential in the transformation process (Leal-Rodriguez et al., 2023).

Learning organization: As Peter Senge (2021) outlined in his book *The Fifth Discipline*, in the long run, the only sustainable source of competitive advantage is the organization's ability to learn faster than the competition. In the context of generative AI, in the relatively early stages of today, players piloting, learning, developing, and deploying business applications at scale successfully will have a competitive advantage. However, as this area matures in the future, many of the applications will become business as usual. Till that time, an organizational culture of experimentation with openness to failures but ensuring a minimum success rate of experiments with scaled business impact will be critical. Companies face digital transformation challenges primarily due to resistance to change, legal and compliance issues, cost perceptions, inadequate ROI data, and unclear alignment with customer research (Solis, 2019).

Concluding Thoughts

This chapter established the relevance and high importance of creating digitally transformed enterprises. A Research and Markets (2020) report indicated that the global digital transformation market is projected to be at $1,009.8 billion by 2025. One of the key enablers of creating digitally transformed enterprises is the role of AI and ML. Digital literacy is growingly important (Davison and Ou, 2017). However, the business impact of AI initiatives, be it AI capabilities in existence for the last 5 to 6 years or the emerging capabilities of generative AI, has been lower than the initial promise. This chapter outlined the required reinventions in AI applications to enable a higher business impact in line with the promise of AI and illustrated that people and organizational recalibrations are required to enable these reinventions.

As business leaders step into an interesting future with an accelerated business impact of AI and generative AI initiatives, three thoughts need to be carefully considered. Firstly, just like there are well-accepted industry metrics for measuring competitiveness in different aspects, there is a need to measure the state of digitally evolved enterprises. Choi et al. (2024) define digital strategic posture (DSP) as a measure of a firm's overall strategic stance toward investing in information technology (IT) initiatives relative to that of rival firms. It is necessary to measure metrics not specific to IT initiatives only but also broader investment in AI initiatives with quantification on the magnitude of the incremental business impact either in driving productivity gains and/or enabling business applications that were not possible before, thereby driving incremental revenues.

Secondly, while in this chapter, the emphasis has been on the end business applications, there are also reinventions required in the transparency, security, and hardware space, for example, potential expanded usage of blockchain for speed, transparency, and security across multiple industries beyond financial services. Immutability and trustworthiness are among the important features of blockchain technology (Pournader et al., 2020).

Thirdly, strong business intelligence and a thorough understanding of the external environment are essential. Market forces such as growth, competition, and regulatory policies spur organizational transformation (Solis, 2019).

In a growingly digital and competitive world, business leaders need to build strong and compelling organizational values in order to succeed. The right alignment of digital architecture, skilled personnel, supportive leadership, and a strategic reinvention approach are major steps in the right direction.

References

Balasubramanian, N., Ye, Y., & Xu, M. (2022). Substituting human decision-making with machine learning: Implications for organizational learning. *Academy of Management Review, 47*: 448–465.

Brock, J.K, and Wangenheim, F.V. (2019). Demystifying AI: What digital transformation leaders can teach you about realistic artificial intelligence. California Management Review, *61*: 110–34.

Bureau of Economic Analysis (2023). US digital economy: New and revised estimates 2017–2022. Accessed July 3, 2024. Viewable at: https://apps.bea.gov/scb/issues/2023/12-december/1223-digital-economy. htm?_gl=1*jggj89*_ga*MTc0NTUxNzM1MC4xNzIwMDIyNTUz*_ga_J4698JNNFT* MTcyMDAyMjU1My4xLjEuMTcyMDAyMjk5My42MC4wLjA.

Progressive Policy Institute (2024). The US Digital Economy on its own would be the world's eighth largest economy. Viewable at https://www.progressivepolicy.orq/bloqs/trade-fact-of-the-week-the-u-s-digital -economy-on-its-own-would-be-the-worlds-eighth-largest-economy/

Choi, I., Cantor, D.E; Han, K., and George, J.F. (2024). Dual Pathways of Value Creation from Digital Strategic Posture: Contingent Effects of Competitive Actions and Environmental Uncertainty, *MIS Quarterly, 48*(1), 409–426.

Davison, R., and Xj Ou, C. (2017). Digital work in a digitally challenged organization. *Information & Management, 54*, 129–37.

Huang, M-H, and Rust, R.T. (2021) Engaged to a Robot? The Role of AI in Service. *Journal of Service Research, 24*(1), 30–41. https://doi.org/10.1177/1094670520902266.

Leal-Rodríguez, A., Sanchís-Pedregosa, C., Moreno-Moreno, A., and Leal-Millán, A. (2023). Digitalization beyond technology: Proposing an explanatory and predictive model for digital culture in organizations. *Journal of Innovation & Knowledge*, 8: 100409.

McKinsey (2018). Unlocking success in digital transformations. Accessed June 27, 2024. Available at: https://www.mckinsey.com/capabilities/people-and-organizational-performance/our-insights/unlocking-success-in-digital-transformations

McKinsey (2020). The State of AI in 2020. Accessed July 3, 2024. Available at: https://www.mckinsey.com/capabilities/quantumblack/our-insights/global-survey-the-state-of-ai-in-2020

Munoz, J. M. (2021). The great recalibration: Ways companies reconfigure to find digital success. *California Management Review Insights*. Accessed July 3, 2021. Available at: https://cmr.berkeley.edu/2021/11/the-great-recalibration-ways-companies-reconfigure-to-find-digital-success/

Oliver Wyman (2024). How generative AI is transforming business and society. Accessed July 3, 2024. Available at: https://www.oliverwymanforum.com/global-consumer-sentiment/how-will-ai-affect-global-economics.html

Pournader, M., Shi, Y., Seuring, S., and Koh, S.C.L. (2020). Blockchain Applications in Supply Chains, Transport and Logistics: A Systematic Review of the Literature. *International Journal of Production Research*, 58(7), 2063–2081.

PWC (2017). Sizing the price: What's the real value of AI for your business and how to capitalize? Accessed June 27, 2024. Available at: https://www.pwc.com/gx/en/issues/analytics/assets/pwc-ai-analysis-sizing-the-prize-report.pdf

Reis, J., and Melão, N. (2023). Digital transformation: A meta-review and guidelines for future research. *Heliyon*, 9, e12834

Research and Markets (2020). The world's digital transformation industry 2020–2025: Trend, opportunities and competitive landscape. Accessed June 27, 2024. Available at: https://www.globenewswire.com/news-release/2020/08/14/2078517/0/en/The-World-s-Digital-Transformation-Industry-2020-2025-Trends-Opportunities-and-Competitive-Landscape.html

Selander, L., and Jarvenpaa, S.L. (2016). Digital action repertoires and transforming a social movement organization. *MIS Quarterly*, 40, 331–52. Available online: https://www.jstor.org/stable/26628909

Senge, P. (2006). *The Fifth Element*. Doubleday: NY.

Solis, B. (2019). Digital is an enterprise-wide strategic priority – but there's work to be done. Accessed June 27, 2024. Available at: https://insights.prophet.com/the-state-of-digital-transformation-2018-2019

Taylor, P. (2022). Nominal GDP driven by digitally transformed and other enterprises worldwide 2018–2023. Statistica. Accessed July 3, 2024. Available at: https://www.statista.com/statistics/1134766/nominal-gdp-driven-by-digitally-transformed-enterprises/

Torres, E. N. & Mejia, C. (2017). Asynchronous Video Interviews in the Hospitality Industry: Considerations for Virtual Employee Selection, *International Journal of Hospitality Management*, 61, 4–13. https://doi.org/10.1016/j.ijhm.2016.10.012

Duane Windsor

5 Responsible and Sustainable Planning in Contemporary Organizations

Abstract: The chapter explicates the current status of responsibility and sustainability approaches in contemporary management. There is an emphasis on possible future developments. Business responsibility and sustainability are crucial elements in sustainable development in expected conditions of climate deterioration.

Introduction

This chapter looks at planning for responsibility and sustainability in contemporary organizations. The chapter's subject matter draws together the three topics of responsibility, sustainability, and planning, including implementation, for integration within organizations. The chapter will contrast different views on responsibility. Among the topics examined will be triple bottom line (TBL), environmental-social-governance (ESG) measures, and UN Sustainable Development Goals (SDGs). The chapter will discuss five critical implications for the future direction of responsibility and sustainability planning: planetary sustainability, business and human rights, expanding expectations for positive social contributions, anticorruption reform as an essential social good, and preparation for unexpected events.

The context is constitutional government and the market system. A constitutional government is one of majoritarian democracy within the rule of law. The conventional market system is regulated and mixed in that governments and not-for-profit organizations typically provide social goods in addition to the private goods typically produced by for-profit organizations. Private or governmental, for-profit or not-for-profit organizations should strive for responsibility and sustainability through targeted planning and implementation. Much of the literature focuses on business responsibility and sustainability, so extrapolation to other organizations is frequently necessary. There is considerable literature in the discipline of business and society bearing on these topics (Brown, de Bakker, Bapuji, Higgins, Rehbein, & Spicer, 2022). A key difference between private and governmental organizations is that the responsibility and sustainability of the latter depend on constitutional and statutory authority. While operating within such authority, private organizations have considerably greater discretion for strategic and policy choices.

The definition of planning is the selection of objectives or targets for achieving the organization's desired future and allocating resources to activities to implement plans (Balanced Scorecard Institute, n.d.). This process involves the determination of the organization's purpose (Neri, 2020). It is essential to recognize that in addition to planning,

https://doi.org/10.1515/9783111316987-005

the selection of objectives and the allocation of resources involves organizational processes (Bower, 2016; Mazzola & Kellermanns, 2010), and there is likely to be an evolution over time of the organization, its leadership, and the external systems within which the organization operates (Barnett & Burgelman, 1996; Tafti, Jahani, & Emami, 2012).

Sustainability is the embeddedness of an organization within its external systems that positively impacts the natural ecology, the societies, and the stakeholders of the business (Rasche, Morsing, Moon, & Kourula, 2023). This definition implies a circular interaction in which the organization's contribution to sustainable external systems increases the organization's sustainability. This combination of goals is complex and challenging (Grabs & Garrett, 2023). The reality of multiple external systems requires some balancing of impacts across these dimensions (Rasche et al., 2023).

Hajian and Kashani (2021) trace the developmental history of sustainability from the 1987 Brundtland Report to sustainable development; this developmental history has come to emphasize the TBL components of planet (environment), people (society), and profit (economy). Like sustainability, responsibility suggests TBL performance (Hourneaux, Gabriel, & Gallardo-Vázquez, 2018; Purvis, Mao, & Robinson, 2019; Slaper & Hall, 2011) and multiple ESG measures (Halbritter & Dorfleitner, 2015; Li, Wang, Sueyoshi, & Wang, 2021).

Responsibility is the integration of multiple obligations (especially ecological, social, and stakeholder) into the organization's operations, processes, and strategy (Rasche et al., 2023). The chief guide to organizational responsibility has been corporate social responsibility (CSR). The developmental history includes the beginning ideas of responsibility, the development of business philanthropy, the acceptance and spread of CSR, and the emergence of various counter-proposals (Carroll, 2021). Carroll separated responsibility into four linked domains: economic, legal, ethical, and philanthropic, prioritized from most important to least important. However, he argued that moral considerations infuse all four domains. Philanthropy is discretionary and thus a matter of strategic judgment.

Challenges and Opportunities

Responsibility and sustainability planning embed complex issues of definition and implementation. The concepts of responsibility and sustainability are controversial. Planning and implementation rest on contested foundations.

One conventional conception of responsibility has been voluntary action of no direct economic value to the organization. For a business, this conception is "the firm's consideration of, and response to, issues beyond the narrow economic, technical, and legal requirements of the firm" to accomplish "social benefits along with the traditional economic gains which the firm seeks" (Davis, 1973, p. 312). This conception means: "Behaviors and practices that extend beyond immediate profit maximization goals and are intended to increase social benefits or mitigate social problems for constituencies external to the firm" (Marquis, Glynn, & Davis, 2007, p. 926); "actions that appear to further some social good, beyond the interests of the firm and that which is required by law" (McWilliams & Siegel, 2002, p. 117). There may be strategic reasons, such as developing reputation and social legitimacy, but there is no definite economic value. This voluntary conception shifts to the government the responsibility to adopt mandatory legal requirements for private organizations; otherwise, an organization is legally free to make choices.

A simple distinction between voluntary and mandatory responsibilities must be revised because the distinction ignores moral or normative understanding by owners, managers, and other stakeholders (Frederick, 1986). The most fundamental obligation of any organization is social improvement, for which profit or substitute objectives are a signal concerning resource allocation by the firm (see Wood, 1991). In contrast, Windsor (2013) separates responsibilities into three domains. One domain is a moral duty not to engage in irresponsibility, whether legally regulated or not. A second domain is a moral and citizenship duty to comply with reasonable laws and public policies. The word reasonable conveys a civil disobedience exception to the compliance duty. A third domain is a voluntary domain of engaging in prosocial citizenship activities such as philanthropy and providing social goods. Responsibility – across irresponsibility, compliance, and citizenship domains – is a matter of moral judgment beyond strategic responsiveness or calculation (Mitnick, Windsor, & Wood, 2023).

The concept of responsibility just discussed concerns an organization's duties and obligations toward stakeholders and society at large. Sustainability involves a potentially complicated relationship between sustainable development and organizational sustainability (Barnett, 2004). The two concepts may or may not work together for a business. Sustainable development is the proposition that it is possible to continue economic development and growth for increased social welfare while saving and improving the planet and the natural environment for the human population. The relationship between the planet and people remains to be determined. Organizations may have to sacrifice to support sustainable development; if so, the link to organizational sustainability does not function. The definition of sustainability is arguably vague and contested but not flatly meaningless (citing the argument and language of Ramsey, 2015). While there may be responsibility for environmental sustainability, the direct relationship to sustainable development for businesses especially seems more problematic.

Model for Success

In a business setting, Rasche et al. (2023, see those authors' Figure 1.2 at p. 18) provide a model combining four motivations for sustainability: instrumental, ethical, political, and stakeholder. This model seems reasonably applicable to responsibility. The instrumental motivation is creating firm value: the owners receive sufficient profit for operating the business. The ethical motivation is doing the right thing: proper conduct may conflict with firm value maximization. Depending on the organization's value objectives, these motivations are analogous to nonbusiness organizations. The stakeholder motivation concerns meeting stakeholders' expectations: the various constituencies must receive acceptable value from interacting with the organization. A key difference across organizations is the political motivation of responsibility for the provision of public goods – public goods provision is the purpose of governmental organizations but a voluntary action for private organizations. This chapter restructures the proposed model as follows. Owners receive sufficient value; owners and managers do the right thing ethically; and other stakeholders receive acceptable value, including public goods. That is, organizational sustainability embeds the organization's sustainability within the sustainability of its external environments.

Three Dimensions of Social Responsibility

Figure 5.1 (see below) provides the author's three-dimensioned conception of social responsibility (adapted from Windsor, 2013). The conception uses a distinction between citizenship and good citizenship by Adam Smith: a citizen complies with laws in the center column; a good citizen wishes to promote social welfare in the right-hand column (Smith, *The Theory of Moral Sentiments*, 1759, VI.ii.2, p. 210, sixth ed.). The author then adds moral duties not explicitly regulated by laws in the left-hand column. Beyond legal compliance, such duties include avoiding harm to others, respecting others' rights, not lying or cheating, and keeping promises and contracts or paying appropriate compensation (Goodpaster, 1984). Violations of laws or moral duties constitute social irresponsibility. Good citizenship reflecting moral sentiment rather than moral duty concerning social needs takes concrete forms in alternatives such as creating shared value (CSV) (Menghwar & Daood, 2021) and strategic philanthropy (Liket & Maass, 2016). The conception in Figure 5.1 thus maps broadly onto duties, rights, and needs.

All three dimensions of social responsibility result in outcomes: absence of social responsibility, compliance with laws and policies, and providing social contributions. Wood's (1991) model for corporate social performance (CSP) combines social responsibility principles, social responsiveness processes, and organizational behavior outcomes. The principles are societal legitimacy, public responsibility, and managerial discretion. The organization seeks legitimacy through responsibility, and managers possess sufficient discretion for moral judgment. Processes include environmental assessment, stakeholder management, and social issues management. The outcomes include policies, programs, and, ultimately, social impacts.

Moral Responsibility (Ethics)	Mandatory Compliance (Citizenship)	Good Citizenship (Moral Sentiment)
Ethics implies zero illegitimate harm or social irresponsibility	Compliance with laws and public policies including CSR requirements and taxation	Social contributions Creating shared value (CSV) Strategic philanthropy Social goods provision
DUTIES	RIGHTS	NEEDS

Figure 5.1: Three Dimensions of Social Responsibility.

Five Fundamental Difficulties in Responsibility and Sustainability

The five fundamental difficulties concerning responsibility and sustainability are the nature of public goods, the possibility of "wicked" problems defying ready resolution, the difficulty of separating between stakeholders and society at large, problems in operationalizing and measuring activities and impacts, and the practical requirements for implementation.

First, providing public goods as a political motivation involves two problems. The first is conceptual (Adams & McCormick, 1987). Public goods are a technical concept in public finance economics: a business operating in a market economy will not produce classic public goods. Although citizens want such public goods, no consumer will reveal a genuine willingness to pay; pricing cannot exclude consumers, and there is no way of collecting revenue except through taxation, which is unavailable to a business. The broader concept in public finance economics is "social goods" (Musgrave, 1969), including public goods, merit goods, and arguably common resources management. A "merit good" is a subjective judgment that the market undersupplies something. A shared resource is subject to depletion because it is freely available to all users. The second difficulty is strategic: a business cannot continue to operate if it gives away profits for no return; therefore, practical considerations limit philanthropy and citizenship. One study argues that for-profit organizations may have a comparative efficiency in producing social goods (Kaul & Luo, 2018).

Second, a fundamental difficulty in responsibility and sustainability planning is that the environmental and social problems are increasingly "wicked," defined as the lack of ready solutions and every solution likely leading to more problems (Aronson & Henriques, 2023). Any solution effectively requires CSV so that there is both financial value to the organization and social benefits (Aronson & Henriques, 2023).

Third, while one can identify specific elements of planetary sustainability, separating an organization's stakeholders and society at large can be difficult. Many organizational actions aim at stakeholders and the link to society is more awkward to establish (Barnett, 2019). One proposal that might help sort out this link is recognizing that organizations compete for stakeholders, who, seeking the best options, may advance aggregate social welfare in a market-like process (Priem, Krause, Tantalo, & McFadyen, 2022).

Fourth, there needs to be more operationalizing and measuring activities and impacts. This measurement problem encompasses CSP (Wood, 2010), environmental and social impacts, and ESG elements. The issue inherent in the measurement problem is the balance between the economic viability of the organization and its impacts, negative and positive, on the natural environment and people. ESG (Moats & DeNicola, 2021) is difficult but arguably possible to measure (Howard-Grenville, 2021).

Finally, the fundamental difficulty in responsibility and sustainability planning is implementation, which must occur throughout the organization. Assuming widespread management and employee support, responsibility and sustainability knowledge and procedures must occur across the organization (Windsor, 2021, 2024).

Useful Standards for Responsibility and Sustainability Planning

Various standards help guide organizations with responsibility and sustainability planning and implementation. Five kinds of such standards are essential.

- The UN Global Compact (UNGC), sponsored by the UN Secretary-General, is a voluntary association of organizations, including businesses (https://unglobalcompact.org/). Adherents implement human rights, labor rights, environmental protection, and anticorruption reform principles.
- The Organisation for Economic Co-operation and Development (OECD), including about 38 member countries (2023) committed to democracy and market economy institutions, issues "Guidelines for Multinational Enterprises on Responsible Business Conduct" (1976, updated 2011 and 2023, https://mneguidelines.oecd.org//mne guidelines/) operating across national boundaries.
- The UN SDGs, adopted in 2015 by the UN General Assembly as Agenda 2030 as the desired achievement deadline, are 17 objectives for directing organizational activities (https://sdgs.un.org). Targets include elimination of poverty (SDG 1) and hunger (2); achievement of good health and well-being (3), quality education (4), gender equality (5), clean water and sanitation (6), affordable clean energy (7), and decent work and economic growth (8); reduction in inequalities (10); calls for economic development dimensions (9), sustainable cities and communities (11), responsible consumption and production (12); strong social institutions promoting peace and justice (16) and cross-sector partnerships (17); and environmental actions for climate (13) and life below water (14) and on land (15). Some of these goals can be addressed in part by private organizations. There are criticisms of the SDGs as "bad economics" (McGee & Block, 2022) and not necessarily financially sustainable for organizations (Filho, Dinis, Ruiz-de-Maya et al., 2022).

- The Global Reporting Initiative (GRI) provides sustainability reporting standards, which are now widely used for reporting and periodically updated (https://www. globalreporting.org/standards). GRI standards presently include human rights and environmental due diligence. There are universal, sector, and topic standards.
- The International Organization for Standardization (ISO) provides certification or guidance standards for various topics. These standards help organizations with implementation. In the context of responsibility and sustainability, particularly important are:
  - ISO 14001:2015 Environmental Management Systems is part of the ISO 14000 family of environmental standards.
  - ISO 26000:2010 Guidance on Social Responsibility concerning sustainable development.
  - ISO 37001:2016 Anti-Bribery Management Systems concerning compliance with anticorruption standards.

Most ISO standards come with certification. However, ISO 26000 is guidance only without formal certification. This fact signals underlying difficulties in defining and measuring CSR.

Concluding Thoughts and Future Direction

TBL, ESG, and SDG dimensions indicate that organizations will face multiple considerations in planning, implementation, and resource allocation (Windsor, 2022).

There are five critical implications for the future direction of responsibility and sustainability planning: planetary sustainability, business and human rights, expanding expectations for positive social contributions, anticorruption reform as an essential social good, and preparation for unexpected events.

1. The overriding issue is planetary sustainability. Climate change leads to an existential threat to the natural environment and human populations worldwide. All organizations will face increasing moral and legal obligations to reduce negative environmental impacts and increase positive environmental impacts. Problems are likely to prove "wicked" in character.
2. Respect for business and human rights is a movement gathering support and momentum (Schrempf-Stirling, Van Buren, & Wettstein, 2022) in the direction of some form of judicial enforcement, domestic and international, including against multinational enterprises (O'Brien, 2018). This direction will move rights from voluntary to mandatory compliance. The basic principle is that everyone should have access to judicial remedies to protect human rights.
3. Social and governmental expectations for positive social contributions will increase. There is a shift in theorizing and social expectations from concern with

motives and appropriate activities toward the impacts of environmental and social programs (Griffin, 2016). An impact is an action's negative or positive effect on an organizational stakeholder or the natural environment. The shift emphasizes that action involves going beyond "good intentions" to achieving good results (Barnett, Henriques, & Husted, 2020).

4. A vital contribution by all kinds of organizations is anticorruption reform, in accordance with the anticorruption principle (number 10) of the UNGC and the UN Convention Against Corruption (UNCAC) in force in December 2005. Corruption – the demand for and supply of bribery in various forms – undermines democracy and economic growth. All citizens have a right to a clean and honest government.

5. Organizations should prepare for unexpected events such as the COVID-19 pandemic. Planning is complex because such events cannot be readily predicted, especially concerning timing, location, and impacts.

References

Adams, R. D., & McCormick, K. (1987). Private goods, club goods and public goods as a continuum. *Review of Social Economy, 45*(2), 192–199. https://www.jstor.org/stable/29769372

Aronson, O., & Henriques, I. (2023). Shared value creation in equivocal CSR environments: A configuration approach. *Journal of Business Ethics, 187*, 713–732. https://doi.org/10.1007/s10551-022-05260-5

Balanced Scorecard Institute. (n.d.). Strategic Planning Basics. Retrieved November 13, 2023, from https://balancedscorecard.org/strategic-planning-basics/

Barnett, M. L. (2004). Are globalization and sustainability compatible? A review of the debate between the World Business Council for Sustainable Development and the International Forum on Globalization. *Organization & Environment, 17*(4), 523–532. https://www.jstor.org/stable/26162406

Barnett, M. L. (2019). The business case for corporate social responsibility: A critique and an indirect path forward. *Business & Society, 58*(1), 167–190. https://doi.org/10.1177/0007650316660044

Barnett, M. L., Henriques, I., & Husted, B. W. (2020). Beyond good intentions: Designing CSR initiatives for greater social impact. *Journal of Management, 46*(6), 937–964. https://doi.org/10.1177/0149206319900539

Barnett, W. P., & Burgelman, R. A. (1996). Evolutionary perspectives on strategy. *Strategic Management Journal, 17*(Special Issue), 5–19. https://www.jstor.org/stable/2486901

Bower, J. (2016). Resource allocation theory. In M. Augier & D. Teece (Eds.), *The Palgrave Encyclopedia of Strategic Management* (online). London, UK: Palgrave Macmillan. https://doi.org/10.1057/978-1-349-94848-2_677-1

Brown, J. A., de Bakker, F. G. A., Bapuji, H., Higgins, C., Rehbein, K., & Spicer, A. (2022). Building on its past: The future of business and society scholarship. *Business & Society, 61*(5), 967–979. https://doi.org/10.1177/00076503221097298

Carroll, A. B. (2021). Corporate social responsibility: Perspectives on the CSR construct's development and future. *Business & Society, 60*(6), 1258–1278. https://doi.org/10.1177/00076503211001765

Davis, K. (1973). The case for and against business assumption of social responsibilities. *Academy of Management Journal, 16*(2), 312–322. https://www.jstor.org/stable/255331

Filho, W. L., Dinis, M. A. P., Ruiz-de-Maya, S. et al. (2022). The economics of the UN Sustainable Development Goals: Does sustainability make financial sense? *Discover Sustainability, 3*. Article 20. https://doi.org/10.1007/s43621-022-00088-5

Frederick, W. C. (1986). Toward CSR₃: Why ethical analysis is indispensable and unavoidable in corporate affairs. *California Management Review, 28*(2), 126–155. https://doi.org/10.2307/41165190

Goodpaster, K. E. (1984). Some avenues for ethical analysis in general management. Harvard Business School Note 9-383-007 (revised April 1).

Grabs, J., & Garrett, R. D. (2021). Goal-based private sustainability governance and its paradoxes in the Indonesian palm oil sector. *Journal of Business Ethics, 188*, 467–507. https://doi.org/10.1007/s10551-023-05377-1

Griffin, J. J. (2016). *Managing Corporate Impacts: Co-Creating Value*. Cambridge, UK: Cambridge University Press.

Hajian, M., & Kashani, S. J. (2021). Evolution of the concept of sustainability: From Brundtland Report to sustainable development goals. In C. H. Hussain & J. F. Velasco-Muñoz (Eds.), *Sustainable Resource Management* (pp. 1–24). Amsterdam, the Netherlands: Elsevier. https://doi.org/10.1016/B978-0-12-824342-8.00018-3

Halbritter, G., & Dorfleitner, G. (2015). The wages of social responsibility — where are they? A critical review of ESG investing, *Review of Financial Economics, 26*, 25–35. https://doi.org/10.1016/j.rfe.2015.03.004

Hourneaux, F., Gabriel, M. L., & Gallardo-Vázquez, D. A. (2018). Triple bottom line and sustainable performance measurement in industrial companies. *Revista de Gestão, 25*(4), 413–429. https://www.emerald.com/insight/content/doi/10.1108/REGE-04-2018-0065/full/html

Howard-Grenville, J. (2021, January 22). ESG Impact Is Hard to Measure — But It's Not Impossible. https://hbr.org/2021/01/esg-impact-is-hard-to-measure-but-its-not-impossible

Kaul, A., & Luo, J. (2018). An economic case for CSR: The comparative efficiency of for-profit firms in meeting consumer demand for social goods. *Strategic Management Journal, 39*(6), 1650–1677. https://doi.org/10.1002/smj.2705

Li, T. T., Wang, K., Sueyoshi, T., & Wang, D. D. (2021). ESG: Research progress and future prospects. *Sustainability, 13*(21), 11663. https://doi.org/10.3390/su132111663

Liket, K., & Maas, K. (2016). Strategic philanthropy: Corporate measurement of philanthropic impacts as a requirement for a "happy marriage" of business and society. *Business & Society, 55*(6), 889–921. https://doi.org/10.1177/0007650314565356

Marquis, C., Glynn, M. A., & Davis, G. F. (2007). Community isomorphism and corporate social action. *Academy of Management Review, 32*(3), 925–945. https://doi.org/10.5465/amr.2007.25275683

Mazzola, P., & Kellermanns, F. W. (Eds.). (2010). *Handbook of Research on Strategy Process*. Cheltenham, UK & Northampton, MA: Edward Elgar.

McGee, R. W., & Block, W. E. (2022). Is the AACSB requiring member schools to teach bad economics? *Journal of Accounting, Ethics and Public Policy, 23*(2), 383–403. https://jaepp.org/index.php/jaepp/article/view/46

McWilliams, A., & Siegel, D. (2001). Corporate social responsibility: A theory of the firm perspective. *Academy of Management Review, 26*(1), 117–127. https://doi.org/10.2307/259398

Menghwar, P. S., & Daood, A. (2021). Creating shared value: A systematic review, synthesis and integrative perspective. *International Journal of Management Reviews, 23*(4), 466–485. https://doi.org/10.1111/ijmr.12252

Mitnick, B. M., Windsor, D., & Wood, D. J. (2023). Moral CSR. *Business & Society, 62*(1), 192–220. https://doi.org/10.1177/00076503221086881

Moats, M. C., & DeNicola, P. (PricewaterhouseCoopers LLP). (2021, December 15). The Corporate Director's Guide to ESG. https://corpgov.law.harvard.edu/2021/12/15/the-corporate-directors-guide-to-esg/

Musgrave, R. A. (1969). Provision for social goods. In J. Margolis & H. Guitton (Eds.), *Public Economics: An Analysis of Public Production and Consumption and Their Relations to the Private Sectors* (pp. 124–144). London, UK: Macmillan.

Neri, S. (2020). Corporate purpose. In S. Idowu, R. Schmidpeter, N. Capaldi, L. Zu, M. Del Baldo, & R. Abreu (Eds.), *Encyclopedia of Sustainable Management* (pp. 847–856). Cham, Switzerland: Springer. https://doi.org/10.1007/978-3-030-02006-4_1077-1

O'Brien, C. M. (2018). *Business and Human Rights: A handbook for legal practitioners*. Council of Europe. https://rm.coe.int/business-and-human-rights-a-handbook-of-legal-practitioners/168092323f

Priem, R. L., Krause, R., Tantalo, C., & McFadyen, M. A. (2022). Promoting long-term shareholder value by "competing" for essential stakeholders: A new, multisided market logic for top managers. *Academy of Management Perspectives, 36*(1), 93–110. https://doi.org/10.5465/amp.2018.0048

Purvis, B., Mao, Y. & Robinson, D. (2019). Three pillars of sustainability: in search of conceptual origins. *Sustainability Science, 14*, 681–695. https://doi.org/10.1007/s11625-018-0627-5

Ramsey, J. L. (2015). On not defining sustainability. *Journal of Agricultural and Environmental Ethics, 28*, 1075–1087. https://doi.org/10.1007/s10806-015-9578-3

Rasche, A., Morsing, M., Moon, J., & Kourula, A. (2023). Corporate sustainability – What it is and why it matters. In Rasche et al. (Eds.), *Corporate Sustainability: Managing Responsible Business in a Globalised World* (2nd ed., pp. 1–26). Cambridge, UK: Cambridge University Press. https://doi.org/10.1017/9781009118644.002

Scherer, A. G., & Palazzo, G. (2011). The new political role of business in a globalized world – A review of a new perspective on CSR and its implications for the firm, governance, and democracy. *Journal of Management Studies, 48*(4), 899–931. https://doi.org/10.1111/j.1467-6486.2010.00950.x

Schrempf-Stirling, J., Van Buren, H. J., & Wettstein, F. (2022). Human rights: A promising perspective for business & society. *Business & Society, 61*(5), 1282–1321. https://doi.org/10.1177/00076503211068425

Slaper, T. F., & Hall, T. J. (2011). The triple bottom line: What is it and how does it work? *Indiana Business Review, 86*(1), 4–8. http://www.ibrc.indiana.edu/ibr/2011/spring/article2.html

Tafti, S. F., Jahani, M., & Emami, S. A. (2012). Explaining evolutionary trend of strategic planning from traditional economy to innovation economy. *Procedia – Social and Behavioral Sciences, 58*, 56–65. https://doi.org/10.1016/j.sbspro.2012.09.978

Windsor, D. (2013). Corporate social responsibility and irresponsibility: A positive theory approach. *Journal of Business Research, 66*(10), 1937–1944. http://dx.doi.org/10.1016/j.jbusres.2013.02.016.

Windsor, D. (2021). Cross-functional integration in sustainability-driven business practice. In S. Markovic, C. Sancha, & A. Lindgreen (Eds.), *Handbook of Sustainability-Driven Business Strategies in Practice* (pp. 432–453). Cheltenham, UK & Northampton, MA: Edward Elgar. https://doi.org/10.4337/9781789908350.00040

Windsor, D. (2022). Theories of the firm: The logic of multiple criteria for assessing outcomes. In M. Pirson, D. M. Wasieleski, & E. L. Steckler (Eds.), *Alternative Theories of the Firm* (pp. 72–102). New York, NY & London, UK: Routledge.

Windsor, D. (2024). Cross-functional collaboration on corporate social responsibility knowledge. In S. Markovic, A. Lindgreen, N. Koporcic, & M. Micevski (Eds.), *Approaches to Corporate Social Responsibility* (pp. 3–25). New York, NY & London, UK: Routledge. DOI:10.4324/9781003255833-2

Wood, D. J. (1991). Corporate social performance revisited. *Academy of Management Review, 16*(4), 691–718. https://doi.org/10.2307/258977

Wood, D. J. (2010). Measuring corporate social performance: A review. *International Journal of Management Reviews, 12*(1), 50–84. https://doi.org/10.1111/j.1468-2370.2009.00274.x

Evolution of Leading

Romie Frederick Littrell

6 Preferred Managerial Leader Behavior: Implicit and Explicit Theories

Abstract: This chapter explores the historical and contemporary perspectives on leadership theories, focusing on the distinction between leader-centric and follower-centric approaches. It compares two well-researched models of explicit and implicit leadership behavior: Robert House's model of implicit leadership dimensions and Ralph Stogdill's model of preferred leader behavior dimensions from the LBDQXII survey. The manuscript concludes by emphasizing the importance of understanding both implicit and explicit leadership behaviors to develop a comprehensive view of how leaders influence and inspire their teams in today's complex and diverse world.

Introduction

Managerial leader behavior is an important consideration in the contemporary workplace. It sets the foundation of the organization's operations and can have a profound impact on business outcome. Theories on its best practices have evolved and expanded over time.

As an example, in his work (1990) *Handbook of Leadership: A Survey of Theory and Research*, Bernard Bass outlined a set of characteristics that distinguish effective leadership theories. These characteristics provide a framework for evaluating and comparing different leadership theories, helping us understand their strengths, limitations, and applicability in various contexts.

Bass' Characteristics Of Leadership Theories

Bass's paradigm is as follows:
1. Scope: The breadth of the theory's focus, encompassing individual, team, organizational, or societal levels of analysis.
2. Domain: The range of leadership phenomena addressed by the theory, including motivation, communication, decision-making, conflict resolution, and change management.
3. Variables: The specific factors or constructs considered by the theory in explaining leadership effectiveness.
4. Antecedents: The external factors or conditions that influence the emergence or success of leadership.

https://doi.org/10.1515/9783111316987-006

5. Processes: The mechanisms or pathways through which leadership exerts its influence on followers, groups, or organizations.
6. Outcomes: The desired or intended results of leadership, such as performance, satisfaction, innovation, or organizational change.
7. Contingency: The extent to which the theory recognizes the situational factors that moderate the relationship between leadership and outcomes.
8. Predictability: The ability of the theory to provide accurate and reliable predictions about leadership effectiveness.
9. Generality: The applicability of the theory to different contexts, cultures, and leadership roles.
10. Testability: The extent to which the theory can be empirically tested, and its propositions verified or refuted.
11. Utility: The practical value and usefulness of the theory in informing leadership practice and development.
12. Evolving Nature: The recognition that leadership theories are dynamic and may require adaptation as new research emerges and societal contexts change.

By considering these characteristics, individuals and organizations can critically evaluate different leadership theories and select those that best align with their specific needs and circumstances.

Historical Perspective

Throughout history, numerous authors have delved into the intricate realm of leadership, offering unique perspectives and insights into the qualities, behaviors, and strategies that identify effective leaders. Some notable historical authors who have shaped our understanding of leadership include:

Herodotus, the Greek historian, delved into the complexities of leadership in his seminal work, *The Histories*. While not explicitly presenting a systematic theory of leadership, his observations and analyses of historical figures provide valuable insights into the qualities and behaviors that distinguish effective leaders.

Herodotus' (c. 484 BCE to c. 430–420) View of Leadership

Herodotus' approach to leadership was multifaceted, recognizing the interplay between personal qualities, external factors, and historical context. He emphasized the importance of intelligence, charisma, and strategic thinking but also acknowledged the influence of cultural norms, political structures, and the broader historical landscape.

Herodotus' Key Characteristics of Effective Leaders. Herodotus highlighted several key characteristics of effective leaders:

- **Intelligence**: Leaders should possess intellectual curiosity, analytical skills, and the ability to grasp complex situations.
- **Charisma**: Leaders should exude personal magnetism, inspire confidence, and connect with their followers emotionally.
- **Strategic Thinking**: Leaders should formulate clear goals, devise effective plans, and make calculated decisions to achieve their objectives.
- **Adaptability**: Leaders must be flexible and responsive to changing circumstances, adapting their strategies and approaches as needed.
- **Integrity**: Leaders should embody honesty, fairness, and moral principles to gain trust and respect.
- **Appreciation of Culture**: Leaders should understand and respect the cultural values and traditions of their followers.

Examples of Leadership Styles in Herodotus' *The Histories*

Herodotus' historical narratives provide examples of leaders with contrasting styles:

- Cyrus the Great: The founder of the Achaemenid Empire, Cyrus was portrayed as a benevolent leader who respected his subjects and sought their well-being.
- Cambyses II: Cyrus' successor, Cambyses, was portrayed as a ruthless and impulsive leader who made disastrous decisions, leading to the decline of the empire.
- Darius the Great: Darius, Cyrus' grandson, was portrayed as a wise and moderate leader who restored stability to the empire and implemented effective governance.
- Xerxes I: Darius' son, Xerxes, was portrayed as a power-hungry and arrogant leader who initiated the disastrous Persian Wars against Greece.

Herodotus' insights into leadership offer valuable lessons that resonate across time and cultures. His emphasis on the interplay between personal qualities, external factors, and historical context highlights the multifaceted nature of leadership. While not providing a prescriptive theory, Herodotus' writings serve as a rich source of inspiration and guidance for those seeking to develop their leadership skills and make a positive impact on the world.

Niccolò Machiavelli's (1469 to 1527) View of Leadership

In his seminal work, *The Prince*, Machiavelli outlined a pragmatic approach to leadership, emphasizing the importance of power, cunning, and ruthlessness in achieving one's political objectives. He argued that leaders must be willing to adapt their principles and methods depending on the situation, even if it means resorting to deception or manipulation.

Sun Tzu's (544 to 496 BCE) View of Leadership

Sun Tzu's *The Art of War* is a timeless classic that delves into the art of strategic leadership, particularly in the context of warfare. He emphasizes the importance of strategic thinking, preparation, and psychological warfare, advocating for decisive action and the ability to outmaneuver one's opponents.

James MacGregor Burns' (1918 to 2014) View of Leadership

In his 1978 book *Leadership*, Burns introduced the concept of transformational leadership, which focuses on inspiring and empowering followers to achieve more than thought possible. He argued that transformational leaders foster a shared vision, create a sense of collective purpose, and motivate followers to transcend their self-interest for the greater good.

Warren Bennis' (1925 to 2019) View of Leadership

Bennis, a renowned leadership scholar, emphasized the importance of self-awareness, adaptability, and the ability to learn and grow as a leader. In his 1989 book *On Becoming a Leader*, he stressed the need for leaders to continuously refine their skills, adapt to changing circumstances, and cultivate a sense of self-mastery.

Simon Sinek's (1973 to present) View of Leadership

Sinek's work focuses on the power of a strong "why" to inspire and motivate followers. In his 2009 book *Start With Why*, he argues that great leaders articulate a compelling purpose that resonates with their audience, enabling them to build a shared vision and inspire others to follow their lead.

Brené Brown's (1962 to present) View of Leadership

Brown, a research professor and author, emphasizes the importance of vulnerability, authenticity, and courage in effective leadership. In her 2012 book *Daring Greatly*, she argues that leaders who embrace their imperfections and allow themselves to be seen as human can foster deeper connections and inspire others to take risks and pursue their own leadership journeys.

These historical authors and their works have significantly shaped our understanding of leadership, providing valuable insights into the qualities, behaviors, and mindsets that distinguish effective leaders. Their contributions continue to inspire and inform individuals seeking to develop their leadership skills and make a meaningful impact on the world around them.

The Great Man Theory of Leadership

The Great Man Theory, also known as the *leadership trait theory*, is a prominent leadership theory that emphasizes the innate and inherent qualities of individuals who make them effective leaders. It suggests that leaders are born with certain traits or characteristics that set them apart from others and naturally enable them to rise to positions of power and influence.

Origins and Proponents. The Great Man Theory emerged in the 19th century, gaining prominence with the works of philosopher and historian Thomas Carlyle. Carlyle famously proclaimed, "The history of the world is but the biography of great men." He argued that history was shaped by the actions of exceptional individuals, not by social, economic, or political factors.

Other notable proponents of the Great Man Theory include:
- William James: American psychologist and philosopher who proposed that the unique physiological makeup of individuals determines their leadership potential.
- Francis Galton: British scientist and social Darwinist who emphasized the role of genetics in shaping leadership traits.

Core Assumptions

The Great Man Theory rests on several key assumptions:
- Leadership is an innate quality: Leaders are born with inherent qualities that make them natural leaders.
- Leadership traits are fixed and unchanging: These traits are stable and do not develop or change over time.
- Leadership is a matter of individual charisma: Leaders exert their influence through their personal magnetism and persuasive abilities.
- Leadership is unrelated to external factors: The environment or context does not play a significant role in shaping leadership effectiveness.

Nature vs Nurture

The Great Man Theories of Leadership heavily favor Nature over Nurture in their explanation of leadership potential. The core proposition of these theories is that great leaders are born, not made, meaning they possess innate, inherent traits that set them apart and automatically qualify them for leadership roles. These traits are believed to be stable and unchanging throughout their lives.

This focus on nature stems from several factors:

Historical Context: These theories originated in the 19th century, a time when the role of heredity in human behavior was widely accepted. Thinkers like Thomas Carlyle argued that history was shaped by the actions of "great men" endowed with special qualities.

Focus on Heroism: Great Man theories often portray leaders as heroic figures who rise above the ordinary and lead through charisma, intelligence, and decisiveness. These qualities are seen as inherent rather than learned.

Gender Bias: These theories were formulated at a time when leadership was primarily associated with men. The very term "Great Man" reflects this bias, neglecting the possibility of great female leaders or the influence of social context on leadership emergence.

While the *Nurture* side is largely ignored, some argue that Great Man theorists did not completely disregard environmental factors. They acknowledged the importance of opportunity and historical context in allowing these innate traits to manifest. However, the emphasis clearly remains on inherent qualities rather than acquired skills or learned behaviors.

Here are some citations and references for further exploration:
- Northouse, P. G. (2016). *Leadership: Theory and practice (8th ed.)*. Sage Publications. This textbook provides a comprehensive overview of leadership theories, including the Great Man Theory and its emphasis on nature.
- Hunt, S. E., & Dodge, G. R. (2009). *Leadership: Theory, practice, and development (5th ed.)*. McGraw-Hill/Irwin. Similar to Northouse's book, this text discusses the Great Man Theory alongside other leadership perspectives.
- Juneja, P. (2021, January 26). "Great Man" Theories. Penn State Behrend. This website article offers a concise explanation of the Great Man Theory and its historical context.
- Bennis, W. G. (2007). *Leaders on leadership: Interviews with the greatest living business minds of our time.* Harvard Business Review Press. This book presents interviews with prominent leaders, some of whom challenge the idea of innate leadership qualities and emphasize the role of development and experience.

By delving deeper into these resources, scholars and practitioners can gain a broader understanding of the debate between nature and nurture in leadership and critically evaluate the claims of the Great Man.

Criticism and Limitations: Great Man Theory

The Great Man Theory has been criticized for its deterministic and limited perspective on leadership. Critics argue that it:
- Overemphasizes individual traits: Ignores the role of external factors, such as social structures, cultural norms, and historical events, in shaping leadership opportunities and outcomes.
- Fails to account for situational leadership: Suggests that the same leadership traits are effective in all situations, regardless of the context or challenges faced.
- Limits the potential for leadership development: Imposes a fixed and unchanging view of leadership, hindering the development of leadership skills and capabilities.

Alternative Perspectives

In response to the limitations of the Great Man Theory, more contemporary leadership theories have emerged, emphasizing the importance of situational factors, learned behaviors, and the interaction between leaders and their followers. These theories include:
- **Situational Leadership Theory**: Suggests that effective leadership depends on the leader's ability to adapt their style to the specific situation and the needs of their followers.
- **Transformational Leadership Theory**: Focuses on the ability of leaders to inspire and motivate followers, to create a shared vision, and to foster a sense of empowerment.
- **Servant Leadership Theory**: Emphasizes the servant leader's focus on the needs and growth of their followers, fostering a collaborative and empowering approach to leadership.

While the Great Man Theory has been largely discredited for its oversimplified and deterministic view of leadership, it has played a significant role in shaping our understanding of leadership. It highlighted the importance of individual qualities and traits in leadership, even if it overstated their role in determining leadership success. Contemporary leadership theories have moved beyond the Great Man Theorie's emphasis on innate traits to explore the dynamic interplay between leaders, followers, and context, recognizing that leadership is not solely a matter of individual charisma but rather a complex and multifaceted phenomenon.

Leader-Centric vs Follower-Centric Approaches

Initially, the study of leadership focused on *leader-centric* approaches, which is still a prominent approach in research. An alternative view is the *follower-centric* approach.

Leader-Centric Approaches to Leadership

Leader-centric approaches to leadership focus on the characteristics, behaviors, and traits of individual leaders as the primary determinants of effective leadership. This perspective emphasizes the role of leaders in driving organizational success, shaping organizational culture, and influencing the motivation and performance of their followers.

Key Assumptions of Leader-Centric Approaches

1. Leadership is a top-down process, with leaders exercising authority and control over followers.
2. Effective leaders possess a set of innate or acquired traits that differentiate them from nonleaders.
3. Leaders' behaviors and actions directly impact follower motivation, performance, and organizational outcomes.

Examples of Leader-Centric Leadership Theories

1. *Trait Theories:* These theories emphasize the role of individual characteristics, such as intelligence, charisma, and self-confidence, in determining leadership effectiveness (Stogdill, 1974).
2. *Behavioral Theories:* These theories focus on the specific behaviors and actions that leaders exhibit, such as initiating structure, providing consideration, and setting expectations (Blake & Mouton, 1964; Likert, 1961).
3. *Contingency Theories:* These theories argue that leadership effectiveness depends on the fit between the leader's style and the situational context (Fiedler, 1967; Hersey & Blanchard, 1969).

Criticisms of Leader-Centric Approaches

1. Overemphasis on the leader's role and neglect of the influence of context and characteristics of followers.
2. Oversimplification of leadership, overlooking the complexities of the leader-follower relationship.
3. Tendency to attribute leadership outcomes solely to the leader's traits or actions, overlooking the contributions of followers.

Follower-Centric Approaches to Leadership

Follower-centric approaches shift the focus from the leader to the follower, emphasizing the active role of followers in shaping leadership dynamics and influencing organizational outcomes. This perspective highlights the importance of understanding the motivations, expectations, and behaviors of followers, recognizing their potential to contribute to leadership processes.

Key Assumptions of Follower-Centric Approaches

1. Leadership is a reciprocal process involving the interaction of leaders and followers.
2. Followers are not passive recipients of leadership; they actively shape leadership dynamics through their behaviors and perceptions.
3. Effective leadership involves understanding follower needs, motivations, and capabilities.

Examples of Follower-Centric Leadership Theories

- **Social Identity Theory**: This theory proposes that followers identify with leaders based on shared social categories and group memberships, influencing their perceptions of leadership effectiveness (Haslam, Reicher, & Platow, 2011).
- **Leadership Attribution Theory**: This theory suggests that followers actively construct their perceptions of leadership based on their observations, interpretations, and biases (Meindl, 1995).
- **Shared Leadership Theory**: This theory advocates for a more distributed and democratic approach to leadership, recognizing the potential for leadership to emerge from various sources within an organization (Pearson, Manz, & Sims, 2008).

Benefits of Follower-Centric Approaches

- More nuanced understanding of leadership dynamics that goes beyond the leader-centric perspective.
- Recognition of the active role of followers in shaping leadership and organizational outcomes.
- Potential for developing more effective leadership practices that cater to the needs and capabilities of followers.

Both leader-centric and follower-centric approaches offer valuable insights into the complexities of leadership. While leader-centric approaches provide valuable frameworks for understanding the traits, behaviors, and styles of effective leaders, follower-centric approaches highlight the importance of understanding followers, their perceptions, and their contributions to leadership processes. A balanced and integrated perspective that considers both leaders and followers is essential for developing effective leadership strategies and achieving organizational success.

Suggested Further Reading:
1. Blake, R. R., & Mouton, J. S. (1964). *The managerial grid.* Houston, TX: Gulf Publishing Company.
2. Bass, B. M., & Stogdill, R. M. (1990). *Bass & Stogdill's handbook of leadership: theory, research and managerial applications (3rd ed.).* New York, NY: Free Press.
3. Fiedler, F. E. (1967). *A theory of leadership effectiveness.* McGraw-Hill.
4. Haslam, S. A., Reicher, S. D., & Platow, M. J. (2011). *The new psychology of leadership: Identity, influence, and power.* New York, NY: Psychology Press.
5. Hersey, P., Hersey, P. (1985). *The situational leader.* New York, NY: Warner Books.

In the past few decades in the field of leadership studies, two additional distinct approaches have emerged to examine how individuals perceive and evaluate leadership: implicit and explicit theories of leadership. These approaches differ in their underlying assumptions about the nature of leadership and the methods employed to assess leader effectiveness.

Implicit Theories of Leadership

Implicit theories of leadership (ILTs) are based on the notion that individuals have internalized and acquired mental models or schemas of what constitutes effective leadership. These schemas are formed through personal experiences, observations of others, and societal cultural influences. ILTs are often unconscious and operate automatically, shaping our perceptions of leaders and influencing our behavior towards them.

According to Lord and Maher (1991), ILTs operate through a process of categorization. When encountering a potential leader, individuals match the leader's characteristics against their existing mental models of leadership. If there is a good fit between the leader's attributes and the individual's ILT, the leader is more likely to be perceived as effective and influential.

Explicit Theories of Leadership

Explicit theories of leadership (ELTs), on the other hand, are more deliberate and conscious representations of leadership. They are formed through formal education, leadership training, and personal reflection. ELTs are typically articulated in the form of statements or beliefs about what constitutes effective leadership behavior.

ELTs can be assessed through questionnaires or surveys that ask individuals to rate their preferences for specific leader behaviors. These preferences may be based on personal values, beliefs about organizational effectiveness, or cultural norms.

Leadership Dimensions: Explicit Leadership Theory

In a widely researched ELT, Stogdill (1959, 1963, 1974 pp. 142–155) noted that it was not reasonable to believe that the two factors of *Initiating Structure* and *Consideration* were sufficient to account for all the observable variance in leader behavior relating to group achievement and the variety of social roles. Stogdill's theory suggested the following patterns of behavior are involved in leadership, though not equally important in all situations (the order of the list and the numerals of the factors have no relevance).

1. *Representation* measures to what degree the leader speaks as the representative of the group.
2. *Demand Reconciliation* reflects how well the leader reconciles conflicting demands and reduces disorder to system.
3. *Tolerance of Uncertainty* depicts to what extent the leader is able to tolerate uncertainty and postponement without anxiety or getting upset.
4. *Persuasiveness* measures to what extent the leader uses persuasion and argument effectively and exhibits strong convictions.
5. *Initiation of Structure* measures to what degree the leader clearly defines own role and lets followers know what is expected.
6. *Tolerance of Freedom* reflects to what extent the leader allows followers scope for initiative, decision, and action.
7. *Role Assumption* measures to what degree the leader actively exercises the leadership role rather than surrendering leadership to others.

8. *Consideration* depicts to what extent the leader regards the comfort, well-being, status, and contributions of followers.
9. *Production Emphasis* measures to what degree the leader applies pressure for productive output.
10. *Predictive Accuracy* measures to what extent the leader exhibits foresight and ability to predict outcomes accurately.
11. *Integration* reflects the degree to which the leader maintains a closely knit organization and resolves intermember conflicts.
12. *Superior Orientation* measures to what extent the leader maintains cordial relations with superiors, has influence with them, and is striving for a higher status. *Superior Orientation* is a behavior set not included in many leadership surveys. It is discussed and analyzed in Kerr, Schriesheim, Murphy, and Stogdill (1974) and moderates between leader predictors and follower satisfaction. They found that the greater the perceived upward influence of the supervisor, the greater the positive relationships between the *Consideration* factor and subordinate satisfaction. This will be especially true for subordinates who are highly dependent upon their boss for such things as recognition, freedom, and physical and financial resources.

Comparison of ILTs and ELTs

ILTs and ELTs differ in several key aspects:
- Origin: ILTs arise from personal experiences and societal influences, while ELTs are formed through formal education and training.
- Level of Consciousness: ILTs are often unconscious and operate automatically, while ELTs are more deliberate and conscious.
- Measurement. ILTs are typically measured using projective techniques, while ELTs are assessed through questionnaires or surveys; however, ILTs are increasingly measured by questionnaires and surveys; see, for example, House et al. (2004).

Implications for Business Leadership

Both ILTs and ELTs play a significant role in shaping leadership perceptions and behaviors. ILTs can influence how individuals respond to leaders, whether they are willing to follow their direction, and how they evaluate their performance. ELTs can guide leaders' decision-making and behavior, influencing their approach to leadership and their ability to motivate and engage followers.

Comparsion of Major Models of Leadership Behavior

There are two well-researched models of explicit and implicit leadership behavior: Robert House's (House, et al., 2004) model of implicit leadership dimensions and Ralph Stogdill's (1974) model of preferred leader behavior dimensions from the LBDQXII survey.

Similarities

Both focus on describing leadership behaviors and characteristics. They aim to define the key qualities and actions displayed by leaders (House et al., 1991; Stogdill, 1963).

The dimensions identified in both models are based on empirical research surveying people's perceptions of leaders. The models seek to capture people's implicit beliefs about leadership (Offermann et al., 1994; Schriesheim & Stogdill, 1975).

There is some overlap in the behavioral dimensions identified. For example, House's *Charisma/Values-Based* aligns with Stogdill's *Representation* and both cover inspirational leadership (House et al., 1991; Stogdill, 1974).

Differences

Scope

Stogdill's model is focused specifically on leadership in organizational/workplace settings (Stogdill, 1974). House's model aims to describe leadership perceptions more broadly, across various contexts (House et al., 1991).

Number of dimensions

Stogdill's model has 12 dimensions of leader behavior described above (Stogdill, 1972), while House's has 6 broad dimensions (House et al., 1991). In chapter 11, "Leader Behavior: *Consideration* and *Initiating Structure*", Stogdill (1974, pp. 128–141) discussed the Ohio State Leadership Studies from 1945 through 1970. Several factor analytic studies produced two factors identified as *Consideration* and *Initiation of Structure in Interaction*. Stogdill (1959, 1963, 1974 pp. 142–155) noted that it was not reasonable to believe that the two factors of *Initiating Structure* and *Consideration* were sufficient to account for all the observable variance in leader behavior relating to group achievement and the variety of social roles. Stogdill's theory suggested his patterns of behavior are involved in leadership, though not equally important in all situations (the order of the list and the numerals of the factors have no relevance).

The GLOBE research project (House et al., 2004) identified nine primary leadership dimensions, grouped into six global leadership clusters, along with their associated secondary dimensions. Here's a list of each with annotations.

Descriptions of the GLOBE projects ILT Global Leadership Clusters (House et al, 2004) follow:

Charismatic/Value-Based Leadership:

Primary—Visionary, Inspirational, Self-Sacrificial, Integrity, Decisive, Performance-Oriented.

Secondary—Proactive, Risk-Taking, Original, Ethical, Assertive, Achievement-Oriented.

Team-Oriented Leadership:

Primary—Collaborative Team Orientation, Team Integrator, Diplomatic, Malevolent (reverse scored), Administratively Competent.

Secondary—Supportive, Trusting, Conflict-Avoiding, Humble, Modest.

Participative Leadership:

Primary—Nonparticipative (reverse scored), Autocratic (reverse scored).

Secondary—Consulting with Individuals, Involving Many in Decisions, Delegating Authority.

Humane-Oriented Leadership:

Primary—Benevolent, Altruistic, Sympathetic, Kind, Modest.

Secondary—Developing People, Empowering, Nurturing, Protecting, Mentoring. (Reference: House et al., 2004).

Assertive Leadership:

Primary—Decisive, Tough-Minded, Demanding, Self-Confident, Risk-Taking.

Secondary—Straightforward, Clear, Proactive, Independent, Individualistic.

Socially Oriented Leadership:

Primary—Socially Attractive, Liking for Social Interaction, Gregarious, Socially Adjusted.

Secondary—Extroverted, Cheerful, Enthusiastic, Socially Bold, Optimistic.

Relationships between Dimensions:

Within Clusters: Primary dimensions within a cluster tend to be positively correlated but not perfectly overlapping. For example, a visionary leader might also be inspirational but not necessarily decisive.

Between Clusters: Clusters can interact in complex ways. Charismatic leadership might not be effective without some level of participative decision-making.

Cultural Context: The effectiveness of different dimensions varies across cultures. For example, assertive leadership might be more effective in individualistic cultures, while humane-oriented leadership might be more valued in collectivistic cultures.

Typology

House proposes a typology of leadership styles (directive, transactional, transformational), while Stogdill's model does not classify styles (House et al., 1991; Stogdill, 1963).

Development Method

Stogdill used surveys asking about behaviors of effective leaders (Schriesheim & Stogdill, 1975). House used a broad and in-depth cross-cultural literature review to identify key leadership perceptions (House et al., 2004).

Universal vs. Cultural Contingency

House saw his model as universal (Den Hartog et al., 1999), while Stogdill emphasized his dimensions may vary across cultures (Stogdill, 1974).

In summary, while both models aim to capture implicit leadership perceptions, House takes a broader approach focused on leadership archetypes, whereas Stogdill provides a more granular, contextualized model specific to organizational leadership behaviors (House et al., 1991; Stogdill, 1963). Stogdill emphasizes leadership perceptions may be culturally dependent (Stogdill, 1974), while House suggests more universal leadership prototypes (Den Hartog et al., 1999).

Conclusions

Understanding leadership goes beyond observable actions and conscious decisions. Implicit and explicit leadership behaviors offer different approaches to capturing the full complexity of leading.

Conclusions: Implicit Leadership Theory

ILT focuses on the unconscious beliefs and assumptions individuals hold about leadership attributes and behaviors. These internal schemas, shaped by culture, personal experiences, and social norms, influence how people perceive and evaluate leaders. Researchers (House et al., 2004) identified six basic leadership dimensions with global applicability:
- Task-Oriented: Initiating action, setting goals, planning, and problem-solving.
- Supportive: Building trust, offering help, showing concern for well-being.

- Innovative: Encouraging creativity, being open to new ideas, taking risks.
- Participative: Seeking input, delegating, involving others in decision-making.
- Humane-Oriented: Emphasizing kindness, fairness, social justice, and ethical conduct.
- Autonomous: Granting independence, respecting others' opinions, promoting self-direction.

Contributions of ILT

- **Unveils unconscious biases:** ILT acknowledges that leadership perceptions are subjective and shaped by internal filters. This helps leaders and followers to understand and address personal biases.
- **Provides cultural context:** ILT recognizes that leadership expectations vary across cultures. This promotes culturally sensitive leadership styles and enhances cross-cultural collaboration.
- **Highlights follower perspectives:** ILT emphasizes how followers perceive and respond to leadership behavior, shifting the focus beyond leader actions to the overall leadership dynamic.

Conclusions: Explicit Leadership Theory

ELT focuses on the conscious thoughts and deliberate actions leaders exhibit. It identifies specific leadership behaviors associated with effectiveness, such as:
- Vision and strategy: Articulating a clear vision for the future, setting strategic goals, and aligning team efforts.
- Communication: Delivering clear, concise, and motivating messages to inform and engage team members.
- Decision-making: Making timely and informed decisions while involving stakeholders when appropriate.
- Relationship building: Fostering trust, open communication, and collaboration within the team.
- Delegation and empowerment: Providing opportunities for individual growth and development by assigning challenging tasks and trusting team members to deliver.
- Coaching and mentoring: Offering guidance, feedback, and support to help team members reach their full potential.

Contributions of ELT

- Provides actionable behaviors: ELT offers a practical framework for developing and practicing effective leadership skills.
- Focuses on measurable outcomes: By identifying specific behaviors, ELT facilitates evaluation of leadership effectiveness and its impact on team performance.
- Promotes intentional leadership: ELT encourages leaders to be mindful and deliberate in their actions, driving conscious choices that align with desired outcomes.

By understanding both implicit and explicit leadership behaviors, contemporary leadership theory offers a more comprehensive view of how leaders influence and inspire their teams. Recognizing the interplay between conscious choices and unconscious biases allows leaders to develop a more nuanced and effective approach to leading in today's complex and diverse world.

References and Further Reading

Avolio, B. J., & Bass, B. M. (2004). *Multifactor Leadership Questionnaire (MLQ): Form R and Form 360.* Leadership Instruments Inc.

Avolio, B. J., Bass, B. M., & Jung, D. I. (1999). Re-examination of the relationship between leadership and charisma: A confirmatory factor analysis. *Leadership Quarterly, 10*(1), 41–61.

Aycan, Z. (2006a). Human resource management in Turkey: Historical, cultural, and institutional perspectives. *International Journal of Human Resource Management, 17*(10), 1633–1654.

Bass, B. M. (1990). *Bass & Stogdill's Handbook of Leadership: Theory, Research and Managerial Applications* (3rd ed.). New York: Free Press.

Bass, B. M., & Avolio, B. J. (1994*). Improving Organizational Effectiveness through Transformational Leadership.* Thousand Oaks, CA: Sage.

Bennis, W. (1989). *On Becoming a Leader.* Basic Books.

Brown, B. (2012). *Daring Greatly: How the Courage to Be Vulnerable Transforms the Way We Live, Love, Parent, and Lead.* Avery.

Burns, J. M. (1978). *Leadership.* Harper & Row.

Den Hartog, D. N., House, R. J., Hanges, P. J., Ruiz-Quintanilla, S. A., & Dorfman, P. W. (1999). Culture specific and cross-culturally generalizable implicit leadership theories: Are attributes of charismatic/transformational leadership universally endorsed? *Leadership Quarterly, 10*(2), 219–256.

Dorfman, P. W., Javidan, M., House, R. J., & Hanges, P. J. (2013). *GLOBE: Leadership and Cultural Effectiveness across the World.* Routledge.

House, R. J., Hanges, P. J., Javidan, M., Dorfman, P. W., & Gupta, V. (2004). *GLOBE: Global Leadership and Organizational Behavior Research Project.* Sage Publications.

Doty, William B. (2003). *Herodotus and the Herodotean Writing: The Contexts of Inquiry.* University of Texas Press.

Eagly, A. H., & Carli, L. L. (2003). The leadership gap: What gets between women and the corner office. *Harvard Business Review, 81*(11), 104–119.

Harrison, Thomas (2002). *The Histories: Herodotus.* Cambridge University Press.

Herodotus (1990). *Herodotus: The Histories.* Translated by Aubrey de Selincourt. Revised by Robert Waterfield. Penguin Classics.

House, R.J., & Javidan, M. (2004). *Leadership across Cultures*. Thousand Oaks, CA: Sage Publications.

House, R.J., Hanges, P. J., Javidan, M., Dorfman, P. W., & Gupta, V. (1997). *Culture, Leadership, and Organizational Behavior*. Thousand Oaks, CA: Sage.

House, R.J., Hanges, P. J., Ruiz-Quintanilla, S. A., Dorfman, P. W., Javidan, M., Dickson, M., & Gupta, V. (1999). Cultural influences on leadership and organizations: Project GLOBE. *Advances in Global Leadership*, *1*(2), 171–233.

House, R.J.; Hanges, P.J.; Javidan, M., Dorfman, P.W. & Gupta, V. (2004) *Culture, Leadership, and Organizations: The GLOBE Study of 62 Societies*. Sage Publications.

Lateiner, Donald A. (2011). *The Historical Method of Herodotus*. Princeton University Press.

Littrell, R.F. (2013), Explicit leader behaviour: A review of literature, theory development, and research project results, *Journal of Management Development*, *32*(6), 567–605. https://doi.org/10.1108/JMD-04-2013-0053

Lord, R.G., & Maher, M. A. (1991). *Leadership and Information Processing: Linking Perceptions and Performance*. Boston, MA: Unwin Hyman.

Lord, R.G., Avolio, B. J., & Hunter, J. E. (2014). *Leadership in Work Organizations*. Sage Publications.

Machiavelli, N. (1513). *The Prince*. Penguin Classics.

Northouse, P.G. (2018). *Leadership: Theory and practice*. Sage Publications. (Chapter 3: Theories of Leadership)

Offermann, L.R., Kennedy, J. K., & Wirtz, P. W. (1994). Implicit leadership theories: Content, structure, and generalizability. *Leadership Quarterly*, *5*(1), 43–58.

Schriesheim, C.A., & Stogdill, R. M. (1975). Differences in factor structure across three versions of the Ohio State leadership scales. *Personnel Psychology*, *28*(2), 189–206.

Sinek, S. (2009). *Start with Why: How Great Leaders Inspire Everyone to Do Their Best*. Penguin Business.

Stogdill, R.M. and Coons, A.E. (1957). *Leader behavior: Its description and measurement*. Columbus, OH: Ohio University Bureau of Business Research.

Stogdill, R.M. (1948). Personal factors associated with leadership: A survey of the literature. *Journal of Psychology*, *25*: 35–71.

Stogdill, R.M. (1950). Leadership, membership and organization. *Psychological Bulletin*, *47*, 1–14.

Stogdill, R.M. (1959). *Individual Behavior and Group Achievement*. New York: Oxford

Stogdill, R.M. (1963). *Manual for the Leader Behavior Description Questionnaire-Form XII*. Bureau of Business Research, College of Commerce and Administration, Ohio State University. University Press.

Stogdill, R.M. (1974). *Handbook of Leadership: A Survey of Theory and Research*. New York: The Free Press.

Sun Tzu (1910). *The Art of War*. Penguin Classics.

Uhl-Bien, M., Marion, R., & McKelvey, B. (2014). Leadership as adaptive change: A complex dynamic perspective. *Leadership Quarterly*, *25*(4), 543–575.

Janet Kirby, Joshua Frye, and Anneliese Nash

7 Human Resource Leadership in a Technology-Driven World

Abstract: Human resource management (HRM) has historically been a core competency of organizations, large and small. However, that is where the commonality across the years ends. Innovation has come in rapid fire, barely allowing time to consider adopting changes, let alone putting the innovations that make sense in place. This chapter discusses the most recent developments in HRM including remote work and artificial intelligence. It suggests a process for considering innovation and adoption.

Introduction

The human resource (HR) function had its genesis in response to the labor needs of the modern corporation and large-scale industrial operations in the early 1900s. Industries involved included railroads and steel. The attitude of the labor force was "hard-fisted . . . in which they paid as little as possible, giving minimal attention to working conditions and employees' needs" (Kaufman, 2010 p. 4). Clearly, what was once a form of HR would not be acceptable in current times. Today, HR is used by organizations to gain a competitive advantage and navigate an increasingly high-technology and global marketplace (Miles and Snow, 1984). The 21st century has included a transformative shift in the role of HR from support to being a strategic partner. HR is recognized as the mechanism facilitating connections between organizational success through the resource of human capital.(Kess-Momah et al., 2024). The business climate puts the HR leader out front as a key factor in the relationship between the employer and employee. This means having a seat at the executive level with titles such as Chief Human Resources Officer (CHRO) (Gupta, 2022). In the present time, the CHRO and staff are challenged to respond to the ever-changing internal and external environments. According to the Society of Human Resource Managers (SHRM), technologies that serve to improve compliance with regulatory requirements while at the same time helping to improve organizational health by allowing for faster decisions regarding talent drive HR leaders forward (Zielinski, 2024). There has never been a time in the past that required a highly complex set of demands than the HR leaders of today.

The 21st-century HR function makes use of data analytics, artificial intelligence, and automation to meet these complex demands. Rapidly developing technological advances further complicate the role. This chapter seeks to provide HR leaders with information that serves as a foundation to leverage the strengths of technology to meet the people needs of the organization while still completing the historically transactional work that is the responsibility of HR. The Deloitte Insights 2023 Global Human

https://doi.org/10.1515/9783111316987-007

Capital survey results use the term boundaryless work world, where "work is no longer defined by jobs; the workplace is no longer a specific place . . . and human resources is no longer a siloed function" (Deloitte, 2023, p. 3). Mercer refers to this time as "human-machine teaming." Artificial intelligence (AI) is one part of the equation with "agile talent models" and "human-centric work design" can reshape how work gets done and thereby increase productivity (Mercer, 2024, p.6). In this new environment, while perspectives of ideal workplace operations may have changed, compliance functions, with their abundance of caution, remain an integral part of the contemporary digital organization.

An important issue to navigate is how leaders manage the paradox between versatility, creativity, and compliance functions. Addressing this question will highlight some of the current thinking about how best to develop human resource systems that can embrace and benefit from the opportunities presented by HR technology. The cost of human presence remains a substantial portion of organizational expenditure. There are variables to consider such as company size, budget, and desired business impact. The mobilization of resources to improve the effectiveness of the HR function requires strategic, evidence-based processes.

Challenges and Opportunities

The most critical issues facing HR leaders today include technological innovation and integration, changing workforce dynamics, evolving organizational priorities, heightened focus on employee experience, rise of hybrid work models, emphasis on skill development, and the evolution of leadership (Ayanponle et al., 2024). Cybersecurity emerges as well because of recent and frequent data breaches. In fact, these breaches are as much about human capital and systems as programming or computer hardware (Llorens, 2017). Three broad categories emerge in a review of such lists. The first category that emerges is the leveraging of opportunities resulting from artificial intelligence (AI). The second has to do with data security. The increasing use of cloud storage and outsourcing functions such as screening of employment applications to online companies like Indeed increases the risk of compromising private employee data. The final category relates to leadership development. HR leaders are tasked with supporting a workforce that is weary of change and anxious about the future. Supporting managers whose teams consist of full-time and part-time employees as well as contingent workers in a rapidly changing and technologically-driven world requires innovative approaches.

The first category bridging human resources and technology is generative AI. Rapid development in this area makes it hard to keep abreast of change. To prepare HR leaders to address this challenge, a foundation knowledge of the terms and basic structures of AI can be helpful. Technology is not new to HR. The early human resource information systems (HRISs) are a repository of data relevant to HR including employee information, benefits structures, and payroll. It provided accurate recordkeeping and the ability to generate reports. The human resources management system (HRMS) held data and performed more complex functions including talent management and employee engagement. Today, the practice of human capital management (HCM) requires the usage of an array of technology based in the cloud that provides data storage, collaboration tools, and AI applications such as digital assistants. Consistent with earlier platforms, what data will be needed and how the data will be used are fundamental considerations (Bischoff, n.d.).

Generative AI is a seismic shift with innovation so rapid that managers need to focus on business fundamentals and strategy. At the core, AI, through the ability to be fed massive amounts of data, using layered processing, and identification of patterns, can create new content (Heaslip, 2023). Machine learning (ML) and natural language processing (NLP) are important terminologies that will be useful for the purpose of understanding why AI is relevant to HR. ML gives computers the ability to interpret data and make decisions without specific programming. An example is when a person looks up an item to purchase using a search engine, and then this person's social media pages are filled with this item (Coursera, 2024). NLP is programming in the AI family that allows computers to understand human speech. For example, your Alexa is using NLP, when asked about a sports score or recipe for biscuits (Brown, 2021). Knowledge of these terms can support an increased understanding of how AI and HR intersect. Having data to support the integration of AI into HR needs to be carefully planned for by contemporary managers.

AI can be impactful in every step of the employee life cycle. In its most familiar application, AI plays a role in the recruitment and selection process. AI can screen candidates, send communications to applicants, develop job interview questions, and eliminate some areas of bias in hiring that are inherent, albeit subconsciously, in the human experience. In onboarding, AI can verify employment documents, use chatbots to answer basic new employee questions, and provide credentials and access to systems as appropriate. Software can report on employee activity and output and reflect what additional support a new employee may need. Learning and development can also be delivered and assessed through AI systems (Siocon, 2023).

The opportunities presented by adopting AI in HR processes include improved efficiency, reduced costs, and more informed decision-making. Repetitive tasks like interview scheduling, updates to candidates, and screening of applications are all tools that can allow HR staff to attend to more complex and human-centered activities (Siocon, 2023). The 2023 McKinsey Global Survey on the adoption of AI reports that the recruitment and onboarding processes will be faster, more accurate, and unbiased (Chui et al., 2023). Utilizing AI resources in the employee lifecycle can result in savings and allow direction of limited resources (time and money) to individual employee development. This, in turn, serves the organization through improved engagement and retention.

The results of McKinsey's updated 2023 survey show that the number of respondents using generative AI (Gen AI) in their organizations had doubled to 65% (Singla et al., 2024). Initially Gen AI was being used in Marketing and Sales. However, Exhibit 6 in the report indicates, "Organizations often see meaningful cost reductions from generative AI use in HR" and revenue increases in other areas (Singla et al., 2024, p. 6).

AI's impact is not only on the time spent on employee development but also on the quality. Virtual reality and augmented reality are technological tools that improve training outcomes by giving trainers the ability to expose learners to new material and skill building in multiple formats, supporting learners with various strengths of learning styles. Virtual reality produces real, almost believable work experiences in a synthetic way. Augmented reality's "basic functionality consists of creating links, direct or triggered by user interface, between the real world and the information generated by a device or electronic information." Because of the realistic nature of these tools, employees can train more quickly and to deeper levels (Arena, et al., 2022, p. 1).

A common concern in using AI is the potential impact on the number of colleagues replaced by technology. IBM conducted a study regarding the impact of AI on the workforce and found that even as AI is used increasingly in business, the core competitive advantage an organization has is people (Goldstein, 2023). Another concern is that the skills gap in organizations is present and increasing. HBR posted content from IBM that highlighted important ways HR leaders can take advantage of AI. This information arises from an IBM report from the Institute for Business Value. First on the list is redesigning work beginning with the original purpose and goal of a function. Applying an AI function to an already troublesome process is of no help. Next is investing in talent in technology at the outset. This may mean hiring or reskilling/upskilling existing staff. Finally comes focusing on the skills needed for positions, not just the work experience of the candidate. This may mean leveraging AI for the training of new or existing members of the team. People are responsible for increased productivity, so focusing on employee needs is critical (Goldstein, 2023). Gartner advises HR leaders to debunk the myths that AI will replace people in HR and that HR leaders are holding back on the use of AI because of this concern. Survey responses of HR leaders in January of 2024 revealed that 38% were studying the opportunities for the use of generative AI in HR ("AI in HR", n.d.).

Organizational leaders across all sectors understand the dread of being alerted that data systems at their organizations have been compromised. Another challenge for HR leaders is data security. Multiple factors have resulted in HR being called on to help manage the security of data. Included are the increased and ubiquitous nature of technology and devices in the lives of organizations and their people, a regulatory environment that increasingly develops laws and rules that have to do with employee data security, and recognition of the importance of strong organizational cybersecurity cultures (Warszona, 2020).

HR has and maintains a wide range of data elements on each person who works or ever worked in the organization. It follows that HR leaders are responsible for the security of employee data. Increasingly, HR has a responsibility beyond the security of employee data. The placement of training and development functions for organizations in HR means being responsible for training on cybersecurity even though it is not the unit that "owns" the data. In a recent article on HR and cybersecurity Marsh and McClennan reported that "almost two-thirds (62%) of executives say the greatest threat to their organization's cyber security is the failure of employees to comply with cyber security rules" (Warszona, 2024, p. 1 n.d.). This coexistent long history of managing employee data and responsibility for training places HR leadership at the center of an organization's work with cyber security.

Humans have been creating tools to work since the beginning of time. Sometimes the development is fast and sometimes slower. But, there is no period in human history where advances in technological tools have been as impactful as they are today. The World Economic Forum reports that in 2000, just over half of Americans had broadband access, and today that number is more than 90%. Globally in 2000, less than 7% of the world was online, and today more than half of the people in the world are online (Hillyer, 2020). The response on cell phones is no less remarkable. At the turn of the last century, just 24 years ago, there were 740 million cell phone users, and today there are 8 billion (Hillyer, 2020). Innovations in the workplace have been developing in the same time span at a breakneck pace. Marsh McLennan, in the 2024 business insurance trends study, reports that 52% of companies responding indicate that tech advancements like AI, cloud computing, and "Internet of Things devices" present increased challenges and risks. However, 93% of executives surveyed indicated there was also opportunity in these same developments (Business Insurance Trends Report, 2024).

Information on internet use over the last 20-some years reflects the pace of change in the use of digital technology, and the COVID-19 pandemic pushed the concept of remote work to new levels. A Forbes report indicated that in 2023, 12.7% of employees were working fully remote, and another 28.2% were working in a model where they spent some time working remotely and some working in an office setting (Haan, 2024). The data further reveals that by 2025, the number of Americans who will be working at least some portion of the time remotely will be 32.6 million (Haan, 2024).

A new approach to data management is critical in contemporary organizations. In some organizations, risk management and legal departments overlook the fact that rather than IT, the highest risk category for a breach is HR. In addition, the cyber space for organizations becomes even more complex with the development of regulatory policies that put a higher degree of care on how data is handled, stored, and secured. Examples of these policies include the EU General Data Protection Regulation (GDPR), California Consumer Privacy Act, and the Illinois Biometric Information Privacy Act. This is just the beginning. HR logically becomes the center of cybersecurity because of its historical responsibilities for compliance (Warszona, 2020). Marsh and McClennan reports 62% of executives attribute the greatest data security risk is internal to the organization not from outside forces such as hackers. The greatest risk is because of employee disregard of rules in place for data security "(Warszona, 2020). Developing and maintaining a culture of cyber compliance is an HR function because of its responsibility for conducting training in digital transformation. Organizations, through HR leaders and training, can use the concept of cyber hygiene, which refers to the practices an organization establishes to secure networks for safety and to create a culture of security of data within the organization (Irei, 2023).

HR leaders have areas of strength in addition to compliance that are critical to an organization's competence regarding cybersecurity and the use of technology. Essential to compliance is determining and enforcing employee access to information. This is done successfully through enhancing HR leadership knowledge, strengthening skills and abilities in technology and data security, disseminating knowledge to upskill and reskill employees to manage compliance, and developing leaders to act as champions of technology-driven HR strategy. Advocating for a seat at the cyber security table should be an easy sell for HR leaders. HR needs to be current in areas such as AI, data-driven decision-making, virtual reality and augmented reality, chatbots, and social media. These technologies are powerful tools to improve the functioning of an organization but need to be protected by adoption of best practices with regard to the safety and security of data (Irei, 2023). This also means HR leaders need to consider staffing their departments with people who have both HR and technology expertise. Technology is impacting the definition of jobs. Machine learning is being adopted quickly, and the impact on jobs is that traditional concepts of jobs such as descriptions and duties will transform into superjobs, which are a combination of traditional and technologically driven automation. This does not eliminate the need for things such as judgment or curiosity that are human capabilities (Jares, n.d.).

The impact on productivity is an important consideration. The *Mercer* report on 2024 global talent trends cites productivity as the number one driver of transformation. On a question relating to what the "how" is in the trend, respondents to the survey selected employee up/reskilling and physical and mental well-being initiatives as the top two choices. There is process optimization and workflow management, and generative AI is number four ("Workforce 2.0", 2024). Employees, selecting from a list of options affecting productivity, cite too busy work or work that does not add value as the first choice. Too many interruptions and ineffective work structures are the second and third most chosen options. Addressing these factors will logically rest in collaboration between HR and other organizational departments. HR leaders are in the best position with the set of skills and knowledge to support what leaders as a whole say is needed to improve productivity (Mercer, 2024).

An amalgamation of skills is essential. The skillsets of HR and cybersecurity have not been traditionally present in the same person. Options to boost skillsets include recruitment of outside talent and reskilling/upskilling individuals already in the organization. The most expedient route may be to identify cybersecurity experts in the organization with some of the qualities of an HR professional. Qualities needed in an

HR professional include communication, conflict management, employee engagement, and change management. Earlier references regarding the explosion of artificial intelligence not only strengthen the assertion that HR teams need to increase expertise in technology for work inside the HR functions but also serve as a key link to the success of cybersecurity efforts and technology implementation organization wide. Whether it is taking an HR-minded person and providing support for development of IT knowledge or recruiting someone from IT to strengthen already existing HR-type skills requires a strategic approach on the part of HR leaders. Additionally, foundational knowledge of technology and data security for all HR team members helps support ongoing partnerships throughout the organization.

A focus on growth and development can lead to operational efficiency. Cyber risk and tech adoption challenges in an organization are best managed through the enhancement of training and development resources. AI can be used to strengthen training and development in HR departments. Chatbots, augmented and virtual reality tools, and onboarding specifically emphasizing cybersecurity are all ways to leverage the existing frameworks of the education function of HR teams in the short term. Increases in the complexity and scope of the HR function require strategic thinking on the part of HR leadership regarding the structure and culture of the department. Identifying the skills gap in the HR department with an eye toward aligning with the overall organizational strategies needs to be intentional and urgent. In addition to training and development, HR leadership is often tasked with the development and communication of organization policies and procedures. Coupling AI training technology with clear cybersecurity policies helps to establish accountability of each employee for maintaining the security of their data. Again, HR leadership's knowledge of cybersecurity and commitment to ongoing education for all employees in partnership with IT professionals helps combat the challenges associated with advancing technology (Viser, 2024).

An opportunity for HR leaders in this era of exploding availability and use of technology is in leadership development. Historically, leaders became leaders after being promoted into management because of their high level of technical skills. Recognition of the need to consider other factors such as "soft skills," also known as "people skills" or "interpersonal skills," has evolved over the last several decades. This need is even more important when considering the trend toward automation of many HR functions using AI. This skillset may have earned the soft skill label because of the challenge in quantifying or measuring them and does not diminish the importance. Forbes asserts that these so-called soft skills – "the ability to navigate complex interpersonal dynamics and build strong relationships" – are essential for success (Danao, 2024, p. 1). The emerging presence of AI and cyber-attacks have introduced a higher sense of urgency for the development of leaders in HR.

The last noteworthy challenge relates to leadership development. Earlier sections described the evolution of HR from transactional and managerial to more strategic in nature (Kess-Momah et al., 2024).

From an historical perspective the HR leader has been viewed as more of a manager with transactional duties related to payroll, benefits, and completion of organizational requirements such as preparation of tax forms. As shown in earlier sections on AI and cybersecurity, the HR function is much larger today, driven in part by recent technologies including AI. One way to reinforce the perception of HR at the strategy planning table is to point out the fiscal impact of the HR department so that it is considered an investment rather than a cost.

Advocating for a presence of HR in strategic conversations is an essential quality for the contemporary HR leader. There is a strong business case to be made for HR in the organization strategy conversation. The first thing to remember is that the single biggest expenditure in most organizations is the cost of people such as salaries and benefits. That makes the realm of HR responsible for the single biggest asset of an organization (Wood, 2023). Further emphasis can come from reminding key organizational actors that HR is responsible for recruiting and developing talent, health and safety of employees, and people record keeping (as pointed out in the cybersecurity function, in general). It is the only space in the organization that touches every other department in the organization.

At the strategy planning table, there are some key innovative approaches an HR leader must be knowledgeable about. For instance, digital transformation (DT), a term used to describe a near future state that organizations need to pursue to maintain a competitive advantage, is a noteworthy consideration. This transformation will require leadership that is strong and savvy about technology. This leader would also need to be able to view the organization in its entirety. Done effectively, the transformation must include the whole organization (McCarthy, et al., 2024). HR leadership will be called upon to support navigation through the transformation process. The literature about DT leadership is rather sparse, but there needs to be strong leadership at the whole system level along with a leader who is a technology expert but who can also navigate the human aspects of the transformation in partnership with the whole system leader (McCarthy, et al., 2024). It is important for leadership at all levels of specialty to remember that an organization is a socially built mechanism (McCarthy, et al., 2024).

Model for Success

There are numerous books, articles, and digital publications that track the trajectory of the manager, from the days of Frederick Taylor to Peter Drucker to Tom Peters to Jack Welch to Steve Jobs. The early names on the list were called managers, whereas those latter on the list were called leaders. They presided in a different way, influenced by the times and their own personality. What is true about each person and era is that the way they led or managed was driven more by external forces of society and economics than by their own will (Nordstrom, 2014). The current environment is no different. Advances in technological development are transforming how managers lead as great a shift as was felt in the Industrial Revolution, except that the amount of change that took 100 years in the early 20th century could take 1 year or less today. It is also true that the evolution of today's manager/leader is also seeing activity dictated by something neither inside themselves nor inside their organizations.

Forbes published an article on December 18, 2023, where they identified the eight biggest HR trends for 2024 (Marr, 2024). Generative AI is first on the list. It is interesting that the use of AI is a forgone conclusion, but the work of HR will be to strike a balance between efficiency and the "human qualities that are still essential in business" (Marr, 2024, p. 1). Gen Z will enter the workforce and prepare for the priorities of work-life balance and access to continuous education with strong commitments to diversity, equity, and inclusion. Third on their list was HR tech advances in training using virtual or augmented reality while also protecting the privacy and security of staff personal data. Flexible working arrangements will remain in demand regardless of the challenges remote work poses to the development and maintenance of organizational culture. HR will be challenged to support flexibility and still manage to have meaningful conversations (Marr, 2024). A model for success is to be a continuous learner who taps into resources within and outside the organizations themselves.

Concluding Thoughts and Future Directions

AI is here and is receiving acceptance in organizations in increasing numbers. In 2024, 56% of businesses are using AI to improve and perfect business operations, 51% are turning to AI for help with cybersecurity and fraud management, and AI is being used for recruitment and talent sourcing by 26% of businesses (Matzelle, 2024). Jumping into the AI bandwagon is not a quick fix for a fundamentally flawed plan or strategy. Whether a specific AI tool is helpful or not, the cybersecurity exposure is the same. Deepfakes, algorithm bias, automation-spurred job loss, and uncontrollable self-aware AI are AI risks that leaders must consider when moving forward with adoption (Matzelle, 2024). Evolution is largely about gradual development. In this chapter, the early days of HR were an outgrowth of the Industrial Revolution, where the human element in organizations was one-way. Employees did what they were told or were let go. Managers were concerned only about the product. Scientific management was characterized by individual employees doing one small part of a process and all the parts together became the product. Frederick Taylor's system focused on efficiency and specialization. Management was likewise a separate function with clear delineation from production workers (Khorasani and Almasiford, 2017).

Management theory evolved from the 1910s through Administrative Management in the 1920s and 1930s, where attention was focused on the structure of an organization and a focus on effective management. The Humanistic movement, which intersected management theory and behavior science, arrived in the 1930s and early 1940s and was characterized by interaction between the worker and management. This period continued into the 1970s, with contributions by Mary Parker Follet, Abraham Maslow, and Douglas Macgregor. During this time, the burden for outcome came to rest more on the manager and the need to become concerned about employee motivation. Organization Environment Theory followed, and the impact of the environment on production was added. Scholars in this period included Katz and Kahn, Davis and Powell, and Aldrich and Marsden (Khorasani and Almasiford, 2017

In the present world, the digitization of organizations is underway. Already HR leaders are using artificial intelligence to complete tasks previously completed by humans. This stage in the evolution of management is reflective of where management began with machines doing the work and employees overseeing the process knowledgeably at warp speed. This oversight role is where HR leaders need to focus. Quaquebeke and Gerpott (2023, p. 1) divided leadership development into the "now, new, and next." The now includes digital communication and leading remote or hybrid work arrangements. The new represents the use of algorithms to support leaders so that AI becomes a collaborator with leadership. AI may make suggestions or provide specific details to support a particular employee. Systems can track attendance and work output, notify a leader of the fact an employee may need support, and make suggestions as to what approach might be taken. The next is where AI not only supports leadership but also substitutes human leadership. Already AI resources allow for the use of digital assistants and avatar "friends" (Quaquebeke and Gerpott, 2023, p.4). AI can provide suggestions about seeing to the psychological needs of employees, which are sometimes ignored by a leader because of personal bias or the pressure time of a project.

The HR leader of the future will need to leverage technology to provide the organization with support in both the human and digital contexts. Appropriate skillsets will have to be deftly built to manage this new paradigm and find efficiencies. The successful HR leader will be a dynamic innovator who perceives the organization holistically, understands the convergence of people and technology, and pursues prompt and strategic action to accomplish set organizational goals.

References

2023 Global Human Capital Trends. Deloitte Insights. (n.d.). https://www2.deloitte.com/xe/en/insights/focus/human-capital-trends.html#read-the-chapter)

2024 Global Talent Trends. 2024 Global Talent Trends. (n.d.). https://www.mercer.com/insights/people-strategy/future-of-work/global-talent-trends/

2024 HR Technology Trend Predictions. Deloitte United States. (n.d.). https://www2.deloitte.com/us/en/blog/human-capital-blog/2024/2024-hr-technology-trends.html

Arena, F., Collotta, M., Pau, G., & Termine, F. (2022). An overview of augmented reality. *Computers*, *11*(2), 28. https://doi.org/10.3390/computers11020028

Ayanponle, L. O., Awonuga, K. F., Asuzu, O. F., Daraojimba, R. E., Elufioye, O. A., & Daraojimba, O. D. (2024). A review of innovative HR strategies in enhancing workforce efficiency in the US. *International Journal of Science and Research Archive*, *11*(1), 817–827. https://doi.org/10.30574/ijsra.2024.11.1.0152

Bischoff, B. (n.d.). HRIS vs. HRMS vs. HCM-what's the difference? People Managing People. https://www.oracle.com/human-capital-management/hrms/hris-hrms-hcm/

Brown, S. (2021, April 21). Machine Learning, explained. MIT Sloan. https://mitsloan.mit.edu/ideas-made-to-matter/machine-learning-explained

Chui, M., Hall, B., Singla, A., Sukharevsky, A., & Yee, L. (2023, August 1). The State of AI in 2023: Generative AI's breakout year. McKinsey & Company. https://www.mckinsey.com/capabilities/quantumblack/our-insights/the-state-of-ai-in-2023-generative-ais-breakout-year

Consulting, I. (2023, November 14). Artificial Intelligence and a new era of human resources. IBM Blog. https://www.ibm.com/blog/artificial-intelligence-and-a-new-era-of-human-resources/

Danao, M. (2024a, April 29). 11 essential soft skills in 2024 (with examples). Forbes. https://www.forbes.com/advisor/business/soft-skills-examples/

Gartner. (n.d.). HR technology imperatives for 2024 | gartner. https://www.gartner.com/en/human-resources/trends/2024-hr-technology-imperatives

Golstein, J. (2023, August 14). New IBM study reveals how AI is changing work and what HR leaders should do about it. IBM. https://www.ibm.com/blog/new-ibm-study-reveals-how-ai-is-changing-work-and-what-hr-leaders-should-do-about-it/

Haan, K. (2024, June 10). Remote work statistics and trends in 2024. Forbes. https://www.forbes.com/advisor/business/remote-work-statistics/

Heaslip, E. (2023, October 7). Traditional AI vs. Generative AI: A breakdown. https://www.uschamber.com/co/.https://www.uschamber.com/co/run/technology/traditional-ai-vs-generative-ai

Hillyer, M. (2020, November 18). Here's how technology has changed the world since 2000. World Economic Forum. https://www.weforum.org/agenda/2020/11/heres-how-technology-has-changed-and-changed-us-over-the-past-20-years/

Jares, J. (n.d.). Machine learning and alternative workforces: The future of work has arrived. Workday Enterprise Management Cloud. https://www.workday.com/en-se/pages/stories/machine-learning-alternative-workforces.html

Kaufman, B. E. (2010). *Hired Hands or Human Resources?: Case Studies of HRM Programs and Practices in Early American Industry*. ILR Press.

Kess-Momoh, A. J., Tula, S. T., Bello, B. G., Omotoye, G. B., & Daraojimba, A. I. (2024). Strategic Human Resource Management in the 21st Century: A review of trends and Innovations. *World Journal of Advanced Research and Reviews*, *21*(1), 746–757. https://doi.org/10.30574/wjarr.2024.21.1.0105

Khorasani, S. T., & Almasifard, M. (2017). Evolution of Management Theory within 20 Century: A Systemic Overview of Paradigm Shifts in Management. *International Review of Management and Marketing*, *7*(3), 134–137.

Matzelle, E. (2024, February 29). Top artificial intelligence statistics and facts for 2024. CompTIA Community. https://connect.comptia.org/blog/artificial-intelligence-statistics-facts

McCarthy, P., Sammon, D., & Alhassan, I. (2024). The characteristics of Digital Transformation Leadership: Theorizing the practitioner voice. *Business Horizons*, *67*(4), 411–423. https://doi.org/10.1016/j.bushor.2024.03.005

Mercer. (n.d.). Workforce 2.0 Unlocking human potential in a machine-augmented world. 2024 Global Talent Trends. https://www.mercer.com/insights/people-strategy/future-of-work/global-talent-trends/

Miles, R., & Snow, C. (1984). Designing strategic human resources systems. *Organizational Dynamics*, *13*(1), 36–52.

Nordstrom, D. S. and T. (2014, September 15). The evolution of the manager . . . and what it means for you. Forbes. https://www.forbes.com/sites/davidsturt/2014/09/11/the-evolution-of-the-manager-and-what-it-means-for-you/

Quaquebeke, N. V., & Gerpott, F. H. (2023). The now, new, and next of Digital Leadership: How Artificial Intelligence (AI) will take over and change leadership as we know it. *Journal of Leadership & Organizational Studies*, *30*(3), 265–275. https://doi.org/10.1177/15480518231181731

Singla, A., Hall, B., Chui, M., Yee, L., & Sukharevsky, A. (2024, May 30). *The state of AI in early 2024: Gen AI adoption spikes and starts to generate value*. Quatam Black AI by McKinsey. https://www.mckinsey.com/capabilities/quantumblack/our-insights/the-state-of-ai?stcr=D65B59511D5A4090A48ACEA19F2A2068&cid=other-eml-rld-mip-mck&hlkid=da804ec9c5674aad82892ee0d3472402&hctky=1926&hdpid=8ce3b68f-0b59-40bd-a478-12ed993bce6f

Siocon, G. (2023, November 20). Ways ai is changing HR departments. *Business News Daily*. https://www.businessnewsdaily.com/how-ai-is-changing-hr

Solutions, H. P. (2024, January 3). Revolutionizing human resources: The AI advantage in 2024. LinkedIn. https://www.linkedin.com/pulse/revolutionizing-human-resources-ai-advantage-f1osc?trk=organization_guest_main-feed-card_feed-article-content#:~:text=Workforce%20Planning%20and%20Analytics%3A%20AI,skills%20development%2C%20and%20succession%20planning

Visier, inc: Workforce trends 2024 – 10 workforce trends 2024. Visier, Inc | Workforce Trends 2024 – 10 Workforce Trends 2024. (n.d.).

Warszona, B. (n.d.). HR's increasingly important role in Cyber Risk Management. Marsh McLennan. https://www.marshmclennan.com/insights/publications/2020/july/hr-s-increasingly-important-role-in-cyber-risk-management.html

What is natural language processing? definition and examples. Coursera. (n.d.). https://www.coursera.org/articles/natural-language-processing

Wood, C. (2023, December 18). HR's New Frontier: The case for strategic business partnership. SHRM. https://www.shrm-atlanta.org/2023/12/hrs-new-frontier-the-case-for-strategic-business-partnership/

Zielinski, D. (2024, January 11). HR technology in 2024: Genai, analytics, and skills tech. SHRM. https://www.shrm.org/topics-tools/news/technology/hr-tech-trends-2024

Romie Frederick Littrell

8 Preferred Managerial Leader Behavior in a Global and Diverse World

Abstract: This chapter aims to analyze preferred managerial leader behaviors across different societal and national cultures, and how these preferences influence leadership effectiveness in multinational organizations. It explores relevant theories and frameworks related to leadership and culture, examines preferred leadership styles in various cultural contexts, discusses cross-cultural leadership challenges, and provides strategies for developing effective cross-cultural leaders. The chapter concludes by discussing implications for international management, including recruitment, leadership development, and performance management in multinational corporations.

Introduction

The bases for this research report are studies concerning preferred leader behavior across societal culture carried out by R.F. Littrell and colleagues under the auspices of the Center for Cross Cultural Comparisons, an international voluntary association of researchers interested in research concerning leader behavior across cultures. A considerable number of references are from this organization. Additionally, Prof. Littrell is a CCI representative for Russia for the GLOBE2020 project.

Theoretical Background

To comprehend preferred managerial leader behaviors across cultures, it is essential to explore relevant theories and frameworks that form the foundation of cross-cultural leadership research. This section discusses key concepts that have shaped our understanding of leadership in diverse cultural contexts within the global society.

Implicit Leadership Theory and Explicit Leadership Theory

Implicit Leadership Theory (ILT) posits that individuals have preconceived notions about the traits and behaviors that characterize effective leaders (Lord & Maher, 1991). These implicit beliefs are shaped by cultural values, personal experiences, and societal norms. In contrast, Explicit Leadership Theory (ELT) focuses on observable leadership behaviors and their measurable outcomes (Yukl, 2013). Both ILT and ELT

https://doi.org/10.1515/9783111316987-008

contribute to our understanding of how leadership is perceived and enacted across cultures.

Littrell (2013) emphasizes the importance of understanding both implicit and explicit leadership theories in cross-cultural contexts, as each significantly influences leadership expectations and perceptions of leader effectiveness across different societies.

Hofstede's Cultural Dimensions

Geert Hofstede's cultural value dimensions theory (Hofstede, 1980, 2001) has been instrumental in understanding cultural differences and their impact on leadership preferences. Hofstede initially identified four dimensions of national culture: power distance, individualism-collectivism, masculinity-femininity, and uncertainty avoidance. Later, he added two more dimensions: long-term orientation and indulgence-restraint (Hofstede et al., 2010).

Littrell (2012) notes that Hofstede's dimensions provide a valuable framework for analyzing how cultural values influence leadership expectations and behaviors. For instance, in high power distance cultures, leaders are expected to be more directive and authoritative, while in low power distance cultures, participative leadership is often preferred.

The GLOBE Project

The Global Leadership and Organizational Behavior Effectiveness (GLOBE) project, led by House and colleagues (House et al., 2004), expanded Hofstede's work by examining leadership across 62 societies. The GLOBE project identified nine cultural dimensions and defined six global leadership dimensions: charismatic/value-based, team-oriented, participative, humane-oriented, autonomous, and self-protective leadership.

Littrell et al. (2018) highlight the importance of the GLOBE project in providing a comprehensive framework for understanding leadership preferences across cultures. They note that the project's findings have significant implications for developing culturally appropriate leadership styles in multinational organizations.

Cultural Intelligence (CQ) Framework

The Cultural Intelligence (CQ) framework, developed by Earley and Ang (2003), focuses on an individual's capability to function effectively in culturally diverse settings. CQ comprises four dimensions: metacognitive CQ, cognitive CQ, motivational CQ, and behavioral CQ.

Here are definitions for the four facets of cultural intelligence (CQ):

Metacognitive CQ: "The mental capability to acquire and understand cultural knowledge, including awareness of cultural assumptions and the ability to plan, monitor, and revise mental models of cultural norms" (Ang et al., 2007).

Cognitive CQ: "The knowledge of cultural norms, practices, and conventions in different cultural settings, acquired through education and personal experiences" (Van Dyne et al., 2012).

Motivational CQ: "The capability to direct attention and energy toward learning about and functioning in culturally diverse situations, including intrinsic interest and confidence in cross-cultural effectiveness" (Earley & Ang, 2003).

Behavioral CQ: "The capability to exhibit appropriate verbal and nonverbal actions when interacting with people from different cultures, including the ability to adapt behavior to different cultural contexts" (Ang & Van Dyne, 2008).

L.N. Littrell and Salas (2005) emphasize the relevance of CQ in developing effective cross-cultural leaders. They argue that leaders with high CQ are better equipped to navigate the complexities of diverse cultural environments and adapt their leadership styles accordingly.

Preferred Managerial Leader Behavior Across Cultures

Preferred managerial leader behaviors vary significantly across cultures, reflecting the underlying values and norms of different societies. This section examines some notable patterns in leadership preferences across cultural contexts.

Participative Leadership in Individualistic Cultures

Research has shown that participative leadership is generally more preferred and effective in individualistic cultures, such as those found in North America and Western Europe (Tung, 1993). Participative leadership involves sharing decision-making power with subordinates and encouraging their input.

Littrell (2010) observes that in individualistic cultures, employees often expect to be consulted and involved in decision-making processes. This preference aligns with the cultural values of individual autonomy and self-expression associated with individualistic societies.

Paternalistic Leadership in Collectivist Cultures

In contrast to the preference for participative leadership in individualistic cultures, many collectivist cultures, particularly in Asia, the Middle East, and Latin America, tend to favor paternalistic leadership styles (Pellegrini & Scandura, 2008). Paternalistic leadership combines strong discipline and authority with fatherly benevolence and moral integrity (Farh & Cheng, 2000).

Littrell and Valentin (2005) note that paternalistic leadership can be highly effective in collectivist cultures, where there is a greater emphasis on hierarchical relationships and respect for authority. They argue that this leadership style aligns with the cultural values of harmony and group-oriented decision-making prevalent in these societies.

Charismatic Leadership Across Cultures

While the specific behaviors associated with charismatic leadership may vary, the GLOBE study found that charismatic/value-based leadership was universally endorsed across cultures (House et al., 2004). This leadership style emphasizes visionary, inspirational, and performance-oriented behaviors.

Littrell (2013) points out that while charismatic leadership is generally well received across cultures, its manifestation and interpretation can differ significantly. For example, in some cultures, charismatic leaders may be expected to demonstrate strong, assertive behaviors, while in others, more subtle and group-oriented charismatic behaviors may be preferred.

Gender and Leadership Preferences

Cultural attitudes toward gender roles also influence preferred leadership behaviors. The GLOBE study found significant variations in gender egalitarianism across cultures, which affects leadership opportunities for women and expectations of leader behavior based on gender (House et al., 2004).

Littrell et al. (2018) highlight the importance of understanding gender-related leadership preferences in cross-cultural contexts. They note that in some cultures, leadership is still predominantly associated with masculine traits, while in others, there is a growing acceptance of diverse leadership styles regardless of gender.

Cross-Cultural Leadership Challenges

Leaders operating in multicultural environments face numerous challenges stemming from cultural differences. This section explores some of the key obstacles encountered by cross-cultural leaders.

Communication Barriers

Effective communication is crucial for leadership, but cultural differences can create significant barriers. These barriers include language differences, varying communication styles (e.g., direct vs. indirect), and differing interpretations of nonverbal cues (Adler & Gundersen, 2007).

Hall (1976) indicated that high-context and low-context communication styles offer valuable insights into cultural differences in communication and their impact on leader effectiveness. In high-context cultures, communication relies heavily on implicit information, shared understanding, and nonverbal cues, while low-context cultures favor explicit, direct communication (Hall, 1976). Leaders who understand and adapt to these cultural communication styles are likely to be more effective in cross-cultural settings (Northouse, 2018). For instance, a leader from a low-context culture working in a high-context environment may need to pay more attention to nonverbal cues and relationship-building to communicate effectively. Conversely, leaders from high-context cultures may need to be more explicit and direct when working in low-context settings to avoid misunderstandings. Research has shown that leaders who can adjust their communication style to match the cultural context demonstrate higher levels of cultural intelligence and are more likely to succeed in global leadership roles (Rockstuhl et al., 2011).

Littrell (2002) emphasizes the importance of developing cross-cultural communication skills for effective leadership. He argues that leaders must be aware of cultural differences in communication styles and adapt their approach accordingly to ensure clear and effective communication with diverse team members.

Varying Expectations of Leader Behavior

As discussed earlier, expectations of appropriate leader behavior can vary dramatically across cultures. Leaders must navigate these differing expectations, which can be particularly challenging in multicultural teams.

Littrell and Cruz (2013) highlight the importance of understanding and managing these varying expectations. They suggest that leaders should be flexible in their approach, adapting their leadership style to align with local cultural norms while maintaining consistency in core organizational values.

Adapting to Different Cultural Norms

Leaders must also adapt their behaviors to align with local cultural norms while maintaining their authenticity and organizational values. This balancing act can be particularly challenging when cultural norms conflict with personal or organizational values.

Littrell (2012) argues that successful cross-cultural leaders must develop cultural intelligence to navigate these challenges effectively. He suggests that leaders should strive to understand the underlying cultural values that drive different norms and expectations, allowing them to adapt their behavior appropriately without compromising their integrity.

Developing Effective Cross-Cultural Leaders

Given the challenges of cross-cultural leadership, organizations must invest in developing leaders capable of operating effectively across diverse cultural contexts. This section explores strategies for cultivating cross-cultural leadership skills.

Cultural Intelligence Training

Cultural Intelligence (CQ) training has emerged as a valuable tool for developing cross-cultural leadership capabilities. CQ training programs focus on enhancing leaders' ability to recognize cultural differences, acquire cultural knowledge, maintain motivation for cross-cultural interactions, and adapt their behaviors appropriately (Earley & Ang, 2003).

L.N. Littrell and Salas (2005) emphasize the importance of CQ training in developing effective cross-cultural leaders. They argue that such training should be comprehensive, addressing all four components of CQ: metacognitive, cognitive, motivational, and behavioral.

Experiential Learning

Experiential learning opportunities, such as international assignments or cross-cultural team projects, can be highly effective in developing cross-cultural leadership skills. These experiences allow leaders to immerse themselves in different cultural contexts, challenge their assumptions, and develop practical skills for navigating cultural differences (Caligiuri & Tarique, 2012).

Littrell (2013) advocates for the use of experiential learning in cross-cultural leadership development. He suggests that organizations should provide structured opportunities for leaders to engage in cross-cultural experiences, coupled with reflection and feedback, to maximize learning.

Mentoring and Coaching

Cross-cultural mentoring and coaching programs can provide leaders with personalized guidance and support as they develop their cross-cultural leadership skills in a global and diverse world. These programs can pair leaders with experienced mentors who have successfully navigated diverse cultural contexts or provide access to coaches specializing in cross-cultural leadership development.

Littrell et al. (2018) highlight the value of mentoring and coaching in cross-cultural leadership development. They argue that these approaches can provide leaders with context-specific insights and strategies for navigating complex cross-cultural situations.

Implications for International Management

Understanding preferred managerial leader behaviors across cultures has significant implications for international management practices. This section explores how these insights can inform key areas of human resource management in multinational corporations (MNCs).

Recruitment and Selection

Knowledge of cultural variations in leadership preferences should inform recruitment and selection processes for international leadership positions. MNCs should consider candidates' cultural intelligence, adaptability, and experience with diverse cultures alongside traditional leadership competencies (Caligiuri & Tarique, 2012).

Littrell (2010) emphasizes the importance of incorporating cultural considerations into leadership selection processes. He suggests using assessment tools that evaluate cultural intelligence and cross-cultural leadership potential to identify suitable candidates for global leadership roles.

Leadership Development

Leadership development programs in MNCs should incorporate cross-cultural elements to prepare leaders for the challenges of global leadership. This may include cultural awareness training, opportunities for international experience, and development of specific cross-cultural competencies.

Littrell and Cruz (2013) argue for the integration of cross-cultural leadership development into broader leadership programs. They suggest that organizations should develop leadership competency models that reflect the diverse leadership requirements across different cultural contexts.

Performance Management

Performance management systems should account for cultural differences in leadership expectations and effectiveness. This may involve developing culturally appropriate performance criteria and considering cultural context when evaluating leadership effectiveness.

Littrell (2012) highlights the need for culturally sensitive performance management practices. He suggests that organizations should adapt their performance evaluation criteria and feedback processes to align with local cultural norms while maintaining consistency in core organizational values.

Conclusion

This chapter has explored the complex landscape of preferred managerial leader behaviors across cultures, drawing on key theoretical frameworks and empirical research. The topic is of increasing importance as a result of heightened globalization and increased diversity in the workplace. The findings highlight the significant influence of cultural values and norms on leadership expectations and effectiveness. While some leadership behaviors, such as charismatic leadership, appear to have universal appeal, the specific manifestations and interpretations of these behaviors vary considerably across cultures.

The challenges faced by cross-cultural leaders underscore the need for organizations to invest in developing leaders capable of navigating diverse cultural contexts in a globalized society. Strategies such as cultural intelligence training, experiential learning, and fostering inclusive organizational cultures can play a crucial role in building effective cross-cultural leadership capabilities.

For international management practitioners, these insights have important implications for various aspects of human resource management, including recruitment, leadership development, performance management, and succession planning. By recognizing and adapting to cultural variations in leadership preferences, multinational corporations can enhance their ability to develop and deploy effective leaders across diverse global operations.

As the business world continues to become increasingly interconnected and multicultural, the ability to lead effectively across cultures will become even more critical. Future research should continue to explore the nuances of cross-cultural leadership, including the impact of technological advancements on global leadership practices and the evolving nature of cultural influences in an increasingly globalized world.

References

Adler, N. J., & Gundersen, A. (2007). *International Dimensions of Organizational Behavior* (5th ed.). South-Western Cengage Learning.

Ang, S., & Van Dyne, L. (2008). Conceptualization of cultural intelligence: Definition, distinctiveness, and nomological network. In S. Ang & L. Van Dyne (Eds.), *Handbook of Cultural Intelligence: Theory, Measurement, and Applications* (pp. 3–15). M.E. Sharpe.

Ang, S., Van Dyne, L., Koh, C., Ng, K. Y., Templer, K. J., Tay, C., & Chandrasekar, N. A. (2007). Cultural intelligence: Its measurement and effects on cultural judgment and decision making, cultural adaptation and task performance. *Management and Organization Review, 3*(3), 335–371.

Caligiuri, P., & Tarique, I. (2012). Dynamic cross-cultural competencies and global leadership effectiveness. *Journal of World Business, 47*(4), 612–622.

Earley, P. C., & Ang, S. (2003). *Cultural Intelligence: Individual Interactions across Cultures*. Stanford University Press.

Farh, J. L., & Cheng, B. S. (2000). A cultural analysis of paternalistic leadership in Chinese organizations. In J. T. Li, A. S. Tsui, & E. Weldon (Eds.), *Management and Organizations in the Chinese Context* (pp. 84–127). Palgrave Macmillan.

Hall, E. T. (1976). *Beyond Culture*. Anchor Books.

Hofstede, G. (1980). *Culture's Consequences: International Differences in Work-related Values*. Sage Publications.

Hofstede, G. (2001). *Culture's Consequences: Comparing Values, Behaviors, Institutions, and Organizations across Nations* (2nd ed.). Sage Publications.

Hofstede, G., Hofstede, G. J., & Minkov, M. (2010). *Cultures and Organizations: Software of the Mind* (3rd ed.). McGraw-Hill.

House, R. J., Hanges, P. J., Javidan, M., Dorfman, P. W., & Gupta, V. (Eds.). (2004). Culture, leadership, and organizations: *The GLOBE study of 62 societies*. Sage Publications.

Littrell, Lisa N. & Salas, E. (2005). A review of cross-cultural training: Best practices, guidelines, and research needs. *Human Resource Development Review, 4*(3), 305–334. https://doi.org/10.1177/1534484305278348

Littrell, R. F. (2002). Desirable leadership behaviours of multi-cultural managers in China. *Journal of Management Development, 21*(1), 5–74.

Littrell, R. F. (2010). Comparative value priorities of Chinese and New Zealand businesspeople and their relationships to preferred managerial leader behaviour. PhD thesis, Auckland University of Technology, Auckland, New Zealand.

Littrell, R. F. (2012). Cultural value dimension theories: Hofstede—A work in progress. *AIB Insights, 12*(4), 3–6.

Littrell, R. F. (2013). Explicit leader behaviour: A review of literature, theory development, and research project results. *Journal of Management Development, 32*(6), 567–605.

Littrell, R. F., & Cruz, E. G. (2013). North and South Latin America: Influence of cultural values on preferred leader behaviour. *Journal of Management Development, 32*(6), 629–656.

Littrell, R. F., & Valentin, L. N. (2005). Preferred leadership behaviours: exploratory results from Romania, Germany, and the UK. *Journal of Management Development, 24*(5), 421–442.

Littrell, R. F., Alon, I., & Chan, K. W. (2018). Regional differences in managerial leader behaviour preferences in China. *Cross Cultural & Strategic Management,* 25(4), 578–605.

Lord, R. G., & Maher, K. J. (1991). *Leadership and Information Processing: Linking Perceptions and Performance.* Unwin Hyman.

Nishii, L. H., & Mayer, D. M. (2009). Do inclusive leaders help to reduce turnover in diverse groups? The moderating role of leader-member exchange in the diversity to turnover relationship. *Journal of Applied Psychology, 94*(6), 1412–1426.

Northouse, P. G. (2018). *Leadership: Theory and Practice* (8th ed.). SAGE Publications.

Pellegrini, E. K., & Scandura, T. A. (2008). Paternalistic leadership: A review and agenda for future research. *Journal of Management, 34*(3), 566–593.

Rockstuhl, T., Seiler, S., Ang, S., Van Dyne, L., & Annen, H. (2011). Beyond general intelligence (IQ) and emotional intelligence (EQ): The role of cultural intelligence (CQ) on cross-border leadership effectiveness in a globalized world. *Journal of Social Issues, 67*(4), 825–840.

Tung, R. L. (1993). Managing cross-national and intra-national diversity. *Human Resource Management, 32*(4), 461–477.

Van Dyne, L., Ang, S., Ng, K. Y., Rockstuhl, T., Tan, M. L., & Koh, C. (2012). Sub-dimensions of the four factor model of cultural intelligence: Expanding the conceptualization and measurement of cultural intelligence. *Social and Personality Psychology Compass, 6*(4), 295–313.

Yukl, G. (2013). *Leadership in Organizations* (8th ed.). Pearson.

Lama Blaique

9 Navigating the Digital Frontier: A Model for Effective Leadership and Virtual Teams

Abstract: Major factors such as globalization and the COVID-19 pandemic have necessitated both global and virtual teams within the workplace. The leadership challenge is thus very high for managing these teams because of the increased potential for misunderstandings and conflicts. This chapter aims at offering several recommendations that would assist leaders in successfully managing these increasingly popular types of teams in the organizational setting.

Introduction

Virtual teams (VTs) have been receiving research attention for more than two decades (Bagga et al., 2023; Townsend, DeMarie, and Hendrickson, 1998). VTs can be defined as teams that are scattered across frontiers and work together using information and communication technologies (ICTs) to achieve organizational tasks or projects (Connelly and Turel, 2016). The emergence of VTs can be attributed to globalization, advancements in technology, and the unprecedented COVID-19 pandemic (Townsend et al., 1998; Blaique et al., 2022). VTs are becoming increasingly popular because of the large advantages they offer compared to face-to-face teams. Some of these advantages include accessing talent from different geographical locations, decreasing transportation and other costs, and offering greater flexibility for employees (Ismail et al., 2023).

Although the concept of VTs is not totally new, the outbreak of the COVID-19 virus played a major role in the increased popularity of this mode of work (Venkatesh, 2020). This new shift to VTs has stimulated interest in examining how VTs can operate effectively in work practices, leading to the need for more research in the field (Bailey and Breslin, 2021; Blaique and Pinnington, 2023; Waizenegger et al., 2020).

Leadership, or e-leadership, has been recognized as a crucial factor contributing to VTs success in the existing literature (Gilson et al., 2015; Larson and DeChurch, 2020). Previous studies identified many challenges that e-leaders face because of the exceptional characteristics of VTs, such as balancing local priorities with the overall objectives of the VT and fostering a shared organizational culture despite geographical separation (Chai and Park, 2022; Lechner and Tobias Mortlock, 2022).

However, in the current period of transitioning to remote or hybrid work and nontraditional work settings, the relevance of these challenges and whether they are the only ones faced by newly transitioned e-leaders remains uncertain.

Even though the implications of the COVID-19 pandemic on organizations and work is waning, big corporations in various industries, such as Barclays, PwC, Unile-

https://doi.org/10.1515/9783111316987-009

ver, Facebook, Twitter, and McKinsey & Company, indicate that the new types of VTs will be used post pandemic (Boland et al., 2020). Companies are enjoying the advantages of VTs such as large-scale digital transformations that challenge traditional management practices and necessitate new working practices for both team members and team leaders are on the rise (Carnevale and Hatak, 2020; Carroll and Conboy, 2020; Youssef et al., 2023; Venkatesh, 2020).

While a limited number of studies have investigated the transformation of regular face-to-face teams to virtual teams as a direct result of the COVID-19 pandemic (Waizenegger et al., 2020), the sudden shift to virtual work resulting from the pandemic, along with the emergence of hybrid work models, necessitate unconventional leadership practices (Feitosa and Salas, 2020). Therefore, the aim of this book chapter is to uncover several factors related to enhancing and facilitating effective leadership of VTs.

This chapter investigates leadership practices related to VTs in an attempt to understand how leaders of traditional, physically collocated teams can transition successfully into e-leaders. The chapter offers several contributions that are valuable for human resources managers, general management scholars, practitioners, and educators seeking to apply existing VT knowledge to the current virtual work context that many individuals are experiencing.

The first section of this chapter describes the challenges and opportunities resulting from VTs and introduces the concept of e-leadership in relation to VTs. Then, the recent literature on VT reconfiguration is presented followed by a recently proposed model for effective leadership of VTs. The final section of this chapter concludes by offering practical managerial implications and future directions for research.

Challenges and Opportunities of Virtual Teams

Virtual teams (VTs) typically consist of individuals who collaborate on interdependent tasks and rely heavily on technology for communication (Connelly and Turel, 2016). Virtual teams offer several advantages, such as promoting work-life balance, reducing travel time, decreasing workplace stress, minimizing sick leave, and enhancing employee satisfaction. These benefits contribute to effective employee recruitment and retention schemes (Green and Roberts, 2010).

However, the literature cites several challenges related to leading VTs. Leaders of virtual teams (VTs) face distinct challenges compared to leaders of traditional face-to-face workplaces (Santos, 2013). Leaders are faced with obstacles such as managing members remotely, establishing trust among the members with less personal interaction, and utilizing technology to foster virtual collaboration (Neufeld et al., 2010). The inability of leaders and members to physically socialize may limit the leadership impact on the members (Liao, 2017). Leaders may encounter difficulties in setting up,

designing, managing, and financially operating VTs, which can lead to reduced efficiency and productivity (Gibson and Gibbs, 2006). The growing reliance on teams, tele-
work, and distributed leadership necessitates several electronic communication skills
that leaders must learn. E-leadership involves the proper utilization and integration
of electronic and traditional communication practices. Additionally, collaboration and
communication skills are essential for e-leaders (Wart et al., 2019). The next section
presents an in-depth explanation of the concept of e-leadership.

Model For Success

E-Leadership

Leadership is considered a major criterion for high-performing teams, specifically virtual ones (Ismail et al., 2022; Larson and DeChurch, 2020). This topic is significant
since a large majority of companies opted for a hybrid mode of work after the pandemic ended. Therefore, in this section the topic of leadership is closely investigated
in the context of VTs. The goal is to unravel how leaders can advance VTs as a new
mode of work post-COVID-19. E-leaders play a significant role in VTs functioning by
affecting how teams overcome obstacles and adapt to challenges (Gilson et al., 2015).
Reports from several companies such as McKinsey & Co. and Deloitte state several
hardships faced by traditional leaders transitioning into VT e-leadership, such as promoting novel styles of leadership, managing work-life challenges, and safeguarding
the well-being of VT members (Comella-Dorda et al., 2020; Deloitte, 2020). While past
studies on VT have researched ICT-related interactions among virtual team members
(Kayworth and Leidner, 2002), the new configurations of VTs call for exploring novel
e-leadership practices that will aid leaders in guiding their followers in the evolving
work environment (Carroll and Conboy, 2020). E-leadership has been an important
subject of research in the context of virtual teams (VTs) (Wart et al., 2019). Scholars
have explored various aspects that may affect VT performance, such as leaders' trust,
collaboration, and behavior (Flavian et al., 2019; Thomas et al., 2007). The next sections present two sets of factors that may advance e-leadership among virtual teams,
namely socio-emotional and task-related factors.

Socio-Emotional Factors of E-Leadership

1. Trust is considered a main challenge for both the leader and followers, specifically when discussing VTs (Bullock and Tucker Klein, 2011). Trust is defined as the
   degree of confidence a person has in another person's capability and willingness
   to act in an ethical and predictable manner (Nyhan, 2000). Specifically, this chap-

ter focuses on leaders' perceived trust and how it can foster efficient VTs. In addition to trust, a leader's behavior is expected to affect VTs members' performance and contribute to establishing trust among team members, including the leader (Duarte and Snyder, 2006). It is important to note that developing trust is usually a responsibility that falls on the shoulders of the leader of the VT (Elyousfi et al., 2021).

2. A leader's behavior plays a crucial role in virtual teams (VTs), particularly in terms of enabling the capabilities of the team (Hoegl and Muethel, 2016). Scholars studying virtual leaders have stressed the significance of a leader's behavior in addressing the challenges faced by VTs (Gilson et al., 2015). The behavior of the leader can be categorized into either task or relationship-oriented behavior (Liao et al., 2017). Task-oriented leadership behavior highlights the importance of achieving certain goals, while relationship-oriented leadership behaviors aim to support and assist subordinates, fostering a sense of belonging and comfort within the work group (Mikkelson et al., 2015). Leaders are expected to engage with the entire team as well as have individual interactions with each member within VTs (Liao et al., 2017). It is important for team leaders to recognize and encourage shared leadership within the team, as underestimating their teams' willingness to contribute to leadership can decrease the effectiveness of VT leadership (Hoegl and Muethel, 2016). Delegation is an important component when leading VTs since there would be limited face-to-face interactions. The empowerment of team members in VTs has a greater impact on team performance as well (Kirkman et al., 2004). In addition, successful VT leaders demonstrate empathy toward members of the team and foster unity by creating a positive social climate, since team unity is positively linked to group effectiveness (Kayworth and Leidner, 2002).

Task-Related Factors of E-Leadership

In addition to the socioemotional factors discussed earlier, the literature highlights the importance of task-related factors of e-leaders. These factors have become significant recently due to the sudden rush to virtual work caused by the pandemic (Garro-Abarca et al., 2021).

1. Leader communication and coordination play a crucial role in virtual teams (VTs). Leaders who exhibit efficient and constant communication with their followers are expected to receive strong employee performance. Given the absence of physical meetings, leaders of VTs may adopt a more informal communication style with the aim of offering effective communication that would influence the VTs members (Saafein and Shaykhian, 2014). Computer-based communication is linked to an increase in idea generation as opposed to face-to-face communication (Rutkowski et al., 2007). Effective VTs leaders are capable of offering regular,

timely, and adequate communication while clearly explaining the duties and responsibilities of their team members, which ultimately enhances team performance (Kayworth and Leidner, 2002).

2. Digital well-being: The well-being of virtual teams has been receiving increasing attention in recent studies (Adamovic, 2018; Carnevale and Hatak, 2020). The selection of relevant and proper ICTs has been highlighted in the literature as playing a significant role in team members' digital well-being (Dennis, Fuller, and Valacich, 2008). The choice of ICTs should be related to their degree of synchronicity and the type of task being performed (DeLuca and Valacich, 2006). The e-leader is responsible for deciding which ICTs would be suitable for a virtual team (Zander et al., 2013). The COVID-19 pandemic has highlighted the importance of appropriate ICT selection due to situations like 'Zoom fatigue,' indicating the potential impact of using unsuitable ICTs on workers' well-being and performance (Sugden, 2020). This may be associated with technostress, which refers to the stress linked to ICT-based work (Tarafdar, Pullins, and Ragu-Nathan, 2015). Leaders should be mindful of the possibility that VT members may experience technostress, particularly when face-to-face interactions are mostly replaced by online interactions. A graphical presentation of what has been discussed in this section is provided in Figure 9.1.

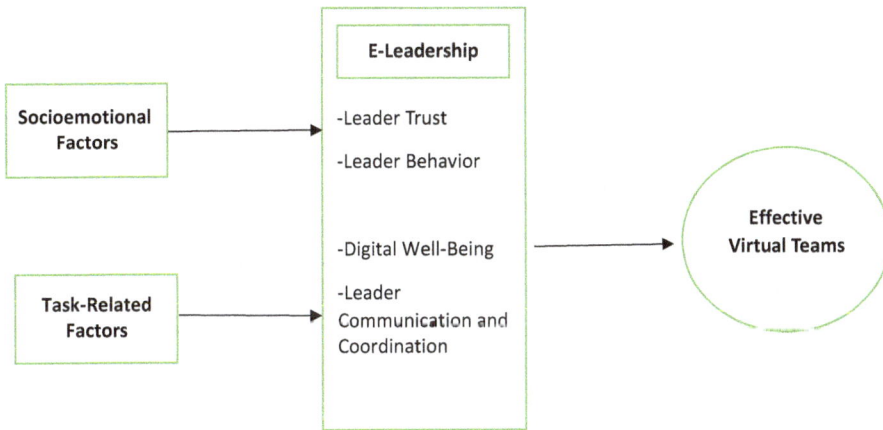

Figure 9.1: Conceptual Model.
Source: Author's own creation

Concluding Thoughts and Future Directions

Practical Implications

First, it is becoming increasingly evident that to navigate the challenge of effective VTs successfully and establish strong and adaptable leadership, cohesive team efforts are essential for the organization's functioning. Complicated problems often call for collaborative group efforts and significant resources, and VTs are no exception. Leaders should be aware of how team members are interacting with one another and their ability to work effectively and harmoniously and identify necessary actions to enhance team performance.

Second, it is recommended that VTs utilize up-to-date information and communication technologies to facilitate interaction, enabling members to effectively collaborate even when geographically separated. Since information technology may be the backbone of VTs functionality, leaders should receive appropriate training for stronger and more effective VTs leadership. Leaders are advised to share their ICT knowledge with their followers to empower them to be effective team members.

Third, following the discussion on the importance of addressing the digital well-being of VT members, e-leaders should assist their team members in selecting appropriate information and communication technologies for their tasks. They should also recognize that in contexts of crises such as the COVID-19 pandemic, there may be additional (unseen/unrecognized) organizational demands placed on team members without overlooking the increased need for adequate resources to perform the necessary tasks. Neglecting such issues could result in challenges like burnout and techno-stress for the followers. Therefore, e-leaders should be aware and acknowledge the unique demands of working in virtual teams and ensure that their team members have the appropriate resources, which may differ from those in a face-to-face team setting.

Fourth, promoting communication and collaboration within VTs is more difficult due to the inherent challenges discussed earlier. E-leaders should proactively identify ways to enhance continual collaboration and communication among VT members. They should try to develop a culture of trust and relationship based on existing social connections between the members.

Future Studies

This chapter presents a useful model that can be used by educators, leaders, and practitioners to compare advanced, effective, and successful VT management. Future studies can investigate the concept of virtual teams by considering other existing frameworks in the literature. The model can also include other factors in addition to socioemotional and take-oriented factors discussed in this chapter, as previous studies have also suggested that VTs performance can be influenced by factors such as culture, personality, and more (Connelly and Turel, 2016). Thus, future studies can also consider incorporating these factors within the model.

The pandemic has necessitated a reconfiguration of the workplace, prompting the establishment of new workplace settings and the need for new research to enhance theoretical and practical understandings of how leaders can foster effective VTs. Acknowledging the significance of e-leadership in the effective functioning of VTs, as recognized in the VT literature (Carroll and Conboy, 2020; Larson and DeChurch, 2020), this chapter proposes a model of effective e-leadership. The proposed model identifies two sets of factors that provide insights for traditional face-to-face team leaders transitioning into VT leadership, enabling them to create high-performing and sustainable VTs. Therefore, this book chapter contributes to a fresh perspective in this domain by identifying several socio-emotional factors, namely, leader trust, communication, coordination, and behavior, as well as task-related factors: digital well-being and enhancing innovation and creativity. The current chapter also provides practical implications for various stakeholders, particularly leaders of traditional teams who have shifted into VT leadership without adequate preparation. It also provides guidance for professional bodies and managers, who should adapt organizational policies to align with the nature of VTs.

References

Adamovic, M. (2018). An employee-focused human resource management perspective for the management of global virtual teams. *The International Journal of Human Resource Management, 29*(14), 2159–2187.

Bagga, S. K., Gera, S., & Haque, S. N. (2023). The mediating role of organizational culture: Transformational leadership and change management in virtual teams. *Asia Pacific Management Review, 28*(2), 120–131.

Bailey, K., & Breslin, D. (2021). The COVID-19 Pandemic: what can we learn from past research in organizations and management? *International Journal of Management Reviews, 23*(1), 3–6. https://doi.org/10.1111/ijmr.12237

Blaique, L., & Pinnington, A. (2023). *Virtual Work Challenges and Opportunities in the Asia-Pacific Region: The Role of Organizational Virtual Work Climate.* Elgar Companion to Managing People Across the Asia-Pacific, 269–288.

Blaique, L., Abu-Salim, T., Asad Mir, F., & Omahony, B. (2022). The impact of social and organisational capital on service innovation capability during COVID-19: the mediating role of strategic environmental scanning. *European Journal of Innovation Management.*

Boland, B., De Smet, A., Palter, R., & Sanghvi, A. (2020). *Reimagining the office and work life after COVID-19.* McKinsey & Company. https://www.mckinsey.com/business-functions/organization/our-insights/reimagining-the-office-and-work-life-after-covid-19#

Bullock, C. & TuckerKlein, J. (2011), *Virtual Work Environments in the Post-Recession Era,* Brandman University, California.

Carnevale, J. B., & Hatak, I. (2020). Employee adjustment and well-being in the era of COVID-19: implications for human resource management. *Journal of Business Research, 116,* 183–187.

Carroll, N., & Conboy, K. (2020). Normalising the "new normal": changing tech-driven work practices under pandemic time pressure. *International Journal of Information Management, 55*, Article 102186.

Chai, D. S., & Park, S. (2022). The increased use of virtual teams during the Covid-19 pandemic: implications for psychological well-being. *Human Resource Development International, 25*(2), 199–218.

Comella-Dorda, S., Garg, L., Thareja, S., & Vasquez-McCall, B. (2020). *Revisiting agile teams after an abrupt shift to remote*. McKinsey & Company. https://www.mckinsey.com/business-functions/organization/our-insights/revisiting-agile-teams-after-an-abrupt-shift-to-remote.

Connelly, C.E. & Turel, O. (2016), Effects of team emotional authenticity on virtual team performance, *Frontiers in Psychology, 7*, 1336.

Deloitte. (2020). Leading virtual teams: Eight principles for mastering virtual leadership of teams [Human Capital]. https://www2.deloitte.com/global/en/pages/about-deloitte/articles/covid-19/leading-virtual-teams.html

DeLuca, D., & Valacich, J. S. (2006). Virtual teams in and out of synchronicity. *Information Technology & People, 19*(4), 323–344.

Dennis, A. R., Fuller, R. M., & Valacich, J. S. (2008). Media, tasks, and communication processes: a theory of media synchronicity. *MIS Quarterly, 32*(3), 575–600.

Duarte, D.L. and Snyder, N.T. (2006), *Mastering Virtual Teams: Strategies, Tools, and Techniques that Succeed*, 3rd ed., Jossey-Bass, San Francisco, California.

Elyousfi, F., Anand, A., & Dalmasso, A. (2021). Impact of e-leadership and team dynamics on virtual team performance in a public organization. *International Journal of Public Sector Management.*

Flavian, C., Guinal_ıu, M. and Jordan, P. (2019), Antecedents and consequences of trust on a virtual team leader, *European Journal of Management and Business Economics, 28*(1), 2–24.

Fletcher, G., & Griffiths, M. (2020). Digital transformation during a lockdown. *International Journal of Information Management, 55*, Article 102185.

Garro-Abarca, V., Palos-Sanchez, P., & Aguayo-Camacho, M. (2021). Virtual teams in times of pandemic: Factors that influence performance. *Frontiers in Psychology, 12*, 624637.

Gibson, C.B. and Gibbs, J.L. (2006), Unpacking the concept of virtuality: the effects of geographic dispersion, electronic dependence, dynamic structure, and national diversity on team innovation, *Administrative Science Quarterly, 51*(3), 451–495.

Gilson, L. L., Maynard, M. T., Jones Young, N. C., Vartiainen, M., & Hakonen, M. (2015). Virtual teams research: 10 years, 10 themes, and 10 opportunities. *Journal of Management, 41*(5), 1313–1337.

Green, D.D. and Roberts, G.E. (2010), Personnel implications of public sector virtual organizations, *Public Personnel Management, 39*(1), 47–57.

Hoegl, M. and Muethel, M. (2016), Enabling shared leadership in virtual project teams: a practitioners' guide, *Project Management Journal, 47*(1), 7–12.

Ismail, H., Blaique, L., & Syagha, O. (2023). The drivers and barriers of telecommuting: The case of Lebanon during COVID-19. *International Social Science Journal*. In Print.

Ismail, H. N., Kertechian, K. S., & Blaique, L. (2022). Visionary leadership, organizational trust, organizational pride, and organizational citizenship behaviour: a sequential mediation model. *Human Resource Development International*, 1–28.

Jasper, J. (2020, June 27). What does England's lockdown easing mean for office workers? The Guardian. https://www.theguardian.com/business/2020/jun/27/what-does-englands-lockdown-easing-mean-for-office-workers

Kayworth, T. R., & Leidner, D. E. (2002). Leadership effectiveness in global virtual teams. *Journal of Management Information Systems, 18*(3), 7–40.

Kirkman, B.L., Rosen, B., Tesluk, P.E. and Gibson, C.B. (2004), The impact of team empowerment on virtual team performance: the moderating role of face-to-face interaction, *Academy of Management Journal, 47*(2), 175–192.

Larson, L., & DeChurch, L. A. (2020). Leading teams in the digital age: four perspectives on technology and what they mean for leading teams. *The Leadership Quarterly*, *31*(1), Article 101377.

Lechner, A., & Tobias Mortlock, J. M. (2022). How to create psychological safety in virtual teams. *Organizational dynamics*, *51*(2).

Liao, C. (2017), Leadership in virtual teams: a multilevel perspective, *Human Resource Management Review*, *27*(4), 648–659.

Mikkelson, A.C., York, J.A. and Arritola, J. (2015), Communication competence, leadership behaviors, and employee outcomes in supervisor-employee relationships, *Business and Professional Communication Quarterly*, *78*(3), 336–354.

Neufeld, D.J., Wan, Z. and Fang, Y. (2010), Remote leadership, communication effectiveness and leader performance, *Group Decision and Negotiation*, *19*(3), 227–246.

Nyhan, R.C. (2000), Changing the paradigm: trust and its role in public sector organizations, *The American Review of Public Administration*, *30*(1), 87–109.

PWC's US Remote Work Survey (2021). https://www.pwc.com/us/en/services/consulting/business-transformation/library/covid-19-us-remote-work-survey.html

Rutkowski, A.-F., Saunders, C., Vogel, D. and Van Genuchten, M. (2007), "Is it already 4 a.m. in your time zone?" Focus immersion and temporal dissociation in virtual teams, *Small Group Research*, *38*(1), 98–129.

Saafein, O. and Shaykhian, G.A. (2014), Factors affecting virtual team performance in telecommunication support environment, *Telematics and Informatics*, *31*(3), 459–462.

Santos, J. (2013), Designing and leading virtual teams, Faculty and Research Working paper, available at: https://flora.insead.edu/fichiersti_wp/inseadwp2013/2013-76.pdf

Sugden, J. (2020). Zoom fatigue is real. *The Wall Street Journal*. https://www.wsj.com/articles/zoom-fatigue-is-real-11587652460

Tarafdar, M., Pullins, E. B., & Ragu-Nathan, T. S. (2015). Technostress: negative effect on performance and possible mitigations: effect of technostress on performance. *Information Systems Journal*, *25*(2), 103–132.

Thomas, D.M., Bostrom, R.P. and Gouge, M. (2007), Making knowledge work in virtual teams, *Communications of the ACM*, *50*(11), 85–90.

Townsend, A. M., DeMarie, S. M., & Hendrickson, A. R. (1998). Virtual teams: technology and the workplace of the future. *The Academy of Management Executive (1993)*, *12*(3), 17–29.

Venkatesh, V. (2020). Impacts of COVID-19: a research agenda to support people in their fight. *International Journal of Information Management*, *55*, Article 102197.

Van Wart, M., Roman, A., Wang, X. and Liu, C. (2019), Operationalizing the definition of e-leadership: identifying the elements of e-leadership, *International Review of Administrative Sciences*, *85*(1), 80–97.

Waizenegger, L., McKenna, B., Cai, W., & Bendz, T. (2020). An affordance perspective of team collaboration and enforced working from home during COVID-19. *European Journal of Information Systems*, *29*(4), 429–442.

Youssef, M. F., Eid, A. F., & Khodeir, L. M. (2023). Challenges affecting efficient management of virtual teams in construction in times of the COVID-19 pandemic. *Ain Shams Engineering Journal*, *14*(7), 102008.

Zander, L., Zettinig, P., & Mäkelä, K. (2013). Leading global virtual teams to success. *Organizational Dynamics*, *42*(3), 228–237.

Evolution of Organizing

Abhishek Kumbhat and J. Mark Munoz

10 Reorganization of Enterprise Business Models with an AI and Blockchain–First Approach

Abstract: This chapter highlights how fundamentally transformative technologies like AI and blockchain of current times are challenging and revolutionizing business models. Instead of a boardroom discussion, the article focuses on giving a very practical perspective for leadership in building an organization-wide mindset for the adoption of such technologies to reorganize business models.

Introduction

The first generation of economy, driven by centuries-long industrial development, was transformed into an information era through digitization in less than a century. This second-generation economy of the information era further fueled the rise of the conceptual age of creativity and entrepreneurial attitude (Pink, 2005; Blank, 2015; Kumbhat, 2017), thereby making these digital startups a significant contributor to the world economy and a vital driver of the socioeconomic prosperity of each country. Additionally, with decades of information empowerment, these digital enterprises became the source of trust, authority, and reliability for the end consumers.

Such a technology transformation journey has never remained static, has always challenged its previous state of digitization, and has continuously transformed businesses and how they are managed. In recent years, new-age technologies have ushered in a transformative wave across industries, empowering new business models to disrupt the established ones and compelling enterprises to rethink and reorganize their business models. Artificial intelligence (AI) and blockchain technologies are central to this transformation, which drives innovation, enhances operational efficiency, and builds decentralized businesses. This is leading to the rise of the third generation of the economy.

Artificial intelligence (AI) is redefining the capabilities of businesses by enabling them to analyze large datasets, make informed decisions, and automate complex processes. The global AI market size was estimated to be about $196 billion in 2023 (Grand View Research, 2024). AI technologies, such as machine learning, natural language processing, and computer vision, provide enterprises with the tools to enhance customer experiences, optimize supply chains, and innovate product development (Tulsani & Sahatiya, 2023). A McKinsey report (2018) indicated that AI is widely used in service operations, product or service development, and sales and marketing, especially in sectors such as telecom, high-tech, and financial services. Research indicates

https://doi.org/10.1515/9783111316987-010

that AI can significantly boost productivity and economic growth by augmenting human capabilities and creating new business opportunities (Bughin et al., 2018).

Similarly, blockchain technology has been on the rise, with its decentralized and immutable nature offering unparalleled security and transparency and making it a critical component for modern enterprise infrastructures. Fortune Business Insights (2024) reported that the global blockchain-as-a-service (BaaS) market size was at $1.90 billion in 2019 and is expected to reach $24.94 billion in 2027 with a CAGR of 39.5% during the period. By ensuring data integrity and facilitating trustless transactions, blockchain can streamline various business processes, including supply chain management, financial transactions, and contract execution (Iansiti & Lakhani, 2017).

It has been noted that integrating blockchain with AI can lead to the creation of more secure and efficient systems, enhancing overall business resilience. The convergence of AI and blockchain fosters the development of innovative business models that leverage the strengths of both technologies. For instance, AI-driven predictive analytics combined with blockchain's secure data storage can enhance decision-making processes in sectors like finance, healthcare, and logistics (Treleaven, Brown, & Yang, 2017). Additionally, blockchain-based smart contracts can automate and enforce business agreements, reducing the need for intermediaries and minimizing operational costs (Tapscott & Tapscott, 2016).

Considering the potential AI and blockchain technologies bring to disrupt the current economy, enterprises cannot ignore them. Therefore, it becomes critical for business leaders to understand the fundamentals of such transformative technologies in their enterprise context and explore the potential use cases to disrupt their business models. More so, such leaders shall adopt an AI and blockchain–first approach mindset to explore an opportunity or address a business challenge, enabling their enterprises to unlock new growth opportunities, streamline processes, and improve security.

This chapter explores how these technologies are reshaping enterprise operations and offers insights into the strategic considerations essential for leveraging their full potential. This chapter starts with the basics of these fundamentally transformative technologies to enable business leaders to understand the changing role of enterprises in this third-generation economy. Furthermore, this chapter offers fundamental principles of AI and blockchain technologies to empower business leaders to establish true use cases of such technologies for the strategic transformation of enterprises. Additionally, this chapter delves into typical implementation challenges and strategies for successfully adopting such technologies.

Understanding AI and Blockchain in Digitization

For Artificial Intelligence

For decades, organizations have been achieving operational efficiency using rule-based robotic process automation (RPA) techniques and comprehending raw data for better business decisions using statistical data analytics techniques. However, in recent years, AI has become one of the most abused words – from startup pitches to board meetings. Publicly available language models like OpenAI boosted usage by making the technology accessible to everyone. This led to unprecedented growth of social media content – sharing messages like, '*AI is magical and can do everything and fit into every role*', '*the world is about to achieve singularity*', and '*AI will take all our jobs*' – reflecting fictionally optimistic and fear-based marketing content. Irrespective of such distractive and impractical marketing stories around artificial intelligence, true benefits and practical use cases of underlying tech cannot be ignored, especially for industries like fintech (Kumbhat, 2024) and cybersecurity (CyberNX, 2024).

Most AI technologies are not definitive but rather iterative processes that need to be refined. Three key buckets of AI use cases are (a) process automation, (b) optimizing tasks assisting humans in cognitive and sensory activities, and (c) personalized recommendations and services. From the implementation perspective, business leaders are empowered to explore options like building proof-of-concepts through API-based third-party models, customizable open-source models, and developing their own AI models. However, applicable implementation time, cost, return on investment, and own intellectual property development should be key parameters in selecting the right option.

For Blockchain

Tech enterprises, for decades, in our "Centralized" Web 2.0 world, have been the sources of trust, authority, and reliability. These enterprises have fueled the growth of technology that is in use today in centralized systems around us, where a single entity controls the data and processes. Enterprises worldwide are evolving from a Web 2.0 world to a Web 3.0 of decentralized systems. This change has been marked by the shift from centralized systems to decentralized systems, where control is distributed across a network. As a result, these same enterprises are now being questioned for the same trust, authority, and centralization they founded.

Blockchain is a technology with elevated security protocols using a cryptographic ledger (IBM, 2017; IBM, 2017a). The technology is expected to contribute about $1.76 trillion to the global GDP by 2030 (PWC, 2020; PWC, 2020a). Blockchain's decentralized nature eliminates the need for intermediaries, thus enhancing transparency and reducing the potential for fraud. Blockchain plays an important role in managing information asymmetry (Cong and He, 2019). Its broad applications include audits, quality assurance, securities and commodities trading, supply chain management, and smart contracts, among others (Uzialko, 2023). For example, in the supply chain sector, blockchain can provide an immutable record of the journey of goods, ensuring authenticity and reducing the risk of counterfeits. Similarly, in the financial sector, blockchain-based smart contracts can automate and enforce agreements without the need for third parties, thus reducing costs and increasing efficiency. An Accenture (2017) report indicated that blockchain technology can reduce infrastructure cost by as much as 30% in the case of eight of the largest investment banks.

In the era of Web 3.0, blockchain technology has emerged as a powerful disruptor, challenging traditional enterprise business models (Kumbhat, 2023). Kumbhat (2023) specifically shared examples of such disruption within the gaming and fintech industry. Business leaders are now tasked with understanding and harnessing the potential of this fundamentally transformative technology to drive innovation and maintain a competitive edge.

Changing Strategies and Roles of Enterprises – The Rise of EEE 2.0

When businesses and business models of technology enterprises face a threat from new technologies, primarily open-source solutions or based on open standards, the Embrace-Extend-Extinguish Strategy (EEE Strategy) is a widespread strategy used by such enterprises (Woodard and West, 2011). As a part of this strategy, a market leader, as a good corporate citizen, first embraces the common standard, which presents a threat to its own power. It participates and makes positive sounds and noises to communicate its embracement. Thereafter, being involved in the community, it identifies shortcomings in the common standard, and as a member, it proposes to add some bells and whistles. However, as a for-profit company, it extends the common standard with proprietary extensions. Ultimately, with its market leader position and extensive marketing push, everybody migrates to its version of the standard with its proprietary extensions. A new proprietary standard is evolved with a combination of open common standards and proprietary extensions of the enterprise. Thereby, the open standard is extinguished, and the market leader is back in control. The second generation of the economy of tech enterprises has seen Microsoft using such strategies in browser and operating system business wars.

However, in the recent times of creativity, entrepreneurship, and the third generation of economy empowered by new-age technologies, the typical strategy of Embrace-Extend-Extinguish (EEE 1.0 as a three-step journey) cannot be implemented by tech enterprises to address such business challenges. Instead, the authors propose

EEE 2.0 as three options, whereby organizations in the current times have to explore either of the three options: Excuse, Extinguish, or Embrace.

Amid the proposed two sets of transformative technologies, while organizations should review the long-term impact of automation and large data models through artificial intelligence, it is equally critical to strike the right balance between Web 2.0 and Web 3.0 in the rise of a decentralized world. Enterprises must navigate challenges such as regulatory compliance, integration with legacy systems, and developing new business models. However, within the context of EEE 2.0, these firms will often find significant challenges in opting for "Excuse" in light of the organization's sustainability and "Extinguish" in light of massive entrepreneurial businesses offering competition. Thereby, practically, most organizations are left with only the option of "Embrace" as an option out of the EEE 2.0 strategy. Figure 10.1 illustrates the shift in the process.

EEE 1.0 (Steps to Regain Market Dominance)

Embrace ⟶ *Extend* ⟶ *Extinguish*

EEE 2.0 (Optional Paths for Sustainability)

| *Excuse*   or | *Extinguish*   or | *Embrace*

Figure 10.1: The shift in the enterprise EEE strategy.

From the model shown in Figure 10.1, enterprise attributes and competencies are forced to rise to a new level, with three essential attributes:

- **Learning Orientation.** Enterprises must invest in understanding an array of fundamentally transformative technologies. This requires a continuous learning and innovation culture, where employees shall be encouraged to explore and experiment with new ideas.
- **Research-Driven.** Enterprises need extensive research to find successful use cases of AI and blockchain technologies. This involves studying industry best practices, engaging with academic research, and collaborating with technology partners to develop and test such new-age technology applications.
- **Adaptation Preparedness.** Business leaders gain and explore use cases of such transformative technologies in their business context while aligning with strategic goals in an effective and seamless manner. This requires strategic planning, change management, and rapidly adapting to evolving market conditions.

Since enterprises vary in skills, resources, and technological access, the ability to successfully navigate changes in this environment will differ across firms. Those who can effectively leverage AI and blockchain technologies will be well positioned to thrive in the digital age. At the same time, those who fail to adapt may find themselves at a competitive disadvantage.

Fundamental Use Cases of AI and Blockchain

At a time when there is a plethora of content developers and social media explosion, whereby everybody claims to be an expert and thought leader, it can be challenging for business leaders to filter out marketing-driven and hyped content. Finding experienced practitioners and true use cases based on the fundamentals of these technologies is extremely difficult. The authors propose that businesses focus on fundamental use cases of these technologies to look at every opportunity and challenge from the lens of an AI and blockchain–first approach to identify where to use and where not to use such technologies.

Fundamental Use Cases of AI

– Divide and Conquer (Automation of operational tasks)

From the outset, the business operations may look complex and challenging to automate. A standard advice for businesses is to look at their day-to-day operational activities, divide them into microtasks, and evaluate each microtask for automation. Such an approach allows businesses to find low-hanging fruits for automation and achieve success with the 80:20 principle. Such automation will commence through a rule-based engine and then migrate to artificial intelligence to achieve efficiency and deliver unexpected outcomes.

– Effective Assistance for Cognitive and Sensory Tasks

AI-based technologies like computer vision, natural language processing, text-to-speech, transcription, large language models, and generative AI have surprisingly initiated the automation of tasks that need the cognitive and sensory skills of human beings. As these technologies enabled through AI models take a significant amount of training data and effort to fine-tune, such tasks should be completed as human-in-loop or as an effective assistance to human workers. AI technologies may enhance employee creativity with higher job skills (Jia et al., 2024). Activities like object detection from images/videos, document processing, and content generation are the most frequent use cases.

– Computationally Challenging Analytical Tasks

There have been instances where businesses are either not collecting or ignoring micro details of business operations, primarily related to user experiences and activities, in the inability to use such data. In the current stage of various machine learning algorithms and big data technologies, businesses can be motivated to collect such micro details not only to offer deeply personalized products and services to their customers (Agrawal et al., 2018) but also to make their processes more efficient by knowing more detailed execution breakages.

While the above three fundamental instances will allow business leaders to look at their business context differently, businesses must recognize the resources, effort, and cost required for such tasks if seen from a short-term outcome perspective. On a practical note, the authors would like to caution business leaders to avoid force-fit AI use cases just for the sake of it. For example:

- For a short-term and temporary project, the effort required for AI implementation to achieve practically beneficial returns cannot be justified.
- For mission-critical use cases like healthcare, the outcome of AI implementation need to be done only as a recommendation rather than automated actions. Human-in-loop is a better strategy for such instances.
- For projects involving sensitive data like personally identifiable information (PII), firm-specific data, regulated data, and trade secrets, businesses need to be careful in selecting the mode of implementation and avoid putting such data on public or third-party models. Enterprise AI use cases should be well architected for data privacy and protection.

Fundamental Use Cases of Blockchain

For enterprises to find true use cases and applications of blockchain, they need to understand the foundational principles of blockchain. Business leaders can utilize such fundamental principles to drive transformative change. At first, considering blockchain as a secure data store, four areas need attention:

– **Immutable Traceability**
Instead of considering blockchain as completely immutable, the actual situation is that it is immutably traceable. Blockchain's inherent immutability enables secure logging, auditing, and integrity control systems, compared to typical file logging for audit trails. Fintech, supply chain, real estate, and gambling can leverage blockchain for enhanced security, regulatory compliance, and transparent traceability.

– **First Mile of Trust**
While blockchain can ensure immutable traceability of data and information (digital assets) put into it, such digital assets must be validated and verified by an authority at the time of first entry into the blockchain. Therefore, such a first mile of trust at the first entry is critical to building credibility and reliability. Additionally, there has to be a custodian for underlying assets before digitizing the assets. This feature would benefit financial services, real estate, and healthcare industries.

– **Operator and Asset Separation**
By leveraging blockchain, enterprises can enable end-users to have ownership and control over their digital assets, including data and credentials. This will allow a never-foreseeable separation of operator and assets, allowing end-users to log into

the operator-managed systems with identity (login credentials) and assets as a modality. Industries like gaming, healthcare, and pharma can benefit from this approach by enhancing data security, privacy, and interoperability.

– Programmable Assets

Programmable assets like smart contracts can automate and enforce business agreements, reducing the need for intermediaries and minimizing operational costs. Smart contracts and concepts like zero-knowledge proofs enable automated asset utilization while maintaining security. Financial services and real estate industries can benefit from blockchain's ability to streamline processes, reduce manual intervention, and enhance efficiency.

Overcoming Implementation Challenges

While adopting AI and blockchain–first approach of next-generation transformation in enterprise settings seems appealing at the outset of the context, it comes with its share of challenges, primarily related to change management. Business leaders must address these hurdles with a three-pronged activity alignment: [1] fostering a culture of openness, innovation, and collaboration; [2] addressing technical considerations for AI and blockchain adoption; and [3] navigating potential regulatory challenges. This approach will ensure successful implementation.

– Mindset Shift

Business leaders should foster a culture of openness, innovation, and collaboration to integrate such new-age technologies into existing business models effectively. More specifically, whenever a business is exploring an opportunity or facing a challenge, business leaders shall look at such an opportunity or challenge with a different lens of AI and blockchain–first approach to come up with appropriate approaches and solutions. For instance, in case of AI adoption, instead of worrying about human-job replacements, businesses need to think about bringing efficiencies and performing humanly impossible tasks of high computing. While adopting blockchain technology, business leaders have to think beyond commonly hyped use cases like cryptocurrencies and NFTs. Instead, they need to focus on shifting from a centralized mindset to embrace.

– Technological and Business Considerations

Data availability for training, hallucination, and scalability for enterprises are the most common technical considerations for the appropriate adoption of artificial intelligence. In contrast, interoperability between various blockchain networks, scalability, and integrating legacy systems with the balance of Web 2.0 and Web 3.0 are critical technical challenges for blockchain adoption. Transformative powers and dependency on large language models like those from OpenAI or large public chains like Ethereum for the adoption of AI and blockchain, respectively, are additional business challenges. In light of the nondefinitive outcomes of artificial intelligence and regulatory uncertainties of blockchain use cases in the short term, business leaders need careful decisions on strategy alignment and investment allocation in talent and infrastructure resources.

– **Regulatory Uncertainty**
As the adoption of AI and blockchain continues to expand, regulatory frameworks are still evolving. Data privacy, data residency, machine bias, and human employability are the most critical regulatory challenges of AI adoption. Regulators are equally concerned about blockchain adoption, considering decentralized data controls and the use of cryptocurrencies for illicit cross-border transactions. Business leaders must stay informed and actively engage with regulators to navigate potential regulatory challenges and ensure compliance.

Strategies for Successful Adoption

AI and blockchain are growing as effective tools in enterprise transformation. These technologies will grow even more prominently in the years to come. Three (3) approaches are essential for optimizing digital solutions and transformation through AI and blockchain.

– **Preparing for Adoption**:
Building competencies in AI and blockchain is a time-consuming and resource-intensive process. Strategic planning and early allocation of resources can significantly enhance the chances of success. Business leaders should invest in educating themselves and their teams about these technologies, their potential, and their industry implications. Developing internal expertise and fostering an innovative culture are crucial preparatory steps.

– **Shifting-Left in Approach:**
Business leaders should consider involving experts early in the project lifecycle to ensure smooth adoption. Collaboration with external partners, startups, and industry consortia can help accelerate such implementation and mitigate risks

– **Accelerating Go-To-Market:**
Business leaders should identify and prioritize high-impact use cases and develop a phased approach for such a technology adoption. More so, working with partners that have contextual digital accelerators can help enterprises achieve faster go-to-market. Quick wins and early successes will help build momentum and gain buy-in from stakeholders across the organization.

Conclusion

The transformative power of AI and blockchain technologies marks the dawn of a new era in the evolution of enterprise business models. It has moved the management practice into a new frontier where technology is a key factor for business success. Moving from the industrial age to the information era and now into the age of AI and blockchain, business leaders and contemporary managers are presented with unprecedented opportunities to innovate, streamline operations, and enhance security. AI's ability to analyze large datasets and automate complex processes, combined with blockchain's unparalleled security and transparency, creates a robust foundation for the third-generation economy.

As businesses embrace these technologies, leaders must also navigate the challenges of decentralization, trust, and authority. Understanding the fundamentals of AI and blockchain is crucial for business leaders, enabling them to identify and implement transformative use cases. The shift from centralized Web 2.0 models to decentralized Web 3.0 systems demands a strategic approach that balances innovation with practical implementation. More so, such technological advancements have forced leaders to rethink their business models and take on an uncharted path toward transformation.

Business leaders that successfully integrate AI and blockchain into their enterprise context will be better positioned to lead in the digital age of the future. By cultivating a culture of continuous learning, contextualizing technological know-how in business operations, and preparing for unexpected regulatory changes, businesses can harness the full potential of these technologies. Embracing an AI and blockchain–first approach is not only a strategy for growth but also a necessity for staying competitive in fast-evolving market conditions.

In conclusion, in an evolved management landscape, reorganizing enterprise business models with an AI and blockchain–first mindset offers a pathway to sustained innovation and economic growth. This chapter provided a comprehensive framework for understanding and leveraging these transformative technologies and offered business leaders fresh insights that would be helpful in navigating and thriving in the digital landscape of the future.

References

Accenture (2017). Blockchain technology could reduce investment banks infrastructure costs by 30%, according to Accenture report. Accessed June 27, 2024. Available at: https://newsroom.accenture.com/news/2017/blockchain-technology-could-reduce-investment-banks-infrastructure-costs-by-30-percent-according-to-accenture-report#:~:text=17%2C%202017%20%E2%80%93%20Blockchain%20technology%20could,is%20part%20of%20Aon%20Hewitt

Agrawal, A., Gans, J. S., & Goldfarb, A. (2018). *Prediction Machines: The Simple Economics of Artificial Intelligence*. Harvard Business Review Press.

Blank, S. (2015). The Global Startup Ecosystem Ranking 2015, *The Startup Ecosystem Report Series*, Compass. co (formerly Startup Genome). Retrieved on August 02, 2020 from http://startup-ecosystem.compass. co/ser2015/

Bughin, J., Seong, J., Manyika, J., Chui, M., & Joshi, R. (2018). *Notes from the AI Frontier: Applications and Value of Deep Learning*. McKinsey Global Institute.

Cong, L. W., & He, Z. (2019). Blockchain Disruption and Smart Contracts. *The Review of Financial Studies*, *32*(5), 1754–1797.

CyberNX Insights (2024). Pros and Cons of AI for Cybersecurity: Strengthening Defense, Understanding Risks. Retrieved on June 20, 2024 from https://www.cybernx.com/b-pros-and-cons-of-ai-for-cybersecurity-strengthening-defense-understanding-risks

Fortune Business Insights (2024). Hardware and software IT services. Accessed June 27, 2024. Available at: https://www.fortunebusinessinsights.com/blockchain-as-a-service-baas-market-102721

Grand View Research (2024). Artificial Intelligence Market Size, Share and Trends Analysis Report. Accessed on June 27, 2024. Available at: https://www.grandviewresearch.com/industry-analysis/artificial-intelligence-ai-market

Iansiti, M., & Lakhani, K. R. (2017). The Truth About Blockchain. *Harvard Business Review*, *95*(1), 118–127.

IBM. (2017). *Blockchain Basics: Introduction to Distributed Ledgers*.

IBM. (2017a). Blockchain security: What keeps your transaction data safe? Accessed June 6, 2023. Available at: https://www.ibm.com/case-studies/energy-blockchain-labs-inc

Jia, N., Luo, X., & Fang, Z. 2024. When And How Artificial Intelligence Augments Employee Creativity. *Academy of Management Journal*, *67*(1), 5–32.

Kumbhat, A. (2017). Startup – Fashion or Fad – Youth Attractiveness – presentation at Startup Oasis Event, India. Retrieved on January 01, 2018 from http://newinyou.com/2017/09/startup-youth-attractiveness/

Kumbhat, A. (2023). Notes from Blockchain – Challenging Enterprise Business Models. Blockchain Expo – TechEx North America 2023.

Kumbhat, A. (2024). Notes from Practical Examples of how fintech can use AI first approach to improve their products and operations. Innovation Series at Fintech Saudi, Kingdom of Saudi Arabia.

McKinsey (2018). Notes from the AI frontier: AI adoption advances, but foundational barriers remain. Accessed June 27, 2024. Available at: https://www.mckinsey.com/~/media/McKinsey/Featured%20Insights/Artificial%20Intelligence/AI%20adoption%20advances%20but%20foundational%20barriers%20remain/Notes-from-the-AI-frontier-AI-adoption-advances-but-foundational-barriers-remain.ashx

Pink, D. H. (2005). *A Whole New Mind – Why Right-Brainers Will Rule the Future*. Penguin Group Publishing, USA.

PWC. (2020). *Time for Trust: The Trillion-Dollar Reason to Rethink Blockchain*.

PwC. (2020a). Time for trust: How blockchain will transform business and the economy. Accessed June 6, 2023. Available at: https://www.pwc.com/gx/en/industries/tech-nology/publications/blockchain-report-transform-business-economy.html

Tapscott, D., & Tapscott, A. (2016). *Blockchain Revolution: How the Technology Behind Bitcoin Is Changing Money, Business, and the World*. Penguin.

Treleaven, P., Brown, R. G., & Yang, D. (2017). Blockchain Technology in Finance. *Computer*, *50*(9), 14–17.

Tulsani, V., & Sahatiya, P. (2023). Intelligent Systems at Work: A Comprehensive Study of AI Applications in Various Fields. https://doi.org/10.5281/zenodo.8186251

Uzialko, A. (2023). Beyond bitcoin: How blockchain is improving business operations. *Business News Daily*. Accessed June 6, 2023. Available at: https://www.businessnewsdaily.com/10414-blockchain-business-uses.html

Woodard, C. Jason & West, Joel. (2011). Strategic Responses to Standardization: Embrace, Extend or Extinguish?. In Gino Cattani, Simone Ferriani, Lars Frederiksen, Florian Täube, eds., *Advances in Strategic Management*, *28*, 2011, pp. 263–285 (10.1108/S0742-3322(2011)0000028014.)

Diana Heeb Bivona and Kristine Mantey

11 Incorporating Design Thinking Into Data-Driven Strategic Management

Abstract: This chapter discusses how to integrate design thinking into strategic management, i.e., design-led strategy. While essential to strategic decision-making, managers are overwhelmed by the influx of quantitative and qualitative data bombarding organizations today. The chapter examines how managers, individually and collectively, can better use such information to enhance strategy discussions and actions.

Introduction

Ambiguity, complexity, and volatility are just a few hallmarks of the 21st-century global business environment. Change seems to be the only true constant in today's business landscape. Managers must steer their organizations through an ever-shifting environment where technological advancements, geopolitical shifts, and unforeseen disruptions appear every day. Managers report feeling overwhelmed when navigating modern business challenges. Making sound strategic decisions while dealing with a multitude of dynamic environmental factors forces managers to make decisions with incomplete or out-of-date information.

Traditional rigid and linear strategic planning models should be revised in the face of this volatility. No longer do they suffice in the modern business arena where constant disruption requires agility. Backward-in-focus, problem-centric planning models often rely heavily on past 'known' factors (i.e., historical performance data). They apply analytical and quantitative approaches to historical data. Yet, we struggle to make good decisions based on accurate and up-to-date information because of data overload. Drowning in a sea of data has roughly 82% of companies making decisions based on 'stale' or outdated information (Business Wire, 2022).

Today's dynamic environment requires leadership to be proactive and future-oriented, using more than just good historical data when making business decisions. Models that allow organizations to adjust, adapt, and pivot quickly are needed. Integrating design thinking into the strategic process complements the use of big data and offers a new and valuable approach to planning and decision-making.

Design thinking is both a mindset and problem-solving approach that prioritizes empathy, collaboration, curiosity, and experimentation when evaluating problems. This approach involves understanding and defining a problem, identifying potential solutions, prototyping and testing those solutions, and iterating based on feedback on the solutions (Han, 2022). Since its introduction over 60 years ago, when it was first presented as a method for collecting and analyzing market and customer-level data

https://doi.org/10.1515/9783111316987-011

(Beckman & Barry, 2007), design thinking evolved into a versatile problem-solving approach applied across disciplines, including business, education, and healthcare. It has also been adopted to improve strategy development and advance strategic management theory and practice (Johansson-Skoldberg et al., 2013).

Design thinking's benefits across disciplines are notable. The iterative process aligns well with the need for adaptability and allows faster responses to changes in the business environment. Organizations can respond more effectively to changes in the market, technology, and consumer preferences by continuously testing and refining ideas. Managers benefit from the agility provided by design thinking, making informed strategic adjustments in real time rather than waiting for an annual planning cycle.

Combining design thinking with strategic management is beginning to be embraced by organizations integrating the approach into their strategic processes. Companies like Apple, IBM, and Google use design thinking in product design and development, while Nike is using it to innovate its marketing and customer engagement. Airbnb applies design thinking to create intuitive interfaces, enhance customer experiences, and drive business growth. Salesforce sees the benefit of using design thinking to improve its user interfaces, streamline workflows, and enhance overall user experiences. Global consulting companies like McKinsey & Company, Booz Allen Hamilton, and Boston Consulting Group have also incorporated design thinking approaches into their strategic services (Knight et al., 2020).

Integrating design thinking into strategic management is not surprising; companies with solid design thinking practices achieve higher revenues and higher returns for shareholders (Sheppard et al., 2018). Furthermore, incorporating design thinking into strategic management provides organizations with the opportunity to overcome organizational challenges that can impede further growth and development.

Challenges and Opportunities

Design thinking contributes to effective strategic management through its human-centric, iterative, and creative approach to problem-solving and decision-making. The adoption of design thinking leads to the development and implementation of effective strategies and resonates with the organization's needs and preferences. Design thinking can prove beneficial across a variety of situations encountered by modern organizations.

A Shift in Thinking. Linear thinking dominates business processes, which is understandable, given its analytical, methodical, and logical approach to challenges. Moving from point A to point B (in a linear method) and making a straight-line connection in a sequential order when addressing challenges 'makes sense.' Using information learned from a previous situation and applying it to the next problem is sensible. Linear thinking ensures the succinct delivery of accurate information within, and outside, an organization for many problems.

Managers spend considerable time dealing with well-defined issues or problems that benefit from the structured approach linear thinking mandates. However, linear thinking is also limiting and becomes a drawback when it generates instinctive responses or responses limited to past experiences. Linear thinking rarely produces new or different solutions needed to address rapidly changing or complex environments (Rauch & Tackett, 2021). This is where design thinking proves beneficial.

Design thinking, by its nature, promotes the use of divergent thinking. Divergent thinking differs from convergent thinking, which involves narrowing down options to find a single correct solution. Design thinking involves generating a wide variety of possible solutions or ideas in response to an open-ended question or problem. It is characterized by exploring multiple perspectives, considering both conventional and unconventional options, and fostering creativity. Organizations engaging in design thinking ask participants to propose multiple solutions with no limits, barriers, or constraints.

Design thinking allows managers to explore other ideas and solutions to complex problems besides those that worked in previous situations. It pushes leaders to shift away from a tendency to rush and accept predetermined solutions. While both design thinking and linear thinking start at point A, design thinking differs in that it allows for the generation of multiple approaches or solutions to reach point B. It encourages the exploration of more than one alternative by using tools like brainwriting or brainstorming where no idea is discarded. Managers are free to explore a set of potential solutions with a set of parameters established beforehand. This freedom to expand a search allows managers to ask more questions and identify potential issues, threats, or opportunities that may not have come to light had the focus remained narrowly on simply moving from point A to point B.

Innovation Catalyst. In addition to solving business challenges, design thinking can help drive innovation across the organization. Rapid technological advancements, changing consumer expectations, and more competition require companies to continuously innovate to stay competitive. An age-old adage in business is that 'innovation is the lifeblood of the organization.' Regularly generating new ideas and turning them into viable products and services for customers is necessary for the survival of any business.

Design thinking is beneficial to strategic planning because of its ability to foster innovation. Design thinking's nonlinear nature encourages the exploration of ideas and experimentation with different solutions for an organization. Such an open-minded approach helps free teams from traditional constraints and consider unconventional solutions or ideas, driving innovation. Design thinking offers a structured and flexible framework for problem-solving and the creation of new services and products and empowers organizations to look beyond what has worked in the past.

This process generates products and services that resonate with users, even where the organization has a tried and true product or service.

Companies often struggle with driving innovation internally due to the linear thinking processes ingrained in the organization. Design thinking provides a systematic way to break free from established thinking patterns and encourages a culture of experimentation. By integrating design thinking into the strategic process, managers nurture mindsets that value curiosity, embrace ambiguity, and view failures as learning opportunities—all essential for fostering innovation.

Design thinking, by its very nature, presents the organization with multiple solutions to any potential project, problem, product, or service. Each of these solutions results in opportunities to investigate a wide range of options. During exploration, innovation blossoms. As organizations embrace design thinking, the mindset and process become part of the culture. Employees see problems not as roadblocks but rather as opportunities for innovation. Ideas that do not meet the organization's current needs are not wholly discarded but cataloged for future consideration. Allowing space to consider more than one potential solution opens opportunities for continual innovation.

Customer-centric Mindset. Innovation and problem-solving work well with design thinking, but in addition, the process also encourages organizations to cocreate solutions with their customers. Companies guide their customers to better understand their needs and desires by asking questions to better define the problem or opportunity. By involving end-users in the design and innovation process, companies gain valuable feedback and insights, significantly reducing the risk of developing less optimal products or services. Design thinking, in collaboration with customers, better defines and meets customer needs. This collaborative approach strengthens the relationship between company and its customers, resulting in more customer-centric and market-responsive strategies.

Managers responsible for shaping the strategic direction of their organizations can leverage design thinking to instill a customer-centric mindset throughout their teams. This shift toward cocreation and collaboration ensures that strategic decisions are informed by real-world user experiences, leading to products and services that are not only innovative but also aligned with customer expectations.

Humanizing Strategy. One of the benefits of the design thinking process is its ability to humanize the strategy process. Traditional strategic design methods prioritize financial metrics, market share, and operational efficiency in the strategic management process, to the detriment of the human factors involved. It is common for leaders to lean into their knowledge bases gathered from personal observation and know-how during the strategic process. Using and trusting a manager's 'gut' when making decisions is all too common, even though this is not considered a rational approach (Hayashi, 2001). This is a shortsighted approach if leaders refrain from using the products or services they sell or have little to no contact with their customers.

Traditional approaches to strategy are often incomplete because they do not consider the customer's needs at its core (Sheppard et al., 2018). Instead of viewing customer needs as the driver of strategic decision-making, traditional approaches perceive customer needs as the result of those decisions (Knight et al., 2020).

In contrast, a key component of design thinking is its focus on understanding and addressing human needs. By incorporating this human-centric approach into strategy development, leaders better align business goals with their customer's actual needs. Design thinking compels leaders to empathize with end-users. In doing so, they gain valuable insights into customer behavior, desire, and pain points. It encourages leaders to think more intuitively. By integrating design thinking into the process, leadership ensures their strategic decisions resonate with, and meet, their customers' evolving expectations.

Incorporating design thinking into the strategy process promotes a more holistic approach to strategic decision-making. Divergent and convergent thought processes come together, highlighting the use of both analytical and intuitive thinking and combining the best of systematic and people-centered approaches. When armed with this well-rounded approach, managers formulate better strategic decisions and are in the best position to make correct decisions.

Fostering Collaboration. Effective strategy planning and execution requires collaboration across different organizational departments and functions. Traditionally, rigid organizational structures hinder communication and collaboration. Unintentional barriers (i.e., silos) too often serve as roadblocks when attempting to resolve a problem or create a product. Design thinking promotes a cross-functional and collaborative approach, encouraging a culture of interdepartmental cooperation. Design thinking pushes for the formation of multidisciplinary teams, bringing together individuals from different departments so that each contributes unique perspectives and expertise. The diversity of skills and perspectives enriches the problem-solving process by allowing for a wide range of viewpoints to be considered.

Effective strategic decision-making requires deliberate, reflective, and structured thinking. By facilitating a customer-centric, iterative, and interdisciplinary approach to innovation projects, design thinking offers a shared framework and language that can be used across all departments, improving communication across teams (Hölzle & Rhinow, 2019). Breaking down barriers using design thinking allows managers to ensure that strategic decisions are informed by diverse perspectives, resulting in more holistic and robust strategies. Thus, the reduction or potential elimination of organizational barriers coupled with a shared framework and language afforded by design thinking allows an organization's stakeholders to begin to identify problems and work together to generate as many potential solutions as possible (Yorio, 2019).

Risk Mitigation. Every strategic decision involves some level of risk, and mitigating this risk is a constant concern for leadership. Design thinking's emphasis on prototyping and testing provides a powerful mechanism for reducing uncertainty. Rather than relying solely on theoretical models and projections, managers embrace a more hands-on and experiential approach to validate strategic assumptions.

Prototyping and testing enable managers to gather real-world feedback before fully implementing any initiatives. An iterative feedback loop identifies potential pitfalls and areas for improvement, allowing for strategic adjustments before significant resources are committed. Design thinking is a significant risk mitigation tool, where strategic decisions are grounded in practical insights developed through the process rather than through theoretical assumptions.

Complementing Big Data. In this digital age, undergoing frequent transformation, data has been ubiquitous. As a result, the amount of data available to organizations grows exponentially every month. Organizations become consumed, and at times overwhelmed, by data. However, the role of data cannot be overstated in the decision-making process. Data is a critical asset for most organizations, particularly regarding strategic decision-making (Agarwal & Dhar, 2014; Shajalal et al., 2023). When the constant influx of data can be converted into actionable information, managers can make informed and accurate decisions backed by reliable data. The volume, velocity, and variety of available data, however, pose significant challenges requiring effective management practices (Mentsiev et al., 2023). Additionally, and just as importantly (if not more), it requires managers to learn how to administer data, analyze it to improve understanding, and then make changes in response to new insights gained (Ross et al., 2013).

From how end-users interact with products and services, to the cost to produce or deliver, data-driven decisions are crucial to avoiding unintended outcomes. Collecting and promptly analyzing appropriate data can minimize risks in strategic decision-making. Incorporating data-driven insights into strategic decision-making prevents businesses from canceling a promising project or launching a product or service in error. It minimizes losses when the intended goal is not achieved and allows for refinement to better meet the customer's needs.

Depending on the product or service, data from any segment of the organization can be used, such as sales, expenses, or competitive analysis. The most important attributes for this data analysis are accuracy and timeliness. In some cases, a seasonal adjustment is also a relevant factor. When leaders are informed about the cost of a trial relative to the potential loss from a wrong decision, they can make better decisions that limit organizational risk.

Design thinking provides valuable methods to manage big data challenges. Managers should frame problems by using data in a human-centric way and focus on the end-users' and stakeholders' needs and pain points. By clearly defining the problem from a variety of stakeholder perspectives, managers develop solutions aligned with user expectations and organizational goals. The definition of the problem guides organizational data collection, ensuring the data collected is useful in the discrete decision-making process. Design thinking informs organizational data collection to maximize the value of the collected data. When data is collected in this manner, it can directly support decision-making, and if during the process gaps in the data are identified, it affords an opportunity to improve data collection methods.

Design thinking emphasizes the importance of collecting and analyzing key performance indicators (KPIs) in decision-making. When appropriate and timely data is collected, managers leverage these data analytics and insights to inform decisions. Furthermore, managers can apply the iterative approach inherent in design thinking to continuously improve data management processes. Feedback and changing requirements allow for agile analysis of the data, and an iterative cycle allows flexibility and adaptability in the face of evolving big data challenges.

This shift can be challenging, and it would be daunting should implementation be completed all at once. In today's fast-paced data and technology environment, innovation and insights may rapidly change the direction of a data initiative. An underlying set of guiding principles in the data strategy can ensure its implementation remains responsive to change and still remains grounded in a core vision and objective. Designing a continuous learning and collaboration approach allows for a quick-win or fail-fast (Elligers et al., 2023). Making the change during design thinking is a process and not a destination.

Challenges. While there are significant benefits from design thinking, challenges to implementing such an approach within an organization also exist. Successfully incorporating design thinking into an organization depends on management's intent and understanding (Minstrom & Luetjens, 2016).

Design thinking is a time-consuming process to implement – it does not happen overnight. Any organizational change requires leadership and commitment, and design thinking is no exception. Design thinking needs to be integrated into both an organization's culture and systems, which requires a substantial change in the norms and practices of an organization. Organizations often resist change, regardless of its potential upsides. Additionally, the methods and tools used in design thinking to solve problems require employees to engage and participate actively. This can be difficult for some organizations if employees are unaccustomed to actively engaging (Elsbach & Stigliani, 2018).

Several steps can be taken to mitigate these challenges. Success lies in a measured adoption of design thinking. Strategies that allow for gradual cultural integration should be developed. One recommended strategy is beginning with small teams or projects, to build organizational buy-in. Given the hands-on, experiential nature of design thinking, employees will likely need targeted training and workshops to emphasize the value of design thinking. Fostering an environment that encourages active participation in design thinking (by recognizing and rewarding innovative contributions and creating opportunities for hands-on experience) is encouraged.

Another recommended workflow is to revisit organizational processes and procedures to ensure they are flexible and supportive of design thinking. Often, the rigid nature of organizational structures impedes adoption of design thinking. Finally, it is essential the organization maintains open lines of communication about the goals, processes, and expectations of design thinking initiatives. Ensuring communication is open builds trust and reduces internal resistance to change.

Model for Success

Organizations need strategic models allowing them to adjust, adapt, and pivot within the changing business environment quickly. Design thinking's iterative nature allows for processes to be incorporated into an organization's strategic thought process and structure. It allows strategic decisions to remain data-driven while providing an effective framework within which data can be interpreted and used in effective decision-making.

Integrating design thinking into strategic management can be accomplished by taking several proactive steps, starting with ensuring that leadership is committed to making the change. Management must understand and support the adoption of design thinking. This is crucial for overcoming potential resistance and setting the tone for a culture that values creativity, collaboration, and user-centricity.

Communicating the adoption of design thinking in strategic management to the entire organization is necessary. Management needs to foster a culture of communication and transparency – a culture that encourages sharing insights, progress, and challenges associated with incorporating design thinking into strategic decision-making.

Management should embed design thinking into the strategic planning process. Teams should be encouraged to use design thinking methodologies to understand customer needs better, identify opportunities, and redefine problems.

By fostering a culture that values experimentation and is open to taking calculated risks, management can encourage a culture that views failure as an opportunity to learn and innovate. Additionally, an iterative approach to strategy development should be embraced. Teams should be encouraged to develop prototypes of strategic initiatives and test them with relevant stakeholders. Then, the organization can use that feedback to refine and improve strategies.

Managers should instill a customer-centric focus in strategic decision-making, encouraging teams to actively seek and incorporate customer feedback throughout the strategic management process. This ensures that strategies align with the real needs and experiences of the end-users. By forming cross-functional teams, individuals from various departments can be brought together, sharing a diversity of skills and perspectives to enhance the problem-solving process and ensuring a holistic approach to strategic challenges.

Defining key performance indicators aligned with strategic objectives is also essential. Regular assessment regarding the impact of implemented strategies and a willingness to adapt based on feedback and changing market conditions is critical. Also, management should promote a culture of continuous learning and improvement. Managers should encourage teams to reflect on their experiences, share best practices, and incorporate lessons learned into future strategic management processes.

Concluding Thoughts and Future Direction

Integrating design thinking into corporate strategy is not merely a trend but a strategic imperative for C-suite executives in today's business landscape. Design thinking offers a human-centric, iterative, and collaborative approach that addresses the challenges of innovation, customer-centricity, adaptability, and risk mitigation. It complements data-driven strategic decision-making, and it 'humanizes' big data, reminding managers that the data represents customers and stakeholders.

Design thinking will become more prevalent across the wide spectrum of business departments. Integration with emerging technologies such as artificial intelligence (AI), augmented reality (AR), and virtual reality (VR) will result in faster innovation. Integrating design thinking into business processes will enhance the design process and result in more innovative and technologically advanced solutions. Between July and September 2023, the number of enterprises that are in the experimentation and expansion stages of implementing generative AI jumped from 62 to 71 percent, representing one of the fastest mass adoption rates of a new technology (Forrester, 2023). For organizations hoping to adopt design thinking, AI will assist with a number of activities including brainstorming and idea generation, provide collaboration tools to facilitate communication and idea sharing among teams, and facilitate rapid prototyping and simulation.

Organizations will incorporate a design thinking framework into their agile and lean practices, which will allow for the faster iteration of ideas, providing a more rapid capability to respond to changing market dynamics and the more efficient delivery of customer-centric solutions. Design thinking within decision-making systems will result in higher customer satisfaction, fewer low-performing products or services, and a generally better return for shareholders.

As cross-functional collaboration remains a priority for organizations, design thinking assists here as well. The approach encourages collaboration among individuals with diverse skill sets, and companies will realize the value of interdisciplinary teams working together to solve complex problems. By ensuring cross-disciplinary teams collaborate in the process, the rigid structure of decision-making across organizations will be eroded, allowing for faster go-to-market timeframes. Similarly, there will be fewer roadblocks during the innovation cycle.

Finally, the dynamic nature of business environments demands continuous learning and adaptation. Design thinking is the best mindset to encourage organizations to embrace change, learn from failures, and continuously iterate on solutions, irrespective of how they have traditionally approached their business challenges.

Design thinking is not a panacea. It does not displace or nullify existing models of strategic decision-making. However, by embracing design thinking principles, executives can foster a culture of continuous improvement and position their organizations as agile, customer-focused, and innovative leaders in their respective industries. As the business landscape evolves, adopting design thinking is not just an option, but a strategic necessity, for those seeking to thrive in uncertainty and disruption.

References

Agarwal, R., & Dhar, V. (2014). Big data, data science, and analytics: The opportunity and challenge for IS research. *Information Systems Research, 25*(3), 443–448.

Beckman, S., & Barry, M. (Fall 2007). Innovation as a learning process: Embedding design thinking. *California Management Review, 50*(1), 25–57.

Business Wire. (2022, May 11). Over 80 percent of companies rely on stale data for decision-making. https://www.businesswire.com/news/home/20210415005357/en/Over-80-Percent-of-Companies-Rely-on-Stale-Data-for-Decision-Making

Elsbach, K., & Stigliani, I. (2018). Design thinking and organizational culture: A review and framework for future research. *Journal of Management, 44*(6), 2274–2306.

Elligers, J., Karkera, K., Leonard, S., & Kelly, L. (2023, July). Don't just have a data strategy, have an effective data strategy. *Deloitte Insights*, https://www2.deloitte.com/us/en/insights/industry/public-sector/chief-data-officer-government-playbook/2023/federal-data-strategy-implementation-plan.html

Forrester. (2023, November). Forrester: Over the next decade, generative ai will be the fulcrum that accelerates business growth. https://www.forrester.com/press-newsroom/forrester-generative-ai-advantage/.

Hayashi, A.M. (2001, Feb.). When to trust your gut. *Harvard Business Review*, 59–65.

Han, E. (2022). What is design thinking & why is it important? *Harvard Business Insights*. https://online.hbs.edu/blog/post/what-is-design-thinking.

Hölzle, K., & Rhinow, H. (2019). The Dilemmas of Design Thinking in Innovation Projects. *Project Management Journal, 50*(4), 418–430.

Johansson-Skoldberg, U., Woodilla, J., & Cetinkaya, M. (June 2013). Design thinking: Past, present and possible futures. *Creativity and Innovation Management, 22*(2), 121–146.

Knight, E., Daymond, J., & Paroutis, S. (2020). Design-Led strategy: How to bring design thinking into the art of strategic management. *California Management Review, 62*(2), 30–52.

Mentsiev, A., Aygumov, T., & Amirova, E. (2023). Data-driven digital transformation: Challenges and strategies for effective big data management. *Reliability: Theory & Applications, 18*, 526–531.

Minstrom, M. & Luetjens, J. (2016, Sept.). Design thinking in policymaking processes: Opportunities and challenges. *Australian Journal of Public Administration, 75*(3), 391–402.

Rauch, D. E., & Tackett, M. (2021). Design thinking. *JFQ: Joint Force Quarterly, 101*, 11–17.

Ross, J., Beath, C., & Quuadgras, A. (2013, December). You may not need big data after all. *Harvard Business Review*, https://hbr.org/2013/12/you-may-not-need-big-data-after-all.

Shajalal, M.D., Hajek, P., & Abedin, M.Z. (2023). Product backorder prediction using deep neural network on imbalanced data. *International Journal of Production Research, 61*(1), 302–319.

Sheppard, B., Kouyoumjian, G., Sarrazin, H., & Dore, F. (October 2018). The business value of design. *McKinsey Quarterly.* https://www.mckinsey.com/business-functions/mckinsey-design/our-insights/the-business-value-of-design.

Yorio, K. (2019). The right skills for the future. *School Library Journal, 65*(2), 14–15.

Albert Tan and Tay Huay Ling

12 Organizing Essential Supply Chain Skills During a Pandemic

Abstract: This chapter identifies the essential skills and competencies that supply chain managers and leaders in Asia required during the COVID-19 pandemic. Interviews with 22 senior professionals and leaders from 6 countries in Asia were conducted, and secondary analysis of published information was performed. The findings indicate that multidimensional skills and a range of competencies are required to manage complex global supply chains, including problem-solving skills, customer orientation, and soft skills to manage conflicts and expectations with clients.

Introduction

The COVID-19 pandemic has brought unprecedented challenges to global supply chains, resulting in significant disruptions to the production, procurement, and distribution of goods and services. The pandemic has disrupted supply chains globally, causing shortages of essential goods and exposing the vulnerabilities of existing supply chain systems. Undoubtedly, the pandemic has highlighted the importance of reframing the organization of supply chain management for the smooth functioning of the economy. In response, supply chain practitioners had to adapt to the rapidly changing circumstances and organize in new ways to keep the supply chains running. This chapter aims to identify the essential supply chain skills that have become critical during the pandemic through literature reviews, interviewing supply chain practitioners, and secondary data analysis.

This chapter aims to fill a gap in existing research by focusing on the skills and competencies required by supply chain managers and leaders in Asia, specifically during the COVID-19 pandemic. While most studies in this field were conducted in the United States and Europe, it is crucial to consider the unique challenges and opportunities faced by Asian supply chain professionals. The COVID-19 pandemic has brought unprecedented challenges to global supply chains, resulting in significant disruptions to the production, procurement, and distribution of goods and services. The pandemic has disrupted supply chains globally, causing shortages of essential goods and exposing the vulnerabilities of existing supply chain systems. The COVID-19 pandemic has highlighted the need for a comprehensive approach to reskilling supply chain professionals to adapt to the new norm and build the necessary competencies for the future.

Numerous studies conducted throughout the COVID-19 pandemic have focused on examining both the immediate effects of the pandemic on supply chain establishment (Ajmal et al., 2023) and strategies aimed at bolstering their resilience amid the impact

https://doi.org/10.1515/9783111316987-012

of detrimental factors (Shen and Sun, 2023; Moosavi et al., 2022; Karmaker et al., 2021). Specifically, Ali et al. (2023) conducted a study to determine how vulnerability reduction strategies impact firm performance while also evaluating the mediating role of supply chain risk. Through a survey involving 335 representatives from small- and medium-sized textile enterprises in China, the authors provided empirical evidence indicating that implementing vulnerability reduction strategies notably decreases supply chain risks, consequently positively influencing firm performance (Ali et al., 2023). Additionally, the researchers identified a novel vulnerability reduction strategy within the realm of small- and medium-sized enterprises (SMEs) known as the supply chain financing (SCF) strategy. To this end, we take the stand that reimagining supply chains to avoid past traps and meet future needs will require a more comprehensive approach to reskilling the supply chain professionals to build new competency for the new norm.

The study aims to identify the business skills required by supply chain professionals in Asia during the pandemic and suggest key skills and competencies that all supply chain professionals should acquire.

Challenges and Opportunities

Since supply chain management (SCM) is concerned with coordinating the activities of all supply chain members effectively and efficiently, it is critical to create metrics that can be used to measure the results of management efforts for both supply chain members and customers. Performance is defined as the outputs and results of SCM research in the traditional sense (Chen and Paulraj, 2004; Closs and Mollenkopf, 2004). Unlike productivity and effectiveness, efficiency is an inward-looking indicator that displays how effectively resources are employed to accomplish output goals (Lai *et al.*, 2002). A company's competitiveness is related to the growth of its human capital, which includes the development of its employees' abilities and developing core competencies that are unique, distinctive, and difficult to replicate (Barnes and Liao 2012).

It is clear from the literature that supply chain managers must possess a range of multidimensional skills and competencies to manage their complex, global supply chains and deal with a wide variety of issues and challenges effectively and responsively. Skills cover general, context-independent knowledge, while competencies refer to experience-based and context-dependent knowledge (Gammelgaard and Larson, 2001). However, there is a lack of consensus and clarification on these skills and competencies or their grouping.

A plethora of skills and competencies are discussed in the literature from various perspectives (e.g., Dubey and Gunasekaran, 2015; Shou and Wang, 2017). This study reviewed several academic and industry articles to identify the skills and competencies required for supply chain managers to manage and configure their current and future supply chains.

Specifically, we highlight primary skill sets associated with logistics and supply chain practitioners from the literature.

Business Skills: Murphy and Poist (1991) identified business skills as a crucial requirement for senior-level managers. These skills encompass a comprehensive understanding of functional areas within a business and knowledge of diverse subjects such as economics, psychology, and sociology, enabling effective decision-making and problem-solving.

Barnes and Liao (2012) emphasize the significance of developing unique, distinctive, and difficult-to-replicate core competencies, contributing to a company's success in the supply chain domain. They highlight the link between a company's competitiveness and the growth of its human capital, including employees' abilities and core competencies.

Logistics Skills: Murphy and Poist (1991) highlight the importance of logistics skills for managers. These skills involve familiarity with a wide range of large and small logistics industries, providing insights and understanding to navigate challenges associated with different logistical contexts.

Management Skills: Murphy and Poist (1991) also mention that effective logistics management requires a combination of planning, organizing, and interpersonal skills. Managers must be able to plan and coordinate activities among supply chain members, ensuring efficient and seamless operations. Personal characteristics like leadership, communication, and adaptability are also important for their effectiveness in logistics.

Competencies in Supply Chain Management: Dubey and Gunasekaran (2015) identify various dimensions of competencies for supply chain managers, including strategic orientation, operational excellence, collaborative capabilities, and leadership. These competencies are crucial for managing supply chains effectively and achieving competitive advantage.

Tyssen and Fugate (2016) emphasize identifying key competencies in supply chain management, such as strategic orientation, customer focus, process management, and collaboration.

Technology and Digital Skills: Shou and Wang (2017) explore the skills and competencies required for supply chain managers in digitalization and technological advancements. They highlight the importance of digital literacy, data analytics, and the ability to leverage emerging technologies for managing supply chains in the modern digital era.

Verville and Halingten (2018) investigate supply chain professionals' evolving skills and knowledge, highlighting the importance of technology, data analytics, and sustainability in the current business environment.

Skill Gap and Talent Management: Knemeyer and Murphy (2016) address the talent challenge in logistics and supply chain management, emphasizing the importance of attracting and retaining top talent with diverse expertise. However, their study does not delve deeply into specific skill sets or competencies required in the industry.

Lambert and Pohlen (2018) assess the gap between industry expectations and academic curriculum in supply chain skills. They call for collaboration between academia and practitioners to bridge this gap.

In summary, the literature review reveals the significance of various skill sets and competencies in supply chain management. Key requirements are identified as business, logistics, and management skills. Competencies such as strategic orientation, operational excellence, collaboration, and leadership play crucial roles. Additionally, technology and digital skills, as well as addressing skill gaps and talent management, are highlighted in the literature. Additionally, while the existing literature discusses the talent challenge and skill gaps, further research is needed to explore effective strategies for talent acquisition, development, and retention in the supply chain context.

To gain insights into the essential supply chain skills during the pandemic, we interviewed supply chain practitioners from six countries in Asia (Malaysia, Thailand, India, Indonesia, Vietnam, and New Zealand) across different industries. The interviewees were selected based on their experience in supply chain management and active involvement in managing supply chains during the pandemic. We used a semi-structured interview protocol to elicit information on the essential skills required for managing supply chains during the pandemic. The interviews were recorded and transcribed, and we used thematic analysis to identify the common themes and patterns that emerged from the data.

The interviewees were asked to identify potential changes that may impact the skills and competency required by supply chain professionals in the future, especially during the COVID-19 pandemic. Some of the interview questions are listed below:
- What are the key goals and targets you have set for your supply chain staff?
- What are the essential skills or competencies for decision-making for supply chain issues?
- Where do you see yourself in the next 5 years?
- Is there anything that you would like to add to be a competent supply chain manager during the pandemic?

Before the interviews, a list of prospective interviewees representing various organizations was drawn up, and each of these interviewees was contacted via email, inviting them to participate in the interviews. The interviews were conducted on a one-to-one basis and averaged approximately 60 minutes. We have interviewed 24 senior supply chain professionals and leaders from 6 countries in Asia to identify the skill competencies to be successful supply chain professionals. They are from logistics, manufacturing, retail, and e-commerce companies. In addition, a secondary analysis of published information, including interview data on Al-Futtaim Logistics, was conducted to complement the primary interviews.

Model for Success

The logistics industry is a very cost-sensitive and customer-oriented industry. It tries to keep its costs low while meeting customer expectations. During the pandemic, more workers were advised to work from home, but warehouse operations need people to move goods. Thus, the logical option is to explore automation in warehousing together with a warehouse management system. With automation, more data will be available for analysis to optimize its operations. Data analysis is another critical skill for this industry to identify performance gaps and improve. Soft skills are also essential to deal with clients and motivating employees. The logistics sector is a labor-intensive industry in Asia, and soft skills are needed to handle conflicts and manage expectations with clients.

In addition, the industry expects employees to have problem-solving skills and customer orientation. They troubleshoot issues every day, and problem-solving skills are an essential part of the skills to resolve the issues. Since some issues will affect the clients, they must also build good customer relationships. Thus, they need to be customer oriented to retain the clients as the switching cost is low for the logistics industry.

The ongoing pandemic did not deter Al-Futtaim Logistics from running its business operations. Quick and adaptable changes were made. Its CEO, Dr. Raman Kumar, commented, "At Al-Futtaim Logistics, we had a strong business continuity plan in place which allowed us to manage the crisis." He also mentioned, "The biggest challenge we saw was the mindset of our customers, especially when it came to delivery services and the steps that would need to be taken to ensure that everyone was safe. We had to implement a new Heath Safety Environment (HSE) strategy and follow strict protocols to ensure that everyone would be protected in the work place."

The manufacturing industry faces material and labor shortages due to the lockdown to prevent the spread of the virus. Most interviewees have indicated data analysis as a critical skill set to better understand their processes and customers during the pandemic. The data will help to identify sales trends and automate simple decision-making to improve productivity. Many companies use the data from their ERP system to analyze consumer behavior and automate their processes in line with Industry 4.0.

Soft skills are also essential to manage client expectations and collaboration. It had become critical to collaborate and jointly forecast with customers and suppliers during the pandemic period when the supply is uncertain. Siam Cement Group in Thailand changed some of its supply chain design and strategies during the pandemic, as shown in Table 12.1.

Table 12.1: Supply chain design and strategies during the pandemic.

Supply Chain Strategies Before the Pandemic	Supply Chain Strategies During the Pandemic
1. Supply chain efficiency	1. Supply chain redundancy
2. Outsource to lowest cost country	2. Outsource locally or nearshoring
3. Single or dual sourcing to keep costs low	3. Multisourcing to lower supply risks and disruption
4. Centralized warehouse	4. Decentralized warehouse

Table 12.1 shows that the supply chain was previously (before the pandemic) focused on cost-saving; thus, supply chain strategies practiced lean management in the supply chain. In terms of purchasing, offshore sourcing, single supplier, and centralized warehouse were the key strategies for these companies. The challenge for global supply chains during the pandemic was transforming to be more resilient while remaining competitive. Therefore, to meet these challenges, risk mitigation must be considered when redesigning the supply chain network, according to Siam Cement Group. Supply chain strategies *shifted* from cost-saving to redundancy by having multiple *suppliers* from local or nearshore suppliers to mitigate the risk of supply disruption. Partnerships and close collaborations with suppliers and customers are vital during this period. Sharing resources, facilities, and data to strengthen the relationship while lowering potential supply risk is vital. Adopting new technology had become inevitable in Siam Cement Group to enhance operational efficiency, ranging from warehouse operations, such as automated warehouses, to more advanced technology in transportation technology like artificial intelligence (AI), machine learning, and autonomous vehicle driving.

The disruption in the supply chain does not spare the trading and retailing industries. Many traders and retailers ran short of inventory due to the late delivery of goods. Thus, most interviewees indicated the need for proper inventory management during this period. The need to constantly review and adjust their inventory policies and supplier reliability was critical for survival, as indicated by the interviewees. Most of these companies use inventory systems to monitor and plan their inventory. With thousands of SKUs to monitor, it made sense to implement an inventory system to manage their inventory and establish policies to optimize the inventory level.

Most of the interviewees from trading and retailing believe inventory management is critical today, increasing safety stock level to reduce the risk of production slow down or stoppages, thus focusing on supply assurance and shortage management. Shortage management is a strategy that involves looking at how many items are needed by a specific date and guiding purchasing managers to procure them based on this information. Supply assurance constitutes looking at all required parts over a very long horizon, considering possible shortages and obsolescence, and developing supply plans for those parts.

Companies had to review their inventory strategies during the pandemic to drive order flexibility and service performance. These include managing long lead times, inventory positioning, safety stock to counter unexpected demands, and dynamic, localized replenishment models to ensure materials are delivered exactly when needed – not simply when they are forecast.

According to the COO of Chilibeli, Mr Damon Yue, his company reacted quickly to disruption. He required a flexible ecosystem of suppliers and partners that could handle sudden shortfalls or even produce new products. That means setting up alternative sourcing and making the most of technologies to optimize cost, improve visibility across the network, and accelerate reaction times. Those relying on imports shifted inward or closer to their core markets. As for Chilibeli, they were fortunate to be able to source their products within Indonesia. Amid the COVID-19 pandemic, the company needed greater visibility into the supply chains of its suppliers. More companies are applying automation and robotics to make their supply chain more autonomous and adding suppliers in their home markets to ensure business continuity. According to the COO, control tower solutions that integrate data across the entire supply chain, 5G technology, and blockchain offer the supply chain team real-time visibility. Companies can better calibrate supply with forecast demand by comparing internal capacity data with real-time demand signals such as weather data.

The pandemic has accelerated the adoption of digital technologies, making digital literacy an essential skill for supply chain practitioners. Digital tools and platforms have become even more critical for managing supply chains during the pandemic, and it is likely to continue to be so in the postpandemic world. The outcomes concerning the evaluation of the impact of digital technologies on ensuring supply chain resilience within the automotive sector in emerging markets were unveiled in the findings of a comprehensive empirical study conducted by Balakrishnan and Ramanathan (2021). Utilizing primary data obtained from questionnaires distributed among employees of various automotive supply chain entities, such as automobile equipment manufacturers, level 1 component suppliers, and prominent logistics service providers across the Asia-Pacific region, Balakrishnan and Ramanathan (2021) substantiated the pivotal role played by digital supply chain technologies. Their study demonstrated how these technological advancements reinforce supply chain resilience and efficiency within the automotive sector in emerging markets, especially in the post-COVID-19 pandemic context.

Concluding Thoughts and Future Directions

The chapter concludes by summarizing the key findings from the interviewees, highlighting critical business skills necessary during the pandemic. These include leveraging information technologies, reorganizing, increasing inventory and warehouse space redundancy, preparing for crisis and risk management, and making effective decisions and solving problems. The insights from this study have implications for human resource managers, policymakers, and educational and training bodies in designing courses and facilitating skill development for future supply chain professionals.

The chapter contributes to the existing body of knowledge on supply chain management in the Asian context during the COVID-19 pandemic. The findings provide valuable insights for supply chain professionals, industry practitioners, and policymakers seeking to enhance their corporate organizational setup and develop skills and competencies to navigate the challenges posed by disruptions and uncertainties.

Based on the research findings, we recommend the following areas that the supply chain community needs to focus on to support the development of skills and competencies for supply chain professionals in Asia:

1. Emphasize Data Analysis Skills: Supply chain professionals should acquire strong data analysis skills, given the increasing importance of data-driven decision-making. Data analysis skills include collecting, analyzing, and interpreting data to identify patterns, trends, and potential risks. Training programs and educational institutions should incorporate data analytics and supply chain analytics courses to equip professionals with these essential skills.
2. Enhance Technology Proficiency: Supply chain professionals need to be proficient in leveraging information technologies and digital tools to optimize supply chain operations. Technology proficiency includes knowledge of supply chain management systems, warehouse management systems, and transportation management systems. Continuous learning and upskilling in emerging technologies such as artificial intelligence, blockchain, and the Internet of Things (IoT) can also provide a competitive advantage.
3. Strengthen Crisis Management and Risk Mitigation Skills: The COVID-19 pandemic has highlighted the importance of crisis management and risk mitigation in supply chain operations. Supply chain professionals should be trained to develop robust crisis response plans, conduct risk assessments, and implement mitigation strategies. Crisis management and risk mitigation skills include diversifying sourcing strategies, building inventory and warehouse space redundancy, and establishing strong relationships with alternative suppliers.
4. Foster Collaboration and Relationship Management: Effective collaboration and relationship management skills are crucial for supply chain professionals, especially during disruption. Professionals should be trained in fostering strong partnerships with suppliers, customers, and other stakeholders. Collaboration and relationship management include effective communication, negotiation, and con-

flict resolution skills. Developing cross-functional collaboration skills within the organization can also enhance supply chain resilience.

5. Cultivate Flexibility and Adaptability: Supply chain professionals should be prepared to navigate dynamic and uncertain environments. They should develop the ability to quickly adapt to changing circumstances, modify strategies, and implement alternative solutions. This includes fostering a culture of flexibility within the organization and encouraging proactive problem-solving.

6. Decision-making and problem-solving skills are highly valuable, given the multitude and complexity of operational challenges arising during the pandemic.

The COVID-19 pandemic has highlighted the importance of supply chain management and the reskilling and upskilling of supply chain professionals in Asia to meet the challenges of the COVID-19 pandemic and future disruptions.

Through our study, this chapter identified agility, communication, risk management, digital literacy, and adaptability as essential skills for managing supply chains during the pandemic. These skills will continue to be critical in the postpandemic world as supply chain management becomes more complex and challenging. Therefore, supply chain practitioners must continue developing these skills to stay ahead of the curve.

The findings of our study are consistent with previous research on supply chain skills, which have identified agility, communication, risk management, digital literacy, and adaptability as essential skills for managing supply chains (Dubey and Gunasekaran, 2015; Shou and Wang, 2017). However, the pandemic has highlighted the importance of these skills, making them even more critical for supply chain practitioners (Ajmal et al., 2023; Ali et al., 2023).

On the whole, the findings of this study provide a foundation for further research and can serve as a guide for the development of training programs and educational curricula tailored to the needs of supply chain professionals in Asia (Table 12.2). Specifically, the findings from our study will benefit human resource managers in their planning for organizational structures, new hires, and talent retention. At the same time, policymakers and educational and training bodies can also use the findings from this study to design new courses necessary to facilitate skill and knowledge development for future supply chain professionals in Asia.

Table 12.2: List of Companies Interviewed.

Country	Company
India	Mega Group
	Sitics Logistic Solutions Pvt. Ltd.
	Zimmer India
Indonesia	Chilibeli.com

Table 12.2 (continued)

Country	Company
Malaysia	Giant Hypermarket
	GS1 Malaysia Berhad
	PKT Logistics Group
	SNT Global Logistics
New Zealand	Zespri
Thailand	Siam Cement Group Logistics
	Sri Trang Gloves (Thailand) Public Company
	Unilever Thai Trading Ltd.
Vietnam	A.P. Moller Maersk Vietnam Ltd.
	Cargill Vietnam
	Central Retail in Vietnam
	Procter & Gamble Vietnam
	Tiki

India

Mega Group is an Indian conglomerate founded by Kishore Biyani and headquartered in Mumbai, India. Established in 2013, it has the national brand Big Bazaar (floor space approx. 30,000 sq. feet) as part of the retail business and employs about 50,000 people. The group has faced severe challenges to its retail business due to the pandemic, leading to losses in the bottom line. Besides its attempt to shift to e-commerce in a big way, Mega Group has ventured into a smaller-scale business with four brands: Nilgiris, Easy Day (earlier Bharti-Walmart), and Heritage food supply chain.

Sitics Logistic Solutions Pvt. Ltd. was founded by Ajmal et al., 2023. The company was registered in 2007 to provide services with the highest ethical values to customers and employees. The company evolved into a full-fledged logistics organization as the founders were providing services to a few corporations, including MNCs, and saw the huge potential of logistics as a service, as there was a dearth of quality services. The market was vast, but the offered services were inadequate and fragmented.

Zimmer India (zimmerindia.com) is a US company specializing in personalized joint replacement in the healthcare industry. The company imports joints into India from its manufacturing facilities in the UK. Since the business involves very specialized logistics where market trends of items and the nature of demand of different joints need in-depth knowledge for different hospitals specialized in joint replacement, customer-related in-depth information and knowledge is a valuable input for inventory management and logistics.

Indonesia

Chilibeli.com is an online shopping application for daily products such as fruit, vegetables, necessities, and other household needs that carries the concept of social commerce — buying and selling activities that involve social interaction between users in a community through online and offline social networks. Products from farmers and producers of fast-moving customer goods (FMCG) are connected directly to Chilibeli Partners, whose role is to make it easier for people around them to shop easily to get fresh, quality products in an environment.

Malaysia

Giant Hypermarket, established in Malaysia by the early 1970s, is the largest food retailer in Malaysia, categorized in terms of sales and the number of retail outlets. The retailer operates hypermarkets and supermarkets nationwide under the different brands. The supermarkets and hypermarkets brand is well known as a home-grown trusted brand in Malaysia. The brand is well known to local shoppers as a retailer offering products of the best value for money. The brands target the mass market and it is classified as Malaysia's largest supermarket chain.

GS1 Malaysia Berhad is a member of GS1, a nonprofit global supply chain standards organization dedicated to designing and implementing global solutions and standards to improve the efficiency and visibility of supply chains in all sectors worldwide. The GS1 System was introduced in Malaysia in July 1988. GS1 Malaysia Berhad is the only official source for GS1 barcode numbers and standards in Malaysia. GS1 Malaysia Berhad enables its more than 6,000 members of all sizes from over 10 sectors across Malaysia to enhance their efficiency and cost-effectiveness by adopting GS1 global supply chain best practices.

PKT Logistics Group is a socially responsible company providing logistics services by utilizing local human resources, building environmentally friendly warehouses, engaging with the communities, and inspiring other businesses to positively impact people and communities through its activities. Among the industry verticals ventured by the group are automotive logistics, FMCG logistics, F&B logistics, electronic and electrical logistics, frozen and chilled logistics, e-commerce logistics, and port logistics.

SNT Global Logistics offers both B2B and B2C logistics solutions for fast-moving consumer goods (FMCG), retail, e-commerce, consumer electronics, fashion, cosmetics, and skincare companies. With eight warehouses across Malaysia and Singapore, SNT Global has been growing rapidly and plans to expand its business in Asia with its partners. The qcompany has recently expanded its e-commerce services by providing global tracking capabilities for clients.

New Zealand

Zespri is a company that manufactures and supplies food products. It was formed as a cooperative of kiwifruit growers in New Zealand in 1997. Its international headquarters are in Mount Maunganui, New Zealand. Zespri's portfolio of kiwifruit varieties includes SunGold, Green, and Organic. With sales revenues of $3.1 billion, the Zespri™ brand is recognized as the world leader in premium-quality kiwifruit. Based in New Zealand, they are 100 percent owned by current or past kiwifruit growers and employ approximately 550 people globally. Zespri's top competitors include Canada Bread, FreshPoint, Bob's Red Mill, and Chiquita Brands.

Thailand

Siam Cement Group Logistics is a subsidiary company under Siam Cement Group (SCG), Thailand's biggest cement-building materials, chemicals, and packaging business. SCG Logistics services cover inland, multimodal transport, warehousing, and fulfillment for B2B, B2C and -commerce sectors. The company's vision is to become the most dominant 3PL firm with Thailand's strongest and largest network coverage.

Sri Trang Gloves (Thailand) Public Company is a manufacturer and distributor of high-quality natural latex and nitrile examination gloves in Thailand.

Unilever Thai Trading Ltd. is a wholly owned subsidiary of Unilever, the Anglo-Dutch multinational. Unilever is one of the largest fast-moving consumer goods manufacturers in Thailand. The company was first established in Thailand in 1932 as Siam Industries (1932) Ltd., manufacturing soaps, candles, and edible oils and fats. The company was renamed Lever Brothers (Thailand) Ltd. in 1954 and then Unilever Thai Holdings Ltd. in September 1997. The home and personal care/ice cream factory is located in Ladkrabang, where a wide range of consumer products are manufactured. The food factory (Gateway) is located southeast of Bangkok. The operations of Unilever in Thailand are split into Unilever Thai Holdings Ltd. and Unilever Thai Trading Ltd.

Vietnam

A.P. Moller Maersk Vietnam Ltd. is the first 100% foreign-owned company within the Vietnam logistics industry. Since 1991, Maersk Vietnam Ltd. has represented Maersk and Sealand. The company's head office is located in Ho Chi Minh City, employing more than 1,600 people with 11 offices across Vietnam, Cambodia, Myanmar, and Laos. With 30 years of local market experience, the Maersk team is uniquely placed to help connect customers to Asia and the rest of the world through seamless connections to the extensive intra-Asia and global service network.

Cargill Vietnam works alongside farmers, producers, manufacturers, retailers, governments, and other organizations to fulfill the purpose of nourishing the world in a safe, responsible, and sustainable way.

Central Retail in Vietnam was established in 2012 with only the fashion business. Central Retail continued developing and transforming Vietnam's modern trade and retail sector throughout its 9-year operation in Vietnam. Today, the company proudly welcomes an average of 175,000 customers daily at more than 280 malls and stores across 39 provinces nationwide, with a total retail area of more than 1,000,000 square meters, providing employment and career opportunities for nearly 15,000 employees in Vietnam.

Procter & Gamble Vietnam is a subsidiary of Procter & Gamble (P&G), an American multinational corporation with one of the strongest portfolios of trusted, quality, leadership brands. P&G Vietnam was one of the first American companies to invest in Vietnam after the normalization of the diplomatic relations between Vietnam and the United States in 1995. It has achieved double-digit growth for many years and has grown 12 times larger over the last 10 years. The company operates two large-scale manufacturing facilities in Binh Duong province and a general office in HCMC.

Tiki (abbr. for "Tìm kiếm & Tiết kiệm," which means "Search & Save") is the fastest and most trusted B2C e-commerce platform in Vietnam. Tiki is well known for its unique TikiNow service (2-hour delivery), world-class customer service with an 80+ NPS score, and diverse categories of 100% authentic products. Tiki is an all-in-one commercial ecosystem consisting of member companies.

References

Ajmal, M.M., Khan M.K., Shad M.K., AlKatheeri H., and Jabeen, F. (2023). Empirical Examination of Societal, Financial and Technology-Related Challenges Amid COVID-19 in Service Supply Chains.

Ali, 7., Gongbing, B., and Mehreen, A. (2023). Do Vulnerability Mitigation Strategies Influence Firm Performance: The Mediating Role of Supply Chain Risk. *International Journal*.

Balakrishnan, AS, and Ramanathan, U. (2021). The Role of Digital Technologies in Supply Chain Resilience for Emerging Markets' Automotive Sector. *Supply Chain Management: An International Journal*, 26(6), 654–671.

Barnes, J., and Liao, Y. (2012). The effect of individual, network, and collaborative competencies on the supply chain management system. *International Journal of Production Economics*, 140(2), 888–899.

Dubey, R., and Gunasekaran, A. (2015). Supply chain talent: The missing link in supply chain strategy. *Industrial and Commercial Training*, 47(5), 257–264.

Economy: Exploring Drivers Using an Integrated Model. *Sustainable Production and Consumption*, 26, 411–427.

Gammelgaard, B., and Larson, P. D. (2001). Logistics skills and competencies for supply chain management. *Journal of Business Logistics*, *22*(2), 27–50.

Karmaker, C.L., Ahmed, T., Ahmed, S., Ali, S.M., Moktadir, M.A., and Kabir, G. (2021). Improving Supply Chain Sustainability in the Context of COVID-19 Pandemic in an Emerging Economy.

Knemeyer, A. M., & Murphy, P. R. (2016). The talent challenge in logistics and supply chain management. *Journal of Business Logistics*, *37*(1), 1–6.

Lambert, D. M., & Pohlen, T. L. (2018). Supply chain skills: Assessing the business and academic gap. *Journal of Business Logistics*, *39*(1), 7–17.

Moosavi, J., Fathollahi-Fard, A.M., and Dulebenets, M.A. (2022). Supply Chain Disruption During the COVID-19 Pandemic: Recognising Potential Disruption Management Strategies.

Murphy, P. R., and Poist, R. F. (1991). Skill requirements of senior-level logisticians: Practitioner perspectives. *International Journal of Physical Distribution & Logistics Management*, *21*(3), 3–14.

Shen, Z.M., and Sun, Y. (2023). Strengthening Supply Chain Resilience During COVID-19: A Case Study of JD.com. *Journal of Operations Management*, *69*(3), 359–383.

Shou, Y., and Wang, W. (2017). Multidimensional competences of supply chain managers: An empirical study. *Enterprise Information Systems*, *11*(1), 58–74.

Supply Chains: Evidence from Emerging Market. *The International Journal of Logistics Management*, *34*(4), 994–1019.

Tyssen, C., & Fugate, B. (2016). Identifying supply chain management competencies: A mixed method approach. *International Journal of Physical Distribution & Logistics Management*, *46*(6/7), 664–688.

Verville, J., & Halingten, A. (2018). The evolving skills and knowledge of supply chain professionals: A mixed methods investigation. *Journal of Business Logistics*, *39*(1), 69–89.

Evolution of Controlling

Syed Adeel Ahmed, Brendan Moore, and Cathy Rehfus-Wilsek

13 Innovation and Operational Control

Abstract: In this chapter, we cover ways in which leaders manage technology and evaluate vendors for how technology needs for our organizations have changed. Because of recent changes in globalization, risk management, disaster recovery, technological breakthroughs, and organizational cultural shifts, leaders must understand their technology portfolios and information governance plans to adapt strategies in addressing fast-changing industries. We outline as a response to these changes a practical assessment of a comprehensive technology portfolio, assessments of technology upgrade scheduling, and considerations for in-house vs. third-party vendor solution vetting.

Overview

Innovations around operational control are a matter that every business needs to consider when positioning for success in its industry. Operations control involves managing a business's functions, including product or service quality, inventory supply, logistics, production, and overall business operations. Innovation can either be incremental, a minor upgrade or increase in efficiency, or substantial, involving a completely new or unique way of doing things. In this chapter, we explore challenges and opportunities surrounding innovation management and operational control and offer recommendations on how to create an innovative culture in a business enterprise and bring systems thinking into business decisions surrounding quality, inventory, supply logistics, production, and overall business functions and operations.

One prominent quality that leaders focus on when trying to instill innovative practices in their business is creativity. A 2010 study of 1,500 CEOs indicated that leaders rank creativity as the top leadership attribute needed for prosperity, underscoring the critical role of creativity in maintaining a competitive edge (Linker, J, 2011). To tap into creativity, not only do leaders need to be aware of the corporate culture they cultivate for their employees to work in, but they also must integrate systems thinking. Systems thinking underscores the need to approach problems holistically and not merely at a reductionist level, where the whole consists of the sum of the financial costs and efficiencies of the parts. This approach entails viewing relationships between businesses and embracing the diverse viewpoints to problem-solving.

Walmart has been an innovator recently in the healthcare market, competing against CVS and traditional pharmacy care centers. Walmart achieves market transformation by scanning its industry for opportunities and being an early adopter of technology in cost-effective areas (Kelly-Detwiler, 2013). While Walmart has become

https://doi.org/10.1515/9783111316987-013

well known for this approach, business leaders, managers, and entrepreneurs in various fields can explore opportunities within their own industry, find opportunities, and become change agents in their businesses. For any project or innovative solution to succeed in adoption, sponsorship is needed at all management levels and across all employees and departments. This widespread adoption must be communicated and supported from the top down by an executive sponsor, and resistance management techniques can be employed to minimize the effects of resistance to change. Executive sponsorship and CEO sponsorship are crucial for supporting any new approach, idea, or initiative.

Challenges and Opportunities

Whenever executive sponsorship is vital for the success of any new process or company-wide project, the CEO creates an organizational ecosystem that encourages and accepts new ideas and changes, which is reflected in their direct reports. A business development executive should subscribe to the innovation-driven culture and lead their team accordingly (Primetica, 2019). Executive sponsorship is needed for company-wide initiatives like adopting new technology or information governance plans.

Information governance requires the involvement of all stakeholders and leader levels because innovation in operations affecting one department likely affects other departments differently. Feedback from various viewpoints across the organization is necessary to understand the totality of effects. When evaluating an innovation, it is important to look holistically and across the entire industry. Building relationships with other organizations can lead to innovations that meet global demand, not just local market demand. Reverse innovation is an example of this approach.

Reverse innovation involves globalizing solutions found in emerging markets into both developed and emerging markets. Vishal Johri, General Manager of GE Healthcare's Imaging Solutions in 2013, explains that reverse innovation uses the talent and skills of emerging markets to develop products that can be made available globally, rather than the traditional approach of innovating for developed markets and then adapting for emerging markets (Johri, 2013). In this case, an innovation was found through sharing solutions that worked in an international market rather than merely seeking solutions within one market's needs and paradigm. Experimentation through business is central to innovation and to improving operational control.

Resistance to change, limited resources, short-term focus, and organizational silos are significant barriers to innovation (Assink, 2006; Hueske & Guenther, 2015). To overcome these challenges, leaders should actively involve employees, provide training and support, prioritize initiatives, explore partnerships and external funding, communicate long-term benefits, set realistic expectations, establish dedicated teams, and foster open communication and knowledge-sharing (Birkinshaw et al., 2011; Tellis et al., 2009).

Leaders can conduct a company-wide survey asking employees to rate the impact of each barrier and provide examples (Rao & Weintraub, 2013). Based on the findings, leaders can develop targeted strategies such as creating an innovation ambassador program, establishing an innovation budget, setting long-term goals, and creating cross-functional teams.

Leaders should communicate the survey results and strategies to all employees, engage them in implementation, regularly assess the effectiveness of the strategies, and make adjustments as needed. By understanding and addressing these barriers, leaders can create a supportive environment for innovation to thrive, driving long-term success and competitive advantage.

Model for Success

Every product and service developed to its current form is typically accomplished through experimentation. At the heart of every company's ability to innovate lies a process of experimentation that enables the organization to create and refine its products and services. Today, a major development project involves literally thousands of experiments, all with the same objective: to learn, through rounds of organized testing, and to determine whether the product concept or proposed technical solution holds promise for addressing a need or problem (Thomke, 2024). By being curious and encouraging a learner's mindset, companies provide employees and leaders the opportunity to think outside of the box and approach innovations in operations control from a variety of viewpoints and approaches. Google famously allows a certain percentage of each of their employee's work time to be dedicated to passion projects, learning and growth, and project experimentation that might not yield an immediate financial benefit to the company in the short term. Business leaders who understand failure is a necessary part of achieving success through experimentation will embrace it as an iterative process that might lead to an innovative process that provides genuine value to their company.

To achieve success, many failures are necessary and inevitable. Experimentation encompasses success and failure; it is an iterative process of understanding what doesn't work and what does. Both results are equally important for learning, which is the goal of any experiment and experimentation overall (Thomke, 2024). Aside from experimentation, collaboration is another key factor in cultivating innovative business solutions.

According to Michael Lenox, the executive director of the Batten Institute for Entrepreneurship and Innovation at the University of Virginia's Darden School of Business, the dominant model of industrial research and development has shifted from a closed, in-house approach to a more open, collaborative one over the past three decades. He contrasts the old model, exemplified by Xerox PARC and Bell Labs (Dann, 2009), where innovation was driven by a group of intelligent individuals working in isolation, with the current approach adopted by companies like Cisco and Intel, which involves forming partnerships with competitors, universities, and licensing technology. This collaborative approach to innovation has largely replaced the traditional method of allocating funds to an internal R&D lab (Dann, 2009). A prime example of this shift is the development of open-source software, which benefits from a community of developers who test, provide feedback, and create resources at no cost, as opposed to the in-house development process that relies on hired employees within an institution.

While open-source software development has its drawbacks, such as quality control issues, it offers the advantage of a fast iterative development approach that reduces costs for developers. This shift in the innovation landscape has led to the adoption of viable new growth models that prioritize rapid, measured experiments and iterative designs. Scott Anthony, a senior partner at Innosight, proposes five ways to accelerate the search for a viable new-growth model (Anthony, 2013). First, he suggests forming small, focused teams to drive innovation. Second, he emphasizes the importance of pushing to learn in the market, allowing for real-world feedback and insights. Third, Anthony recommends measuring learning rather than results, as the iterative process is more critical than immediate outcomes. Fourth, he advises tying funding to risk reduction instead of adhering to a rigid calendar, ensuring that resources are allocated based on the project's progress in mitigating risks. Finally, he stresses the need for decision-makers to have the right experience to guide the team before the data are clear, enabling them to make informed decisions even in the face of uncertainty.

When utilizing an agile approach as a product development methodology, open communication takes place among team members, sometimes in small groups called 'scrums' throughout the workday. While a more traditional waterfall method of development moves slowly from design to development to implementation, the agile approach breaks down a product's function into modules, and development in this modularized fashion may lead to testing and retesting as various parts are developed separately from the whole (Leau et al., 2012).

The design thinking methodology, as illustrated in Figure 13.1, follows an iterative cycle centered on the user. It begins with the "Empathize" step, where researchers deeply understand user experiences and needs through observations and interviews.

Next is "Define," articulating the core problem statement based on user insights. The "Ideate" phase encourages divergent thinking to generate potential solutions through brainstorming and creative exercises.

The most promising ideas progress to the "Prototype" step, where tangible low- or high-fidelity models are created. In the "Test" phase, these prototypes are evaluated by users, providing valuable feedback.

Crucially, the cyclical flowchart highlights the iterative nature of design thinking. The team may revisit previous steps based on testing insights – redefining the problem, generating new ideas, or refining prototypes. This iteration continues until a user-centric solution emerges.

Through empathy, creativity, and continuous refinement, illustrated in Figure 13.1, design thinking fosters innovation. This user-centric, collaborative approach leads to solutions that genuinely resonate with and address user needs.

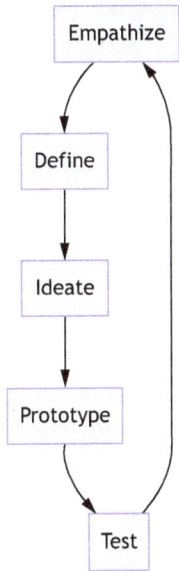

```
┌──────────────┐
│  Empathize   │
└──────────────┘

┌──────────────┐
│  Define      │
└──────────────┘

┌──────────────┐
│  Ideate      │
└──────────────┘

┌──────────────┐
│  Prototype   │
└──────────────┘

┌──────────┐
│  Test    │
└──────────┘
```

Figure 13.1: Design thinking process flowchart (created by coauthor Cathy Rehfus-Wilsek).

Jeanne Liedtka at the University of Virginia's Darden School of Business, 2012, mentions another approach – integration of design thinking. At the business school she teaches, they are studying and incorporating design thinking as an important part of their curriculum, not to replace the finance, accounting, marketing, and operations skills necessary to run a successful business but to complement them with the creative problem-solving skills necessary to invent a new one. Focused questions and design tools were utilized in articulating an approach for creative problem-solving (Liedtka, 2012).

Several key processes are incorporated alongside design tools to generate creative problem-solving approaches. Liedtka and her colleagues have created a simple process that incorporates four key questions and ten design tools to get MBAs and practicing managers comfortable with design thinking. These creative problem-solving solutions include answering questions such as *what is, what if, what wows,* and *what works.*

To encourage creative problem-solving at work, sometimes tasks that seem unproductive, such as daydreaming, allow for the focus on approaching problems in creative ways. Amy Fries, a writer and researcher on the benefits of daydreaming, outlines several ways daydreaming can enhance creativity and problem-solving (Fries, A., 2010). It allows one to envision, model, and simulate in our mind's eye; think uncensored thoughts that are necessary for originality; freely associate to make random connections and come up with novel solutions; and tap into the most complex regions of the brain. By recognizing the value of activities like daydreaming, organizations can foster an environment conducive to creative thinking and innovative problem-solving approaches.

Collaboration software such as Miro allows for collaboration among team members, teams, and departments in a business setting. One can brainstorm and map out relationships between each other's work alongside the work to be done to discover new efficiencies in their operations and processes. Focus groups are a recommended approach to help articulate issues that arise. Any innovation that's adopted company-wide needs input from a variety of departments, as a change in process, product, or service can affect all other areas of the business. Furthermore, leaders and managers should encourage speculative thinking across all management levels and stakeholders. Some recommended ground rules that can be adopted when collecting feedback and brainstorming ideas and solutions include asking "what if" questions and encouraging speculative thinking and accepting risk and a certain amount of failure, as well as providing a forum for idea sharing and giving feedback (Fries, A., 2010). By leveraging collaborative tools, gathering cross-functional input, and fostering an environment that embraces questioning and managed risk-taking, organizations can uncover innovative solutions to operational challenges.

In providing a forum for idea sharing and giving feedback, leaders can create a psychologically safe environment for experimentation, authenticity, and honest feedback to be given. Amy C. Edmondson, a prominent American scholar specializing in leadership, teaming, and organizational learning and Professor of Leadership at Harvard Business School, emphasizes that leaders must prioritize psychological safety to foster open communication and value every individual's contribution (Edmondson, 2012). Practical tips she recommends for fostering psychological safety include facilitating regular open forums for feedback, implementing anonymous suggestion boxes, and encouraging team-building activities that build trust among employees. By taking deliberate steps to cultivate an atmosphere of psychological safety, organizations can unlock the full innovative potential of their workforce through open dialogue, risk-taking, and the free exchange of perspectives.

Furthermore, prioritizing consent over consensus encourages action and experimentation, leading to improved outcomes in uncertain and important situations (Edmondson, 2012). Framing the work and asking what is not going well can encourage open discussion and problem-solving. While focus groups and forums work well for brainstorming and collecting honest feedback, there are several other methods to create a culture of innovation in companies.

Another way to foster creative thinking and innovative solutions to business problems pertains to the acceptance of failures early and often. Venture capitalist and professor Josh Linkner recommends several strategies to develop a culture of innovation (Linker, 2011). These include fueling employee passion for their work, celebrating ideas openly regardless of outcome, fostering autonomy to empower individuals, encouraging courage to take calculated risks, embracing a "fail forward" mentality where failures are treated as learning opportunities, thinking small by pursuing incremental innovations, and maximizing diversity of thought and experience across teams. By proactively implementing such measures to ingrain innovation into the organizational culture, businesses can cultivate an environment where creativity thrives, novel ideas are welcomed, and the inherent value of trial and error is recognized as a catalyst for breakthrough solutions.

Diversity in this context refers to diversity of thought and experience. Leaders may have blind spots surrounding problems that are obvious to frontline workers. Project managers are especially effective at communicating business needs and requirements to product developers and foreseeable development stallers and stoppers to project leads. Tapping into everyone's unique skillset is important. Often, a business with work silos will have wasted talent across its system if employees are not in the habit of cross-functional collaboration. Concerning failing forward, embracing bad news as valuable input can lead to quick problem resolution and positive outcomes. Celebrating wins is important, as is recognizing the courage of employees who share innovative ideas, regardless of whether a finalized version of the idea will eventually become adopted or rejected. As a business leader or manager, being supportive of employees' business solution experimentation is crucial.

Belinda Primetica, President and Chief Strategy Officer at eGlobalTech, identified key actions for leaders to enable innovation (Primetica, 2019). Firstly, she emphasizes asking questions and truly listening to others' perspectives. This open dialogue fosters understanding of challenges and opportunities.

Primetica stresses the importance of comprehending the root cause of a client's problem, not just surface symptoms. This deep dive into complexities uncovers underlying issues, paving the way for innovative solutions.

Additionally, she advocates for trial and error, embracing an experimental mindset where new ideas can be tested and refined iteratively. This approach values learning from both successes and failures.

Cultivating passion within the organization is crucial, according to Primetica. By nurturing shared purpose and enthusiasm, leaders tap into intrinsic motivation and creativity, driving innovation from the ground up.

Finally, networking and fostering connections, both internally and externally, stimulate the cross-pollination of ideas and encourage unconventional solutions through diverse perspectives and collaboration.

Through these strategies, leaders can cultivate an organizational culture that embraces innovation, empowering teams to think creatively, take calculated risks, and drive transformative change.

Utilizing and building a network efficiently is important. As an individual contributor or employee, success is most likely attained through technical expertise, which likely took a long time to develop. However, in the case of business leaders and managers, results are achieved through a team rather than individually, so social skills and soft skills are critical. Being able to motivate the work team and tap into their passion is important.

Concerning employee motivation, psychologist Daniel Pink, in his book *Drive: The Surprising Truth About What Motivates Us*, distinguishes between Motivation 1.0, Motivation 2.0, and Motivation 3.0. Motivation 1.0 and Motivation 2.0 relate to extrinsic rewards that motivate employees (Pink, 2011). These rewards generally relate to an employee's survival, such as increased monetary pay or food. However, to generate and reward creative solutions, tapping into employees' Motivation 3.0 rewards will result in better incentives for creative endeavors.

In contrast to the extrinsic motivation factors of Motivation 1.0 and 2.0, Pink (2011) introduces Motivation 3.0, which operates on the premise that humans are driven by more than just basic survival needs and punishments/rewards. While the traditional Motivation 2.0 approach, originating from early 20th-century scientific management, focused on monetary incentives and control mechanisms, Pink argues this became insufficient as work grew more complex and knowledge based over time. He suggests that relying solely on external rewards and punishments is incompatible with the evolving nature of modern work, which requires autonomy, growth opportunities, and intrinsic motivators to unlock people's full innovative and creative potential (Pink, 2011).

Amabile and Kramer (2011) argue that outdated motivational models focused on extrinsic rewards and punishments are ill suited for the creative, cognitive challenges of contemporary work. Traditional approaches "were designed for people who stand at manufacturing lines, turning out widgets or punching data into computers – routine work that can be motivated through a system of rewards and punishments" (p. 72). However, in industries relying on innovation and problem-solving abilities, these methods are ineffective as "the solution is not simply to give people more rewards to motivate them. More individual creativity and organizational innovation are required" (p. 73). They emphasize the need for new motivational paradigms that tap into intrinsic drivers to fuel the conceptual, inventive efforts demanded in today's business landscape.

An excellent example of a company that has successfully implemented systems thinking is Toyota. Toyota is known for its Toyota Production System (TPS), which is based on the principles of systems thinking and has been widely studied and emulated by businesses across various industries. Figure 13.2 highlights the key considerations in systems thinking.

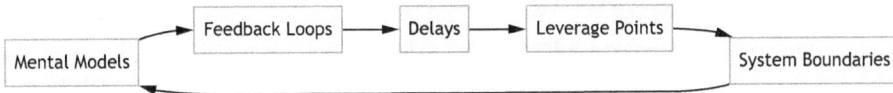

Figure 13.2: Systems Thinking Diagram (created by coauthor Cathy Rehfus-Wilsek).

Figure 13.2 presents a visual representation of the key considerations in systems thinking. The diagram highlights the interconnected nature of various elements within a system, emphasizing the importance of understanding the relationships and interdependencies between these components. It underscores the need to adopt a holistic perspective, recognizing that changes or actions in one part of the system can have ripple effects on other parts. The diagram serves as a reminder that systems thinking involves considering the broader context, identifying patterns and feedback loops, and acknowledging the dynamic and complex nature of systems. This approach contrasts with linear or reductionist thinking, which often fails to capture the intricate interactions and emergent behaviors that arise from the interplay of various system components.

Case Study: Toyota's Application of Systems Thinking

Toyota's approach to systems thinking involves viewing their entire manufacturing process as an interconnected system rather than focusing on individual components or departments in isolation. This holistic perspective allows Toyota to identify and address the root causes of problems rather than simply treating the symptoms.

One key aspect of Toyota's system is the concept of 'jidoka', which means "automation with a human touch." This principle emphasizes the importance of building quality control into the production process rather than relying on postproduction inspections to catch defects. In practice, this means that every employee on the production line has the authority to stop the line if they notice a problem, preventing defects from being passed down the line (Liker, 2004).

Another critical component of Toyota's system is the concept of 'just-in-time' (JIT) production. JIT involves producing only what is needed, when it is needed, and in the quantity needed. This approach minimizes waste, reduces inventory costs, and improves efficiency. To achieve JIT, Toyota relies on a pull system, where each step in the production process only produces what is required by the next step, based on real-time demand.

The success of Toyota's systems thinking approach is evident in its consistent quality, efficiency, and profitability. By viewing its operations as an interconnected system and continuously seeking to improve and optimize that system, Toyota has become a global leader in the automotive industry.

The case study highlights a real-world example of how systems thinking can be applied to drive operational excellence and innovation. It also illustrates the practical benefits of adopting a systems thinking mindset and its implications on quality enhancement, waste reduction, and efficiency improvement.

Challenges and Barriers to Innovation

While resistance to change, limited resources, short-term focus, and organizational silos are significant barriers to innovation in many organizations (Assink, 2006; Hueske & Guenther, 2015), t culture of open communication and knowledge-sharing actively involve employees in the innovation process, provide training and support, prioritize initiatives based on impact and alignment with goals, explore partnerships and external funding, communicate the long-term benefits of innovation, set realistic expectations, establish dedicated innovation teams, and foster a culture of open communication and knowledge-sharing (Birkinshaw et al., 2011; Tellis et al., 2009).

To identify and address specific barriers, leaders should conduct a company-wide survey asking employees to rate the impact of each barrier and provide examples (Rao & Weintraub, 2013). Based on the findings, leaders can develop targeted strategies such as creating an innovation ambassador program, establishing an innovation budget, setting long-term goals, and creating cross-functional teams.

Leaders should communicate the survey results and strategies to all employees, engage them in the implementation process, regularly assess the effectiveness of the strategies, and make adjustments as needed. By understanding and addressing these barriers, leaders can create a supportive environment for innovation to thrive, driving long-term success and competitive advantage.

In today's digital age, technology is crucial for enabling innovation and improving operational control. Companies can leverage automation, data analytics, and digital collaboration tools to streamline processes, gather insights, and foster innovation. Technology also helps companies track and measure the success of their innovation initiatives using key performance indicators (KPIs) such as ROI, time-to-market, customer satisfaction, and employee engagement. To align technology investments with innovation goals, companies should identify key areas where technology can support innovation, assess the current technology landscape, develop an implementation roadmap, establish clear metrics and KPIs, and continuously monitor and evaluate the impact of technology on innovation and operational control.

By leveraging technology and measuring success, companies can create a data-driven culture that fosters innovation, improves operational control, and drives long-term growth. Embracing these elements is essential for companies to position themselves for success and remain competitive in the face of evolving market demands and technological advancements.

Implications to Contemporary Management Practice

In this chapter, challenges and opportunities surrounding innovation management and operational control were explored. Operations control involves managing a business's functions, including product or service quality, inventory supply, logistics, production, and overall business operations. Innovation can either be incremental, a minor upgrade or an increase in efficiency, or substantial, involving a completely new or unique way of doing things.

We explored models that lead to innovation, such as the first-mover advantage that early adopters may find when taking on the risks of a new and different approach. We also discussed how, on a global scale, sometimes reverse innovation approaches can meet market demands when cross-global market demands differ vastly.

Pitfalls were also discussed in the hesitancy of senior executives to lend executive sponsorship to experimentation and innovating solutions found through creative thinking that have the possibility of failure. We offered recommendations pertaining to how to create an innovative culture in business and bring systems thinking into business decisions surrounding quality, inventory, supply logistics, production, and overall business functions and operations. Ultimately, our solution suggests that collaboration, psychological safety, tapping into the intrinsic motivations of employees, and giving space for failure and experimentation are key to success in cultivating innovative and creative solutions to operational control issues and business solutions.

In today's rapidly changing business landscape, innovation is no longer a luxury but a necessity. By implementing the strategies and best practices outlined in this chapter, organizations can position themselves for success and further enhance the products and services available globally rather than further adapting for developed markets. Embracing failure as a necessary part of the innovation process, organizations can position themselves for success and further enhance the products and services available globally rather than further adapting for developed markets. Organizations should also encourage cross-functional collaboration and leverage diverse perspectives, including globalizing solutions available in emerging markets to develop products that can be made available globally. Practical tips for organizations to foster creative thinking and innovative solutions to business problems include facilitating regular open forums for feedback, implementing anonymous suggestion boxes, and encouraging cross-functional collaboration.

In today's rapidly changing business landscape, innovation is no longer a luxury but a necessity for organizations to remain competitive and adapt to evolving market demands and technological advancements. Traditional management practices that were effective for routine, manufacturing-driven work are becoming increasingly obsolete in this new era that demands creativity, cognitive flexibility, and self-directed effort from employees. By implementing the forward-looking strategies and best practices outlined in this chapter – such as embracing failure as part of the innovation process, encouraging cross-functional collaboration, prioritizing psychological safety, and aligning motivation with intrinsic rewards – organizations can redefine their management philosophies. This modern approach unlocks the full innovative potential of the workforce and positions companies for sustained success amid the relentless disruption and progress that defines the contemporary business environment.

References

Amabile, T. M., & Kramer, S. J. (2011). *The Progress Principle: Using Small Wins to Ignite Joy, Engagement, and Creativity at Work*. Harvard Business Press.

Anthony, S. (2013). Five Ways to Innovate Faster, *Harvard Business Review, Innovation*, July 30. https://hbr.org/2013/07/how-to-innovate-faster

Assink, M. (2006). Inhibitors of disruptive innovation capability: a conceptual model. *European Journal of Innovation Management*, 9(2), 215–233.

Birkinshaw, J., Bouquet, C., & Barsoux, J. L. (2011). The 5 myths of innovation. *MIT Sloan Management Review*, 52(2), 43–50.

Dann, J. (2009). Darden Prof: Tap Outside Resources to Rev Your Innovation Engine, *CBS News, Leadership, Moneywatch*, July 14. https://www.cbsnews.com/news/darden-prof-tap-outside-resources-to-rev-your-innovation-engine/

Edmondson, A. (2012). *Teaming: How Organizations Learn, Innovate, and Compete in the Knowledge Economy 1st Edition*. Publisher Jossey-Bass, March.

Fries, A. (2010). Sparking Creativity in the Workplace, *Psychology Today*, February 9. https://www.psychologytoday.com/intl/blog/the-power-of-daydreaming/201002/sparking-creativity-in-the-workplace

Hueske, A. K., & Guenther, E. (2015). What hampers innovation? External stakeholders, the organization, groups and individuals: a systematic review of empirical barrier research. *Management Review Quarterly*, 65(2), 113–148.

Johri, V. (2013). Leaders today have to be comfortable with ambiguity, *Business Standard, Companies*, January 21. https://www.business-standard.com/article/management/-leaders-today-have-to-be-comfortable-with-ambiguity-110030900116_1.html

Kelly-Detwiler, P. (2013). How Walmart and G.E. Are Leading a Transformation in the Energy Market, *Forbes, Innovation-Sustainability*, September 30. https://www.forbes.com/sites/peterdetwiler/2013/09/30/walmart-ge-and-lighting-a-case-study-in-market-transformation/?sh=6e2b8a154ba3

Leau, Y.B., Loo, W.K., Tham, W.Y. and Tan, S.F. (2012). Software development life cycle AGILE vs traditional approaches. International Conference on Information and Network Technology, 1(7), 162–168.

Liedtka, J. (2012). How To Innovate – Without A Miracle, *Forbes, Entrepreneurs*, November 28. https://www.forbes.com/sites/darden/2012/11/28/how-to-innovate-without-a-miracle/?sh=37e7791579f6

Liker, J. K. (2004). *The Toyota Way: 14 Management Principles from the World's Greatest Manufacturer*. New York: McGraw-Hill.

Linker, J. (2011). 7 Steps to a Culture of Innovation, *Inc., Innovate*, June 16. https://www.inc.com/articles/201106/josh-linkner-7-steps-to-a-culture-of-innovation.html

Pink, D.H. (2011). *Drive: The Surprising Truth About What Motivates Us*. Riverhead Books, April 5.

Primetica, B. (2019). Why Leadership And Innovation Cannot Exist Without Each Other, *Forbes, Leadership*, January 31. https://www.forbes.com/sites/forbesbusinessdevelopmentcouncil/2019/01/31/why-leadership-and-innovation-cannot-exist-without-each-other/amp/

Rao, J., & Weintraub, J. (2013). How innovative is your company's culture? *MIT Sloan Management Review, 54*(3), 29–37.

Tellis, G. J., Prabhu, J. C., & Chandy, R. K. (2009). Radical innovation across nations: The preeminence of corporate culture. *Journal of Marketing, 73*(1), 3–23.

Thomke, S. (2024). How Business Experimentation Fuels Innovation, *Chief Executive*, Retrieved, January 15, 2024. https://chiefexecutive.net/how-business-experimentation-fuels-innovation/

Oliver Degnan

14 Technology Oversight for Optimal Corporate Performance

Abstract: In this chapter, we explore the pivotal role of strategic technology management in driving corporate success. This chapter provides a comprehensive framework for aligning technology with business goals, managing risks, and fostering a tech-savvy corporate culture. By examining case studies and best practices, executives will gain actionable insights to enhance productivity, ensure cybersecurity, and leverage emerging technologies for sustained competitive advantage.

Introduction: The Technology Factor in Business

In recent years, technology has changed the business world. From personal computers and the Internet to AI and cloud computing, technology has redefined how business is conducted. Those who adapt fast to these new technologies get a significant head start over their competitors.

Enterprise resource planning (ERP) systems were introduced in the 1990s. These systems changed internal processes by integrating all functions—finance, HR, and supply chain management—into one system. This integration brought efficiency, accuracy, and decision-making to a whole new level (Davenport, 1998). Over time, ERP systems have evolved and have become more complex and critical to strategic and operational success.

Ensuring technology investments are aligned with business goals and deliver value is the key to good technology governance. This governance involves not only choosing and implementing the right technology but also maintaining it and using it correctly. Without governance and proper oversight, businesses risk wasting resources, exposing themselves to security vulnerabilities, and missing out on opportunities.

Technology governance covers strategic planning, risk management, and performance monitoring. By having clear governance and oversight structures and processes in place, businesses can get the most out of their technology investments and minimize risk. This is critical in this digital age (Weill & Ross, 2004). As businesses become more dependent on technology, robust governance is key to competitive advantage and operational excellence. This chapter will show executives how to govern and effectively oversee technology in their organization.

https://doi.org/10.1515/9783111316987-014

Technology Strategy

Technology should be seen as a strategic enabler, not an end in itself. Aligning technology to business objectives means every technology investment and initiative contributes to the overall business mission. This requires an in-depth understanding of the technology landscape and the business strategy.

For example, a company focused on customer experience might invest in a customer relationship management (CRM) system and data analytics to get insights into customer behavior and preferences. Those insights can then inform marketing, product development, and customer service, which ultimately drives customer satisfaction and loyalty (Payne & Frow, 2005).

Technology can increase productivity and efficiency by automating mundane tasks, simplifying workflows, and enabling better communication and collaboration. AI automation tools can do the data entry so employees can focus on more strategic activities.

Several businesses have shown what good technology oversight can do. Amazon is an example. The company has used data analytics and cloud technology to optimize its supply chain, personalize the customer experience, and drive continuous innovation. This technology-led approach has been key to Amazon's growth and market dominance (Schneider, 2020).

One of the most significant advantages of leveraging technology is the ability to harness data for decision-making. Data-driven strategies allow companies to make informed decisions, predict trends, and respond proactively to market changes. This not only minimizes risks but also opens up new opportunities for growth and innovation.

Consider the impact of artificial intelligence (AI) in various industries. AI-powered tools can analyze vast amounts of data at incredible speeds, providing insights that were previously unattainable. In healthcare, AI is used to predict patient outcomes and personalize treatment plans, significantly improving patient care. In finance, AI algorithms detect fraudulent activities with higher accuracy than traditional methods, safeguarding assets and enhancing trust.

Furthermore, technology facilitates remote work and global collaboration. Cloud-based platforms enable teams to work together seamlessly, regardless of their physical location. This flexibility not only boosts productivity but also attracts top talent who value work-life balance. Companies like Slack and Zoom have revolutionized how individuals communicate and collaborate, making remote work a viable and efficient option.

More power, however, means expanded responsibility. The rapid advancement of technology also brings challenges, such as cybersecurity threats and ethical concerns. Businesses must invest in robust security measures and establish ethical guidelines to protect sensitive information and ensure technology is used responsibly. Chief information officers are challenged to produce comprehensive security measures and company policies and provide adequate employee training to ensure AI can be used efficiently and responsibly.

Ultimately, the key to successful technology integration lies in continuous learning and adaptation. As technology evolves, so must the strategies that leverage it. Organizations that foster a culture of innovation and encourage their employees to embrace new tools, systems, and methodologies will stay ahead of the curve. By viewing technology as a dynamic enabler rather than a static solution, businesses can unlock their full potential and achieve sustainable growth in an ever-changing landscape.

Technology Oversight Framework

In the realm of technology management, establishing good governance and oversight is essential for success (Peterson, 2004). This entails implementing policies, processes, and structures that align technology investments with broader business objectives, ensuring value delivery. Key principles such as accountability, transparency, and strategic alignment underpin effective governance. Frameworks like COBIT (Control Objectives for Information and Related Technologies) offer comprehensive guidance to managers navigating the complexities of technology management (ISACA, 2012). These principles emphasize the importance of proactive planning and action. Accountability ensures clear roles and responsibilities, while transparency fosters trust and collaboration through open communication. Aligning technology initiatives with the overarching business strategy is crucial for driving competitive advantage and achieving organizational goals (Peterson, 2004).

A good technology oversight framework requires clear roles for key stakeholders, including the chief information officer (CIO), chief technology officer (CTO), and other executives. The CIO typically focuses on aligning technology to business goals, overseeing IT operations, and managing risk. The CTO is responsible for technology innovation and new product and service development. When the CIO reports to the CEO, the business objective is to improve competitive advantage, whereas when the CIO reports to the CFO, the focus is more on cost containment (Degnan, 2022). Collaboration between these roles and other executives is essential. For example, the CIO and CFO must collaborate with others to ensure technology investments are financially viable and deliver the expected return on investment. The CIO and chief marketing officer (CMO) must work together on digital marketing initiatives to drive customer engagement and revenue growth (Preston & Karahanna, 2009). Each stakeholder's role is critical to good technology oversight and alignment with business objectives.

Having a technology oversight committee helps to structure technology investments and initiatives. This committee will typically include senior executives, technology leaders, and other key stakeholders, such as outside counsel, to balance internal viewpoints. It will set technology strategy, approve major spending, monitor performance, and manage risk. Regular meetings to review progress, discuss trends, and address issues are crucial. This committee enables cross-functional decision-making and ensures that technology initiatives are aligned with business objectives and deliver maximum value (Weill & Ross, 2004).

Risk and Cybersecurity Management

Technology risks can come from many sources, including cyber threats, system failures, and compliance issues. Identifying these risks is the first step in developing a mitigation strategy. Risk assessments involve evaluating the likelihood and impact of potential threats and vulnerabilities, both internal and external.

Once risks are identified, organizations can implement strategies such as robust security controls, regular audits, and incident response plans. For example, multifactor authentication and encryption can protect sensitive data from unauthorized access, and regular software updates and patches can fix vulnerabilities and prevent cyber-attacks (NIST, 2018).

Cybersecurity is a key part of technology oversight as cyber threats are becoming more frequent and sophisticated. Best practices include a layered security approach, cybersecurity awareness and training, and a proactive approach to threat detection and response. A layered security approach means employing multiple security controls to protect different parts of the IT estate, including firewalls, intrusion detection systems, antivirus software, and secure access controls (ENISA, 2020).

For instance, JPMorgan Chase, one of the largest financial institutions globally, illustrates this multilayered security strategy effectively. Given its constant exposure to cyber threats, the bank has developed a robust security framework to safeguard its extensive IT infrastructure (JPMorgan Chase, 2021).

The first layer includes advanced firewalls that monitor and filter network traffic, allowing only authorized communications. These firewalls act as the initial barrier, blocking unauthorized access attempts right at the gate.

Next, the bank utilizes intrusion detection systems (IDSs) to keep an eye on network traffic for any suspicious activities. These systems are designed to spot unusual patterns or behaviors that might indicate a threat. When such activities are detected, the IDS promptly alerts the security team for swift investigation and response.

Furthermore, JPMorgan Chase employs sophisticated antivirus software across all endpoints to guard against malware, ransomware, and other malicious software. This software is regularly updated to recognize and counteract the latest threats, ensuring the network remains protected (JPMorgan Chase, 2021).

Additionally, secure access controls are a critical aspect of the bank's security strategy. Multifactor authentication (MFA) is mandatory for all employees, requiring multiple forms of identification before access to sensitive systems and data is granted.

This measure ensures that even if one security layer is breached, unauthorized users are still kept out of critical areas.

To maintain and enhance its security posture, JPMorgan Chase also conducts regular security audits and penetration testing. These tests simulate cyber-attacks to identify and address vulnerabilities, allowing the bank to strengthen its defenses continually.

By implementing these diverse controls at different levels, JPMorgan Chase effectively demonstrates how a layered security approach can protect an organization's IT environment from a broad range of cyber threats.

Technology Investment and ROI

When evaluating and prioritizing technology investments, the management team needs to consider the benefits, costs, and risks of each project. This ensures resources are allocated to projects that are aligned with business objectives and give the highest return on investment (ROI). Important factors for consideration include strategic alignment, expected benefits, implementation costs, and risks. For example, a new customer relationship management (CRM) system will have significant upfront costs and challenges. Nevertheless, the benefits, such as better customer insight and improved sales performance, will justify the investment.

Measuring the ROI of technology investments requires tracking key performance indicators (KPIs) that show the impact of the investment on business outcomes. These KPIs can be financial (revenue growth and cost savings) or nonfinancial (customer satisfaction and employee productivity). For example, an enterprise resource planning (ERP) system can streamline business processes, reduce operational costs, and improve decision-making. By tracking metrics such as order processing time and inventory levels, managers can measure the ROI of the ERP system and make data-driven decisions to optimize its use (Dehning & Richardson, 2002).

Innovating with budget constraints necessitates a strategic approach to technology investment. Managers need to prioritize projects that give the most value and manage costs. This means setting clear investment criteria, finding cost savings, and leveraging external resources such as partnerships and grants. For example, cloud computing solutions can provide access to advanced technology and scalable infrastructure without the need for significant capital investment. By taking a strategic and collaborative approach, managers can innovate with budget constraints and drive growth (Marston et al., 2011).

Data Management and Analytics

Data governance is about creating policies, procedures, and standards for managing data assets. It ensures that data is accurate, consistent, secure, and used effectively to support business objectives. Good data governance supports decision-making, compliance, and operational efficiency.

Big data and analytics allow organizations to get value from large volumes of data to inform decision-making and strategy. By analyzing data from multiple sources, such as customer interactions and market trends, organizations can identify patterns and opportunities for improvement. For example, retailers can use big data analytics to optimize inventory management and personalize marketing campaigns, improving customer experience (Davenport, 2014).

Emerging Technologies and Trends

New technologies like artificial intelligence (AI), Internet of Things (IoT), and blockchain are changing businesses worldwide. AI automates processes, makes better decisions, and personalizes experiences. IoT connects devices and systems and provides real-time data and insights to optimize operations. Blockchain provides secure and transparent solutions for transactions and data sharing.

For example, AI-powered chatbots can provide instant customer support, improve satisfaction, and reduce costs. IoT sensors can monitor equipment performance and predict maintenance needs, reducing downtime and increasing productivity. Blockchain can streamline supply chain processes and ensure transparency and trackability from production to delivery (Daugherty & Wilson, 2018).

To successfully adopt and integrate new technologies, managers need a structured approach that includes strategy, stakeholder engagement, and operational enhancement. Organizations should create a technology adoption roadmap, define roles and responsibilities, and allocate resources for implementation and training. By involving employees in the innovation process and providing opportunities for skills development, organizations can drive technology adoption (Westerman et al., 2014).

Building a Tech-Savvy Corporate Culture

Building a tech-savvy culture compels continuous learning and development. Giving employees access to training programs, certifications, and learning resources means they stay up to date with the latest technology and develop new skills. Investing in employee development means the entire organization gets more tech-savvy and competitive.

For example, online courses, workshops, and mentorship programs can help employees gain expertise in emerging tech like AI, data analytics, and cybersecurity. Encouraging attendance at industry conferences and networking events provides valuable opportunities for knowledge sharing and growth. By having a culture of continuous learning, organizations can build a highly skilled and agile workforce (Noe et al., 2014).

Collaboration between IT and other departments is key to successful technology management and innovation. Cross-functional teams with IT professionals, business leaders, and other stakeholders can drive the development and implementation of technology initiatives that are aligned with business goals. This collaborative approach means technology solutions address the needs and challenges of the whole organization. By having a culture of collaboration, organizations can unlock technology (Gratton & Erickson, 2007).

Having an innovative and agile mindset involves encouraging employees to be open to change, try new things, and continually improve. This entails creating an environment that supports risk-taking, rewards innovation, and values diversity of thought. Leadership has a key role in setting the tone for innovation and agility, promoting a culture that is open to new ideas and adaptable to changing circumstances (Rigby et al., 2016).

Vendor Management and Outsourcing

Choosing and managing technology vendors requires evaluating their capabilities, reliability, and alignment with the organization. This involves doing due diligence, negotiating the terms, and setting clear performance expectations. Good vendor management leads to technology that delivers the desired outcomes and supports business goals (Gordon, 2006).

Outsourcing technology can give managers access to specialist skills, reduce costs, and increase flexibility. However, it also brings risks like loss of control, security concerns, and misalignment with business goals. Having a clear outsourcing strategy and choosing the right partners is key to success. By having a robust governance framework and regular communication with the outsourcing partner, managers can mitigate the risks and attain desired outcomes (Lacity & Willcocks, 2014).

Consider a scenario where a midsized retail company outsources its IT infrastructure to a reputable third-party provider. Initially, the company experiences significant cost savings and benefits from the provider's expertise. However, they would soon face challenges when the provider's priorities do not align with their strategic goals, leading to delays in critical projects. To address this, the company needs to establish a dedicated governance team to oversee the outsourcing relationship, set clear performance metrics, and schedule biweekly meetings with the provider. This proactive approach would ensure better goal alignment, improved project delivery, and ultimately maximize the benefits of outsourcing while minimizing its risks.

Performance Metrics and Continuous Improvement

Key performance indicators (KPIs) for technology oversight provide managers with numbers to measure the success and impact of technology projects. These KPIs can be financial (cost savings, revenue growth, ROI) or operational (system uptime, response times, user satisfaction). Monitoring these KPIs provides the foundation for measuring the performance of technology investments and in making data-driven decisions. For example, tracking system uptime and response times will offer insight into the IT infrastructure (Parmenter, 2015).

Tools and techniques for monitoring and evaluation include performance dashboards, benchmarking, and regular audits. Performance dashboards give managers real-time visibility into key metrics so that progress can be tracked and trends seen. Benchmarking compares performance against industry standards and best practices to identify areas for improvement. Regular audits and assessments ensure managers are compliant with policies, standards, and regulations (Kerzner, 2017).

Strategies for continuous improvement and innovation involve creating a culture of learning, experimentation, and feedback. Implementing methodologies like Lean and Six Sigma will support continuous process improvement and operational excellence. Encouraging employees to share ideas and insights through innovation programs and suggestion schemes will stimulate creativity and drive innovation. For example, running regular retrospectives and lessons-learned sessions will help teams identify successes and areas for improvement (Liker, 2004).

Rewarding and recognizing ideas and contributions will encourage employees to think creatively and take risks. By embedding continuous improvement and innovation into the company's culture, managers can stay ahead of the curve and be competitive.

Having the right tools are essential since they can lead to significant operational improvement.

For instance, Google uses a combination of OKRs (Objectives and Key Results) and continuous feedback mechanisms to drive innovation and maintain high performance across its teams (Doerr, 2018).

Conclusion: The Future of Technology Oversight

This chapter has underscored the importance of technology oversight in enhancing business performance. We have examined the strategic value of technology, aligning technology to business goals and risks and cyber security. We have also examined how to evaluate and prioritize technology investments, use data and analytics, and adopt emerging technologies. All of these form a framework for executives to oversee technology and drive business success.

As technology is key to business success, executives need to take a proactive and strategic approach to technology oversight. This requires aligning technology to business objectives, managing risk, creating a culture of innovation, and using data and analytics. By following best practices and continually improving their technology management skills, executives can achieve sustained growth and stay ahead of the competition.

The practice of management has evolved significantly over the past decades. In the past, management was largely hierarchical, with a focus on efficiency and standardization. However, the contemporary business environment demands agility, collaboration, and innovation. Modern managers must navigate rapid technological changes, globalization, and shifting consumer expectations. Critical for success in the present time and in the future are adaptive leadership, fostering a resilient organizational culture, and leveraging digital transformation to create value. Embracing these elements helps businesses to be competitive and responsive in an ever-evolving market.

Consider how management styles have evolved. In the past, top-down approaches were the norm. Managers made decisions, and employees followed orders. The environment has changed, especially during the post–COVID pandemic period. Managers now act as facilitators, encouraging teamwork and creativity.

On top of that, there has been a current shift toward remote work. The shift to remote work has been one of the most significant changes in the workforce in recent years. According to a report by Gallup (2021), about 45% of full-time employees in the United States were working from home at least some of the time during the pandemic, and many companies plan to maintain flexible work arrangements in the near future. This transition, driven by advancements in online meeting solutions and changing employee expectations, has led to a significant increase in remote work adoption. The percentage of employees working remotely has tripled since 2019, with nearly 58% of American workers having the option to work from home 1 to 3 days per week as of 2021 (Gallup, 2021). This trend is expected to continue, and many organizations recognize the benefits of a remote workforce, such as increased productivity, reduced overhead costs, and improved employee satisfaction. In addition, managers improved their leadership skills and learned to trust their teams more and focus on outcomes rather than hours clocked.

Moreover, digital tools have revolutionized how work is conducted. It is now hard to imagine a company without email, project management software, or video conferencing facility. These tools not only streamline operations but also open up opportunities for global collaboration. Under this scenario, a manager in New York can seamlessly coordinate with a team in Tokyo.

Lastly, the importance of emotional intelligence cannot be overstated. In an era where mental health and work-life balance are paramount, leaders who understand and empathize with their team's challenges will thrive. It is growingly important to create a supportive environment where everyone feels valued and motivated to contribute their best.

In essence, the journey from rigid, top-down management to a more fluid, empathetic, and tech-savvy leadership style is a testament to how much the corporate world has transformed. With the right technological tools and appropriate oversight, managers would be well positioned to enhance corporate performance.

References

Cullen, S., Seddon, P. B., & Willcocks, L. P. (2005). Managing outsourcing: The life cycle imperative. *MIS Quarterly Executive, 4*(1), 229–246. https://www.researchgate.net/publication/220496422_Managing_Outsourcing_The_Life_Cycle_Imperative

Daugherty, P. R., & Wilson, H. J. (2018). *Human + Machine: Reimagining Work in the Age of AI.* Harvard Business Review Press.

Davenport, T. H. (1998). Putting the enterprise into the enterprise system. *Harvard Business Review, 76*(4), 121–131. https://hbr.org/1998/07/putting-the-enterprise-into-the-enterprise-system

Davenport, T. H. (2014). *Big Data at Work: Dispelling the Myths, Uncovering the Opportunities.* Harvard Business Review Press.

Degnan, O. (2022). The relationship between the CEO and the CIO and its impact on business performance (Doctoral dissertation). ProQuest Dissertations & Theses database. https://www.proquest.com/docview/2734108479

Dehning, B., & Richardson, V. J. (2002). Returns on investments in information technology: A research synthesis. *Journal of Information Systems, 16*(1), 7–30. https://doi.org/10.2308/jis.2002.16.1.7

Doerr, J. (2018). *Measure what matters: How Google, Bono, and the Gates Foundation rock the world with OKRs.* Penguin Random House. https://doi.org/10.1111/psq.12247

ENISA. (2020). Cybersecurity culture guidelines: Behavioural aspects of cybersecurity. https://www.enisa.europa.eu/publications/cybersecurity-culture-guidelines-behavioural-aspects-of-cybersecurity

Gallup. (2021). State of the global workplace: 2021 report. Retrieved from https://www.gallup.com/workplace/349484/state-of-the-global-workplace.aspx

Gratton, L., & Erickson, T. J. (2007). Eight ways to build collaborative teams. *Harvard Business Review, 85*(11), 100–109. https://hbr.org/2007/11/eight-ways-to-build-collaborative-teams

Gordon, S. R. (2006). Evolving vendor management at SanDisk. *Journal of Corporate Accounting & Finance, 17*(5), 49–54. https://onlinelibrary.wiley.com/doi/abs/10.1002/jcaf.20209

ISACA. (2012). COBIT 5: A business framework for the governance and management of enterprise IT. https://www.isaca.org/bookstore/cobit/cobit-5/wcb5

JPMorgan Chase. (2021). JPMorgan Chase's cybersecurity strategy. Retrieved from https://www.jpmorganchase.com/news-stories/jpmorgan-chase-implements-cybersecurity-strategy.

Kerzner, H. (2017). *Project Management Metrics, KPIs, and Dashboards: A Guide to Measuring and Monitoring Project Performance.* John Wiley & Sons.

Lacity, M. C., & Willcocks, L. P. (2014). Nine keys to world-class BPO. *Strategic Outsourcing: An International Journal, 7*(3), 180–214. https://doi.org/10.1108/SO-07-2014-0016

Liker, J. K. (2004). *The Toyota Way: 14 Management Principles from the World's Greatest Manufacturer.* McGraw-Hill.

Marston, S., Li, Z., Bandyopadhyay, S., Zhang, J., & Ghalsasi, A. (2011). Cloud computing: The business perspective. *Decision Support Systems, 51*(1), 176–189. https://doi.org/10.1016/j.dss.2010.12.006

National Institute of Standards and Technology (NIST). (2018). Cybersecurity framework. https://www.nist.gov/cyberframework

National Institute of Standards and Technology (NIST). (2020). Guide for conducting risk assessments (NIST SP 800–30). https://nvlpubs.nist.gov/nistpubs/Legacy/SP/nistspecialpublication800-30r1.pdf

Noe, R. A., Hollenbeck, J. R., Gerhart, B., & Wright, P. M. (2014). *Fundamentals of Human Resource Management*. McGraw-Hill Education.

Oven, C., & Bechtel, M. (2023). Rethinking How Tech Trends Shape Governance and Oversight. Deloitte United States. https://www2.deloitte.com/us/en/pages/center-for-board-effectiveness/articles/rethinking-how-tech-trends-shape-governance-and-oversight.html

Parmenter, D. (2015). *Key Performance Indicators: Developing, Implementing, and Using Winning KPIs*. John Wiley & Sons.

Payne, A., & Frow, P. (2005). A strategic framework for customer relationship management. *Journal of Marketing, 69*(4), 167–176. https://doi.org/10.1509/jmkg.2005.69.4.167

Peterson, R. (2004). Crafting information technology governance. *Information Systems Management, 21*(4), 7–22. https://doi.org/10.1201/1078/44705.21.4.20040901/84185.2

Porter, M. E., & Heppelmann, J. E. (2015). How smart, connected products are transforming companies. *Harvard Business Review, 93*(10), 96–114. https://hbr.org/2015/10/how-smart-connected-products-are-transforming-companies

Preston, D. S., & Karahanna, E. (2009). Antecedents of IS strategic alignment: A nomological network. *Information Systems Research, 20*(2), 159–179. https://doi.org/10.1287/isre.1070.0159

Schneider, D. (2016). Building a data-driven culture. *Harvard Business Review Digital Articles*. https://hbr.org/2016/04/building-a-data-driven-culture

Schneider, S. (2020). Amazon: The economics of extreme digital concentration (Harvard Business School Case). Harvard Business School. https://www.hbs.edu/faculty/Pages/item.aspx?num=54852

Weill, P., & Ross, J. W. (2004). *IT Governance: How Top Performers Manage IT Decision Rights for Superior Results*. Harvard Business Press.

Westerman, G., Bonnet, D., & McAfee, A. (2014). *Leading Digital: Turning Technology into Business Transformation*. Harvard Business Review Press.

Manjula S. Salimath and Vallari Chandna

15 Strategic Control and its Impact on Efficiency, Speed, and Innovation in Organizations

Abstract: Whether and how smoothly an organization is able to attain its strategic objectives depends on monitoring and evaluative processes that generally fall under the realm of strategic control. Without strategic control mechanisms, organizations can be put in a disastrous position relative to their own goals and their competition. Such a situation would be like running a race blindfolded, with no cues about one's own position on the racetrack, the twists and turns coming ahead, the need to accelerate in comparison to other runners, the remaining distance in the race, or even whether the finish line was reached. Thus, a lack of strategic control mechanisms is problematic for organizations as limited resources require efficient management, and in a competitive industry landscape, efficiency, speed, and innovation are necessary for success. We move on to discuss contemporary technology, artificial intelligence (AI), as offering unique opportunities as well as challenges for organizations with regard to strategic control. We offer a model for success and end with future directions.

Introduction

In this chapter, we discuss the importance of strategic control for organizations. In particular, we discuss the benefits that may result from appropriate levels of strategic controls in terms of efficiency, speed, and innovation. We analyze how artificial intelligence offers a source of great opportunity that can be leveraged as well as the challenges that are presented in its use. We hope that future CEOs will effectively navigate these challenges and benefit from effective use of strategic control mechanisms within their organizations. The rest of the chapter is organized as follows: first, we introduce strategic control mechanisms and how it has evolved over time; second, we discuss their impact over three critical areas, namely efficiency, speed, and innovation; third, we focus on artificial intelligence as an interesting source of opportunity and challenge; fourth, we present a model for success; and fifth, we offer conclusions and future directions.

At the most fundamental level, strategic control is the systematic process of ensuring systemic alignment. While organizations are focused on moving forward on the path to achieving their goals and objectives, strategic control is an oversight mechanism designed to ensure that the organizational activities and practices are actually aligned with the strategic goals and objectives (Eden and Ackermann, 1993). Strategic control operates from the very beginning of the strategic process, thereby ensuring

https://doi.org/10.1515/9783111316987-015

organizations develop strategies aligned with their mission, vision, and values; it continues through the middle, helping organizations monitor and evaluate how effective their strategies really are; and finally, during the implementation and execution stage of a strategy, it helps organizations make adjustments to their strategies as needed (Julian and Scifres, 2002). Strategic controls fulfill three major needs: coordination, motivation, and monitoring (Goold and Quinn, 1990).

From a historical or evolutionary perspective, the concept of strategic control has undergone many changes. In the 1960s and 1970s, management practices emphasized the distinct natures and operations of planning and control separately. However, over time, the field of strategic management came into its own (Cummings and Daellenbach, 2009). This resulted in concepts like strategic fit (Scholz, 1987), competitive advantage (Porter, 1985), and balanced scorecard (Kaplan, 2009) becoming part of the business landscape and the embedded nature of strategic control becoming more prominent. The seminal works on strategic control are from this era of the 1980s and 1990s, which include the insights of Schreyogg and Steinmann (1987), who expanded the scope of strategic control, and Preble (1991), who proposed a comprehensive system of strategic control. Lin et al. (2017) demarcate management control now into two types: strategic and operational.

According to Schendel and Hofer (1979), 'the last "task" in the strategic management process is that of strategic control. Strategic control focuses on the dual questions of: (1) whether the strategy is being implemented as planned; and (2) whether the results produced by the strategy are those intended. The basic criteria used to answer these questions are derived from: (1) the strategy and action plans developed to implement strategy; and (2) the performance results that strategy is expected to produce. If a deviation occurs, then feedback takes place and the strategic management process recycles.' (p. 18).

In the last two decades, as globalization and technological advancements abound, the importance of strategic control has grown (Muralidharan, 2004). It has evolved from the traditional top-down approach to a more dynamic, data-driven process. No longer is control relegated to a secondary position as compared to planning, but rather, it is viewed as a critical function that helps an organization anticipate and proactively shape organizational strategy and performance. Today, strategic control helps organizations deal with the mountains of data generated, whether it is data related to financial performance, operational data such as defect rates, human resources data like employee turnover, or perhaps marketing data such as social media reach, all to ensure that it is able to spot deviations from strategy rapidly. Organizations have to deal with a great deal of environmental complexity. A well-developed strategic control system helps organizations be better equipped in the face of such uncertainty (Julian and Scifres, 2002). Additionally, strategic control has moved beyond looking at just the typical financial metrics typically employed in the past; instead, we now have organizations employing a more holistic approach that focuses on stakeholders as well (Lawrie and Cobbold, 2004).

Strategic control is thus an important mechanism in the arsenal of an organization because it offers valuable and timely feedback and monitoring to set, reset, or change the course of action to the extent that movement toward a particular omitted trajectory is desirable. Overall, strategic control helps to aid organizations in three key aspects: efficiency, speed, and innovation. The varying impacts of these critical factors are discussed below:

Efficiency and Strategic Control: Strategic control helps organizations with efficient resource utilization by assessing how effectively and efficiently resources are deployed across an organization (Phillips, 2007). Additionally, strategic control acts as a mechanism to ensure process optimization for maximum efficiency (Muralidharan, 2004). By identifying inefficiencies in resource utilization or business processes, appropriate adjustments can be made in a timely manner thereby helping the organization to reduce costs and improving overall organizational efficiency. Regardless of how advanced a system of strategic control is being used, one of the most fundamental purposes of strategic control is to identify inefficiencies and reduce wastefulness.

Speed and Strategic Control: With rapid technological advancements and globalization, organizations have to keep up with rapidly evolving market conditions and need to engage in agile decision-making (Julian and Scifres, 2002). Organizations can stay nimble and maintain a strong competitive advantage by adapting their strategy (Denning, 2017). Strategic control enables such agile decision-making while also aiming to aid organizations in being adaptable when it comes to making swift strategic change. By identifying delays and slow responses to changing market conditions, strategic control mechanisms aid the organization in its ability to react with speed in areas that are of strategic importance to the organization. The heightened responsiveness that comes from the appropriate use of strategic control allows organizations to be faster than their competitors when it comes to reacting to opportunities and challenges across the board.

Innovation and Strategic Control: Organizations that seek to learn and grow also benefit from a good strategic control system as the continuous assessment of strategy allows them the opportunity to learn about what works and what does not (Wijethilake, Munir, and Appuhami, 2018). Organizations are constantly working on building and enhancing their dynamic capabilities. With ever-increasing competition, being innovative in their approaches to seize and reconfigure resources is the need of the hour. By identifying areas for innovation and facilitating creative solutions, strategic control mechanisms enable organizations to be at the forefront of technology and competition. Organizations cannot simply be reactive and utilize strategic control to monitor the present but rather must seek to be creative, innovative, and proactive in their approaches.

Challenges and Opportunities

In our current times, with regard to strategic control, we identify one specific area, namely artificial intelligence (AI), as a source of great opportunity. In simple terms, artificial intelligence refers to the capacity of machines or computers to mimic how human/natural intelligence works, by essentially analyzing large volumes of data to recognize patterns and predict outcomes. Indeed, artificial intelligence has revolutionized all aspects of the business experience and is poised to do even more. For example, AI can enable strategic control to be more efficient, fast, and innovative. At the same time, it is also the source of the greatest challenges. Unfettered, artificial intelligence can create more problems than it can resolve. As we elaborate next, this double-edged sword can revolutionize strategic control if utilized and implemented appropriately.

Efficiency through Automation and Analytics: The use of technology to enhance organizational strategy and strategic control is not new and was discussed as far back as the 1980s by Bakos and Treacy (1986). By using artificial intelligence, organizations can automate decision-making processes and utilize analytical techniques to arrive at solutions more efficiently. AI can save labor and resources and offer data-backed predictions that can be verified and validated with different inputs. Today, AI has the capability to analyze the ever-increasing amounts of internal and external data from multiple sources, thereby helping organizations identify inefficiencies as well as opportunities to act upon. This could enable organizations to be more precise with their resource allocation, reduce costs and inefficiencies, and improve processes (Conboy et. al., 2020). For instance, they can analyze the data on social media engagement and reach to better understand deviations from expected performance and, in conjunction with external data about social media usage, better understand content strategy. Another example is in the detection of defects as there are now multiple tools available including those from well-established companies like IBM that help with the detection of defects using AI and visual cues. Further, it can help convince stakeholders of the usefulness of a course of action and get their support. In summary, the use of AI can provide greater analytical agility by automating complex analysis, offering ad hoc and predictive analytics, and empowering organizations to uncover meaningful trends, mitigate risks, and get insights much more efficiently.

Speed through Simulation and Decision Support: Simulations allow managers to better understand how varying scenarios can change outcomes by presenting virtual models and alternate solutions. This ability is especially pertinent in rapidly changing environments and markets with high volatility and uncertainty, where incorrect decisions can result in costly mistakes. Using predictive AI algorithms, potential complications and market issues can be identified in a timely manner, which would allow organizations to be better prepared and adjust their strategies alongside AI (Kiron and

Schrage, 2019). While data-driven decision-making is already widely utilized as a part of strategic control, the speed at which data can be processed and compiled using AI is phenomenal (Lombardi et. al., 2021). Organizations can thus avail of real-time insights and make faster decisions based on the most recent information, as well as simulated scenarios. Thus, AI can aid in providing decision support in a speedy fashion. Such data-driven, informed decisions are less likely to miss important information.

Innovation through Creative Augmentation: The importance of continuous innovation cannot be underestimated for any organization. AI can also aid organizations in their more innovative pursuits by aiding in idea generation and brainstorming (Lavrič and Škraba, 2023). It can help with relatively predictable tasks such as developing multiple scenarios and multiple potential outcomes with great ease (Spaniol and Rowland, 2023) or more complex tasks such as identifying unconventional combinations of ideas or strategic pursuits. Thus, organizations can augment the work of their best and brightest, with AI.

As mentioned earlier, artificial intelligence also poses several challenges, two of which we will discuss further.

The Challenges with Data: Despite the many advantages of AI, at the end of the day, it has been recognized that the AI models rely completely on the data that they have trained on. Hence, if the training data utilized is inaccurate, incomplete, or biased in some way, the output generated from it will be unreliable and unusable (Rana et. al., 2021). In such cases, where the training data itself is not comprehensive, inclusive, representative, and unbiased, rather than supporting and advancing strategic control, the use of AI could be detrimental. Low-quality data is an issue for even the most basic technological systems. For AI models, given their impactful nature, it is critical that biased, low-quality, or flawed data should be kept out of the system. An additional challenge is availing of the needed data. Most organizations do not have all their data readily available; rather, it tends to be within siloed systems or with external partners (Janssen et. al., 2020). This would hinder AI's ability to act as a positive tool of strategic control. AI systems for organizations that handle sensitive and highly confidential data would need to have extremely robust security protocols in place. The exponential increase in cybersecurity attacks and bad-faith actors in recent years has necessitated cybersecurity measures for even the smallest organizations (Chandna and Tiwari, 2023). Additionally, there can also be "old-school" leaks of data such as physically lost phones, which cybersecurity mechanisms could still help with, while human errors such as leaving folders with passwords, for example, can be reduced with better cybersecurity training of employees.

The Challenges with People: Aside from the data issues, there could also be "human issues". Our society is at a crossroads when it comes to AI (Jarrahi, 2018). Organizations may find that employees worry about being completely replaced by AI and thus are not accepting of utilizing the same. They also feel threatened by the relative superiority of AI tools in completing many tasks and are wary or reluctant of incorporating any AI tools even though it may help them become more efficient and save time. Other organizations may be willing but unable to use AI – the infrastructure would require significant expenditure and also necessitate upskilling of employees to be able to utilize such technology (Davenport and Malone, 2021). But organizations that do not integrate AI as part of their strategic control system may find themselves left behind as their competitors utilize AI to improve their strategic approaches and gain a competitive advantage that will be hard for rivals to overcome. While AI is still in the nascent stage, business history is replete with examples of how disruptive technologies pose a challenge for incumbents, which, when ignored, can spell the end of once-successful-giants, as in the case of Blockbuster, which failed to adapt to streaming technology; Kodak, which ignored the rise of digital photography; or, most recently, Bed Bath & Beyond, which never established a satisfactory digital presence.

Model for Success

See Figure 15.1 for a visual representation of the effect of strategic control. As illustrated, the strategic control mechanism is valuable because it has direct effects on organizational efficiency, speed, and innovation. At the same time, artificial intelligence (AI) can become a source of either opportunities that enhance these effects or challenges that diminish the same.

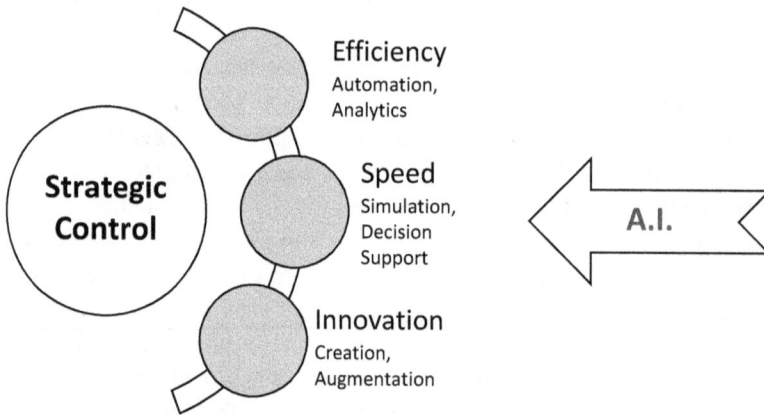

Figure 15.1: How Efficiency, Speed, and Innovation are Affected.

See Figure 15.2 for a summary table in the form of a 3 x 3 matrix juxtaposing the three levels of strategic control and their effect on key organizational outcomes. Herein, we recognize that strategic control should be viewed as existing on a continuum, and for simplicity, we have categorized the continuum into three segments (high, appropriate, and low).

Since there is always a relative rather than an absolute aspect of control (i.e., control can be more, less, or appropriate for the organizational situation), we depict at least nine different scenarios that the matrix gives rise to. These can be used as aids or decisional heuristics for managers.

Efficiency occurs when resources are used wisely, and the input-output ratio is beneficial. That is, more output per unit of input implies greater efficiency. Of course, this requires careful monitoring and control. Taken to an excess, high strategic control means both time and managerial inputs are being expended to a great degree to monitor physical resources, leading to overall inefficiency in the system. With low strategic control, on the flip side, greater physical resource waste and process inefficiencies are likely to occur due to minimal oversight. As such, following research on transaction costs, we suggest that appropriate conditions of strategic control will result in greater process and resource efficiencies for the organization.

Under conditions of high strategic control, speed is sacrificed, because all decisions have to be checked and monitored, creating administrative delays. Yet, at the same time, with low levels of strategic control, many decisions may abound, creating confusion and chaotic situations due to a lack of clarity on the most beneficial solution to follow, slowing down the organization's ability to pursue its goals in a quick and sure way. Hence, in line with decision-making literature, we suggest that appropriate levels of control are important to achieve goals quickly and without wasting valuable time. Especially in competitive industries, speed of response is critical for survival and success.

Likewise, under conditions of high strategic control, innovation becomes stifled, as some creative freedom is necessary for the unrestricted movement of ideas, experimentation, and thinking. However, at low levels of strategic control, the free-floating

Effect on Organization	Strategic Control		
	High	Appropriate	Low
Efficiency	↓	↑	↓
Speed	↓	↑	↓
Innovation	↓	↑	↓

Figure 15.2: Effect of Varying levels of Strategic Control on Organizations.

ideas and wide berth given to try out new solutions can be counterproductive because they are not subject to any restriction, including whether they are central or peripheral to organizational goals. Following prior research on the importance of strategic alignment, we suggest that an appropriate level of strategic control allows for creativity within the bounds of intended trajectories, thereby enabling greater innovation.

Concluding Thoughts and Future Direction

The evidence on whether organizations actually use strategic controls is paradoxical. Despite the ubiquitous acknowledgment of their effectiveness, it is surprising that strategic controls are not as widely prevalent in practice (Goold and Quinn, 1990). It is hoped that as we look into the future, more CEOs will utilize and benefit from strategic control mechanisms within their organizations.

As discussed in earlier sections, a dichotomous approach to strategic control (to have or not) should give way to a more nuanced understanding of it as belonging to a continuum. Yet another related aspect is that there is no one best solution that fits all organizations. Rather, it is important to recognize that the ideal or best way to achieve success is to tailor the varying levels of strategic control to not only different types of organizations but also varying life cycle stages of the same organization over time. Thus, strategic control should be utilized in a dynamic fashion, adapting to many contingencies. This highlights the critical role of the strategic leadership team and managers in keeping the organization on its path, using tools to benchmark and track progress, and motivating employees to higher performance, because an absence of this mechanism can lead to disastrous consequences.

Ethical issues with the use of AI cannot be ignored either. According to the 2023 AI Index Report by the Stanford Institute for Human-Centered Artificial Intelligence (HAI), ethical misuse of AI has risen by 26 times since 2012, which is quite problematic. Deepfake videos intended to propagate misinformation, create distrust, and trigger political chaos have unfortunate consequences that are hard to isolate and difficult to avert. As new developments in AI also pose unanticipated and unintended ethical consequences, the importance of having strategic control over the development and use of AI technologies in organizations should become evident.

In conclusion, organizations benefit in terms of efficiency, speed, and innovation when appropriate levels of strategic controls are used. The potential of AI in augmenting strategic controls via automation, simulation, decision support, and analytics makes it invaluable. At the same time, managers and organizations should be cognizant of the challenges posed, alongside exploring newer ways to leverage the opportunities of AI.

In a world characterized by rapid technological advancements, the practice of management has also evolved to reflect those changes. In a coevolutionary sense, these synergies have enabled management practice to reach a new frontier. To effectively navigate and succeed in a competitive landscape, contemporary managers can attain operational efficiency by planning, organizing, and controlling in a timely and innovative manner.

References

Bakos, J. Y., & Treacy, M. E. (1986). Information technology and corporate strategy: a research perspective. *MIS Quarterly*, 107–119.

Chandna, V., & Tiwari, P. (2023). Cybersecurity and the new firm: Surviving online threats. *Journal of Business Strategy*, *44*(1), 3–12.

Conboy, K., Mikalef, P., Dennehy, D., & Krogstie, J. (2020). Using business analytics to enhance dynamic capabilities in operations research: A case analysis and research agenda. *European Journal of Operational Research*, *281*(3), 656–672.

Cummings, S., & Daellenbach, U. (2009). A guide to the future of strategy? The history of long range planning. *Long Range Planning*, *42*(2), 234–263.

Davenport, T., & Malone, K. (2021). Deployment as a critical business data science discipline. *Harvard Data Science Review*, *3*(1).

Denning, S. (2017). The next frontier for Agile: strategic management. *Strategy & Leadership*, *45*(2), 12–18.

Eden, C., & Ackermann, F. (1993). Evaluating strategy—Its role within the context of strategic control. *Journal of the Operational Research Society*, *44*(9), 853–865.

Goold, M. & Quinn, J. J. (1990). The Paradox of Strategic Controls. *Strategic Management Journal*, *11*(1), 43–57.

Janssen, M., Brous, P., Estevez, E., Barbosa, L. S., & Janowski, T. (2020). Data governance: Organizing data for trustworthy Artificial Intelligence. *Government Information Quarterly*, *37*(3), 101493.

Jarrahi, M. H. (2018). Artificial intelligence and the future of work: Human-AI symbiosis in organizational decision making. *Business Horizons*, *61*(4), 577–586.

Julian, S., & Scifres, E. (2002). An interpretive perspective on the role of strategic control in triggering strategic change. *Journal of Business Strategies*, *19*(2), 141–160.

Kaplan, R. S. (2009). Conceptual foundations of the balanced scorecard. *Handbooks of Management Accounting Research*, *3*, 1253–1269.

Kiron, D., & Schrage, M. (2019). Strategy for and with AI. *MIT Sloan Management Review*, *60*(4).

Lavrič, F., & Škraba, A. (2023). Brainstorming Will Never Be the Same Again—A Human Group Supported by Artificial Intelligence. *Machine Learning and Knowledge Extraction*, *5*(4), 1282–1301.

Lawrie, G., & Cobbold, I. (2004). Third-generation balanced scorecard: evolution of an effective strategic control tool. *International Journal of Productivity and Performance Management*, *53*(7), 611–623.

Lin, Y.H., Chen, C.J. & Lin, B.W. (2017). The influence of strategic control and operational control on new venture performance. *Management Decision*, *55*(5), 1042–1064.

Lombardi, R., Cano-Rubio, M., Schimperna, F., & Trequattrini, R. (2021). The impact of smart technologies on the management and strategic control: a structured literature review. *Management Control Special Issue*, 11–30.

Muralidharan, R. (2004). A framework for designing strategy content controls. *International Journal of Productivity and Performance Management*, *53*(7), 590–601.

Phillips, P. A. (2007). The balanced scorecard and strategic control: a hotel case study analysis. *The Service Industries Journal*, *27*(6), 731–746.

Porter, M. E. (1985). Technology and competitive advantage. *Journal of Business Strategy*, *5*(3), 60–78.

Preble, J. F. (1992). Towards a comprehensive system of strategic control. *Journal of Management Studies*, *29*(4), 391–408.

Rana, N. P., Chatterjee, S., Dwivedi, Y. K., & Akter, S. (2022). Understanding dark side of artificial intelligence (AI) integrated business analytics: assessing firm's operational inefficiency and competitiveness. *European Journal of Information Systems*, *31*(3), 364–387.

Schendel, D. E. & Hofer, C. W. (1979). *Strategic Management*, Little. Brown, Boston.

Scholz, C. (1987). Corporate culture and strategy—The problem of strategic fit. *Long Range Planning*, *20*(4), 78–87.

Schreyögg, G., & Steinmann, H. (1987). Strategic control: A new perspective. *Academy of Management Review*, *12*(1), 91–103.

Spaniol, M. J., & Rowland, N. J. (2023). AI-assisted scenario generation for strategic planning. *Futures & Foresight Science*, e148.

Wijethilake, C., Munir, R., & Appuhami, R. (2018). Environmental innovation strategy and organizational performance: Enabling and controlling uses of management control systems. *Journal of Business Ethics*, *151*, 1139–1160.

List of Figures

https://doi.org/10.1515/9783111316987-016

List of Contributors

Syed Adeel Ahmed, PhD holds a BS in Electronics and Communication Engineering from Osmania University (India) and two MS degrees from the University of New Orleans in Electrical Engineering (MSEE) and Engineering Management (MSENMG). He is a Microsoft-certified professional and business strategy game champion. Dr. Ahmed was awarded his PhD in Engineering and Applied Sciences in 2006 from the University of New Orleans. He has been in the teaching and research profession for over 20 years. He has taught math, physics, engineering, business, and computer science courses at the undergraduate and graduate levels at Tulane University, the University of New Orleans, Xavier University, Southern University of New Orleans, Dillard University, Delgado Community College, and Nunez Community College.

Lama Blaique has a PhD in Business Management from the British University in Dubai. She is Assistant Professor of Business Management at the American University in Dubai. She has over 15 years of experience in the fields of academia and executive research in the Middle East region. Her research interests are in the areas of organizational behavior, human resources, gender and diversity, and leadership. She has several publications in peer-reviewed journals. She serves as a journal reviewer for multiple Scopus-based journals and is a member of the Academy of International Business (AIB).

Dr. Vallari Chandna is a Professor of Management at the Austin E. Cofrin School of Business at the University of Wisconsin -Green Bay. Her current research interests are in strategy and entrepreneurship including digital entrepreneurship, cybersecurity, sustainability, individual and organizational issues in start-ups, and interorganizational relationships. Dr. Chandna's work has been published in the *Journal of Business Research, Technovation, International Journal of Sustainable Entrepreneurship and Corporate Social Responsibility, Business Horizons, Journal of Business Strategies, Management Decision*, and *Electronic Commerce Research*, among others.

Sunando Das is a veteran data science practitioner with two decades of industry experience and regularly presents in leading platforms on AI/ML, personalization, and strategy. His work on AI/ML has received several industry awards. Presently, Sunando leads the Predictive Analytics global center of excellence in the consumer insights team at Unilever.

Dr. Oliver Degnan is a healthcare CIO, entrepreneur, inventor, and author with 20 years of experience leading world-class teams in technology and product innovation, entrepreneurship, and business. As the former SVP and CTO of IBM Watson Health, healthcare CIO of industry leaders ChenMed and Marshfield Clinic, and Chief Architect for Intuit in Silicon Valley, Oliver was awarded multiple technology patents in use today by Fortune 100 companies worldwide. Over the course of his career as a C-suite executive leader in technology and healthcare innovation, Oliver developed a proprietary science-backed system of techniques to empower executive leaders with ultra-productivity and career growth without burnout.

Joshua B. Frye serves as the Director of People Operations for O'Shea Builders in Springfield, IL. He focuses on strategic business functions Including the logistics of employment and continuously improving employee engagement, development, and retention to drive growth. Josh holds a Master of Science degree in Management and Organizational Behavior from Benedictine University. Joshua holds a Senior Professional in Human Resources (SPHR) certification, is recognized as a Scrum Master, certified in DiSC and the Predictive Index, is a Certified Technical Trainer (CTT+), and an ATD certified trainer.

Dr. Diana Heeb Bivona's background is an eclectic mix of business, SME consulting, and higher education experience. She is the author of the textbook *Entre- and Intrapreneurship* and "International

https://doi.org/10.1515/9783111316987-017

Financial Institutions (IFIS): Facilitators or Obstructionists to Globalization?," featured in *Globalization Alternative: Strategies for the New International Economy*, and coeditor of *Managerial Forensics*.

Sara Junio is an experienced leader with over 30 years in operational management, business transformation, and product development in Fortune 1000 companies. She excels in consulting, enhancing operating efficiency, and executing impactful communication campaigns. Skilled in corporate communication, change management, and strategic planning, Sara drives performance and achieves business goals. She holds an Executive MBA from the University of Wisconsin-Milwaukee and is pursuing a doctorate in strategic leadership at Liberty University.

Dr. Abhishek Kumbhat is Founder and CEO of SapidBlue Technologies. He is a technology enthusiast, researcher, and serial entrepreneur with over 20 years of experience in Product Innovation and Technology solutions with New Age Technologies. He has also advised global businesses on innovation, strategy, and technology.

Dr. Janet Kirby is a practitioner-scholar, having held leadership positions in the public and private sectors, and is an organizational consultant with an emphasis on nonprofit strategic planning. She is Assistant Professor of Organizational Leadership at Millikin University focusing on organizational change, innovation, and human resource management.

Huay Ling Tay is an Associate Professor and Head of the International Trade Management Minor at the Singapore University of Social Sciences. She received her PhD from the University of Melbourne. Her research interests include operations and supply chain management, Lean Six Sigma, humanitarian logistics, and sustainability.

Prof. Romie Frederick Littrell is the managing director of the Centre for Cross Cultural Comparisons, a voluntary association of researchers, students, teachers, and practitioners interested in the study of preferred leader behavior across societal/national cultures. He has published widely in major international business management and leadership journals. He is a member of the Academy of International Business, the Academy of Management, the International Association for Cross Cultural Psychology, and a Fellow of the International Association for Intercultural Research.

Kristine Mantey is a finance professional whose consulting has extended across Fortune 500 companies to nonprofits. She is focused on the application of systems engineering techniques in combination with economic modeling across a variety of applications. Her work with homeless service providers was featured in the INCOSE Members Newsletter.

Brendan James Moore, PhD, MS, MA, MPS, is a philosopher and instructional designer currently working on developing a leadership development program at Ochsner Health Systems in New Orleans, Louisiana. His background includes more than 15 years of university ethics teaching at Ohio University and Tulane University and several years of work in the area of information technology, instructional technology, and applied computing systems. Dr. Moore is a former PhD student in the area of philosophy with two Masters' in Philosophy (one from Tulane University and another from Ohio University) in addition to a Master's in Information Technology Management, a Master's in Engineering Management, and a PhD in Engineering and Applied Science. Dr. Moore is passionate about teaching, process improvement, energy efficiency, and philosophy.

Dr. J. Mark Munoz is a tenured Full Professor of Management and International Business at Millikin University in Illinois. He was a former Visiting Fellow at the Kennedy School of Government at Harvard University. He is a recipient of several awards including four Best Research Paper Awards, a Literary Award, two International Book Awards, and the Accreditation Council for Business Schools and Programs (ACBSP) Teaching Excellence Award, among others. He was recognized by the Academy of Global Business Advancement as the 2016 Distinguished Business Dean and recognized for Global Academic Excellence by Amity/IEEE in 2019. Aside from top-tier journal publications, he has authored/edited/coedited over 20 books including *Contemporary Microenterprise: Concepts and Cases, Handbook on the Geopolitics of Business, Global Business Intelligence, Advances in Geoeconomics, Managerial Forensics, Handbook of Artificial Intelligence and Robotic Process Automation: Policy and Government Applications, Economics of Cryptocurrencies, The AI Leader,* and *Digital Entrepreneurship and the Global Economy*. He directs consulting projects worldwide in the areas of strategy formulation, international marketing, international finance, and business development.

Anneliese K. Nash is a human resource professional with experience in nonprofit and healthcare industries. Her practice includes HRIS operations, employee life cycle, and talent development. She holds a Master of Science degree in Management and Organization Behavior and an MBA from Benedictine University.

Dr. Cathy Rehfus-Wilsek, MD, MBA, is an experienced academic medical doctor with over 20 years of global leadership in strategic development, program development and management, and performance/process improvement. She specializes in healthcare and Lean Six Sigma principles and has a proven track record of successfully managing and accrediting healthcare programs. Her expertise spans healthcare business consulting, compliance, and leadership development, with a strong focus on justice, equity, diversity, and inclusion in healthcare.

Dr. Manjula Salimath holds dual doctorates (in Business and Psychology) and is a full professor at the G. Brint Ryan College of Business, University of North Texas. She has published extensively in multiple academic handbooks, monographs, research volumes, and peer-reviewed journals. She is the past president of the Southwest Academy of Management, and her research interests encompass technology and innovation management, ethics, sustainability, international business, and strategy.

Dr. Albert Tan joins the AIM faculty as an Associate Professor and Academic Program Director of the online MBA program. He has a combined 32 years of industry practice and teaching experience in Australia, Singapore, China, Dubai, Indonesia, Malaysia, and Vietnam. Most recently, he was a visiting professor at NUS, Singapore; MIT SCALE Network; Wollongong-Dubai; and Curtin University, Australia, as well as in Indonesia and Vietnam.

Duane Windsor is the Lynette S. Autrey Professor of Management at Rice University's Jones Graduate School of Business. His scholarship emphasizes responsibility, stakeholder theory, and sustainability. His work has been published in various academic journals such as the *Academy of Management Journal, Business and Society, Business Ethics Quarterly, Journal of Business Ethics, Journal of Business Research,* and *Journal of Management Studies*. He served as editor of *Business & Society* (2007–2014).

About the Editor

Dr. J. Mark Munoz is a tenured Full Professor of Management and International Business at Millikin University in Illinois. He was formerly a Visiting Fellow at the Kennedy School of Government at Harvard University. He is a recipient of several awards including four Best Research Paper Awards, a Literary Award, two International Book Awards, and the Accreditation Council for Business Schools and Programs (ACBSP) Teaching Excellence Award. Mark was recognized by the Academy of Global Business Advancement as the 2016 Distinguished Business Dean, and recognized for Global Academic Excellence by Amity/IEEE in 2019. Aside from top-tier journal publications, he has authored/edited/coedited over 25 books including *Contemporary Microenterprise: Concepts and Cases*, *Handbook on the Geopolitics of Business*, *Global Business Intelligence*, and *Digital Entrepreneurship and the Global Economy*. He directs consulting projects worldwide in the areas of strategy formulation, international marketing, international finance, and business development.

https://doi.org/10.1515/9783111316987-018

Index

https://doi.org/10.1515/9783111316987-019